Recovery of the L⟨

Recovery of the Lost Good Object brings together the hugely influential papers and seminars of Eric Brenman, revealing his impact on the development of psychoanalysis and allowing a better understanding of his distinctive voice amongst post-Kleinian analysts.

Gathered together for the first time in one volume, Eric Brenman's papers give the reader a unique insight into the development of his clinical and theoretical thinking. They highlight many issues which are relevant to the present debate about psychoanalytic technique, including:

- The narcissism of the analyst
- Hysteria
- The recovery of the good object relationship
- Meaning and meaningfulness
- Cruelty and narrowmindedness
- The value of reconstruction in adult psychoanalysis

The second half of the book documents three of the clinical seminars and covers the transgenerational transmission of trauma, the analysis of borderline pathology and the psychoanalytical approach to severely deprived patients.

This collection will be welcomed by all psychoanalysts and psycho-therapists, and other members of the helping professions interested in investigating the valuable contribution that Eric Brenman has made to contemporary psychoanalysis.

Eric Brenman trained originally in Medicine and Psychiatry, and then at the British Institute of Psychoanalysis. He is a Senior Training Analyst and Supervisor in the British Psychoanalytic Society, and a past President of the Society.

Gigliola Fornari Spoto trained in Medicine and Psychiatry in Italy and is a Senior Training Analyst in the British Psychoanalytic Society.

THE NEW LIBRARY OF PSYCHOANALYSIS
General Editor Dana Birksted-Breen

The New Library of Psychoanalysis was launched in 1987 in association with the Institute of Psychoanalysis, London. It took over from the International Psychoanalytical Library, which published many of the early translations of the works of Freud and the writings of most of the leading British and Continental psychoanalysts.

The purpose of the New Library of Psychoanalysis is to facilitate a greater and more widespread appreciation of psychoanalysis and to provide a forum for increasing mutual understanding between psychoanalysts and those working in other disciplines such as the social sciences, medicine, philosophy, history, linguistics, literature and the arts. It aims to represent different trends both in British psychoanalysis and in psychoanalysis generally. The New Library of Psychoanalysis is well placed to make available to the English-speaking world psychoanalytic writings from other European countries and to increase the interchange of ideas between British and American psychoanalysts.

The Institute, together with the British Psychoanalytical Society, runs a low-fee psychoanalytic clinic, organizes lectures and scientific events concerned with psychoanalysis and publishes the *International Journal of Psychoanalysis*. It also runs the only UK training course in psychoanalysis that leads to membership of the International Psychoanalytical Association – the body which preserves internationally agreed standards of training, of professional entry, and of professional ethics and practice for psychoanalysis as initiated and developed by Sigmund Freud. Distinguished members of the Institute have included Michael Balint, Wilfred Bion, Ronald Fairbairn, Anna Freud, Ernest Jones, Melanie Klein, John Rickman and Donald Winnicott.

Previous General Editors include David Tuckett, Elizabeth Spillius and Susan Budd. Previous and current Members of the Advisory Board include Christopher Bollas, Ronald Britton, Donald Campbell, Stephen Grosz, John Keene, Eglé Laufer, Juliet Mitchell, Michael Parsons, Rosine Jozef Perelberg, David Taylor, Mary Target, Catalina Bronstein, Sara Flanders and Richard Rusbridger.

ALSO IN THIS SERIES

TITLES IN THE NEW LIBRARY OF PSYCHOANALYSIS TEACHING SERIES

Reading Freud: A Chronological Exploration of Freud's Writings Jean-Michel Quinodoz

THE NEW LIBRARY OF PSYCHOANALYSIS

General Editor: Dana Birksted–Breen

Recovery of the Lost Good Object

Eric Brenman

Edited & introduced by
Gigliola Fornari Spoto

Routledge
Taylor & Francis Group

LONDON AND NEW YORK

First published 2006
by Routledge
27 Church Road, Hove, East Sussex, BN3 2FA

Simultaneously published in the USA and Canada
by Routledge
270 Madison Avenue, New York, NY 10016

Routledge is an imprint of the Taylor & Francis Group, an informa business

© 2006 selection and introduction, Gigliola Fornari Spoto;
introduction to clinical seminars, Franco De Masis;
individual chapters, Eric Brenman

Typeset in Bembo by
Keystroke, 28 High Street, Tettenhall, Wolverhampton
Printed and bound in Great Britain by
TJ International Ltd, Padstow, Cornwall
Cover design by Sandra Heath

British Library Cataloguing in Publication Data
A catalogue record for this book is available from the British Library

Library of Congress Cataloging in Publication Data
Brenman, Eric.
Recovery of the lost good object / Eric Brenman ; edited and introduced
by Gigliola Fornari Spoto.
p. cm. — (The new library of psychoanalysis)
Includes bibliographical references and index.
ISBN13: 978–0–415–40922–3 (hbk : alk. paper)
ISBN10: 0–415–40922–5 (hbk : alk. paper)
ISBN13: 978–0–415–40923–0 (pbk : alk. paper)
ISBN10: 0–415–40923–3 (pbk : alk. paper)
1. Psychoanalysis. I. Fornari Spoto, Gigliola. II. Title. III. Series.
[DNLM: 1. Psychoanalysis. 2. Psychoanalytic Theory.
WM 460 B8373r 2006]
RC501.2.B74 2006
616.89′17—dc22
2006007191

ISBN13: 978–0–415–40922–3 (hbk)
ISBN13: 978–0–415–40923–0 (pbk)

ISBN10: 0–415–40922–5 (hbk)
ISBN10: 0–415–40923–3 (pbk)

I believe with Schopenhauer that one of the strongest motives that lead men to art and science is escape from everyday life with its painful crudity and hopeless dreariness, from the fetters of one's ever-shifting desires . . . into the world of object perception. . . . Each makes this cosmos and its construction the pivot of his emotional life, in order to find in this way the peace and security he cannot find within the all-too-narrow realm of swirling personal experience . . .

> The then 39-year-old Einstein's address at Max Planck's
> 60th birthday (1918)

I am fascinated by your Vergil (sic) – and am steadfastly resisting him. The book shows me clearly what I fled from when I sold myself body and soul to Science – the flight from the I and the WE to the IT.

> Written thanking Hermann Broch in 1945 for his
> book on the poet Virgil

An uneasy feeling comes over me when the inevitable birthday nears. All year long the Sphinx stares at me in reproach and reminds me painfully of the Uncomprehended blotting out the personal aspects of life. Then comes the accursed day when the love shown me by my fellow man reduces me to a state of hopeless helplessness. The Sphinx does not let me free for a moment, and meanwhile I am troubled by a bad conscience, being unable to do justice to all this love because I lack inner freedom and relaxation.

> Written on his 71st birthday (1950)

All quoted in the book *Albert Einstein* by Banesh Hoffmann published by Paladin (1975)

Contents

Introduction

Gigliola Fornari Spoto

I vividly remember first meeting Eric Brenman, about thirty years ago, when, as a young Intern in Psychiatry (and as a future candidate of the British Society), I was asked to be the translator for the seminars which he and Irma were running at the Milan Institute. This was my first contact with 'real life' clinical Kleinian analysis: my analytical knowledge, up to then, was somewhat limited, coloured by a touch of idealization and largely theoretical.

What struck me, at the time, was Eric Brenman's passion for the clinical work, his humanity, his clinical acumen, his capacity to 'take the patient in', to move fluently from the experiential to the theoretical, and to transform the scattered elements of a patient's history and background, as they emerged in the transference, into a complex, intriguing narrative about human conflicts, desires, loving and hateful feelings, in a rounded, never reductionist way, where internal and external reality, past and present, became interwoven and mutually resonant with meaning. You felt the analyst and the patient were two real human beings struggling together, sharing a journey which was never easy but always compelling.

I remember him to be also rather partial to good Italian food and wine, which I took to be part of his natural ability to recognize 'good objects' and tune in with them. My resolve to come to England to train as an analyst was very much strengthened by this good experience and I am grateful to Eric for it.

I felt very pleased and honoured to be asked to be the English editor of his book, a task which I think of, at a personal level, as a 'recovery' of a past good 'psychoanalytical object' and of my Italian roots.

This book is adapted from the one originally published in 2002 in Italy, by the Centro Milanese di Psicoanalisi 'Cesare Musatti', edited by Roberto

Basile, Paola Capozzi, Franco De Masi, Patrizia Gammaro Moroni, Dino Lanzara and Federico Rocca: it was meant as a tribute to Eric Brenman as a remarkable clinician and psychoanalytical thinker, who fostered and nurtured their psychoanalytical development.

Several analysts from the Milan Institute had been attending clinical supervision seminars, run by Eric Brenman throughout the 1970s, 1980s and 1990s, when Italian psychoanalysis, always receptive to psychoanalytical ideas from other countries, was consolidating a stronger and more distinctive sense of identity. The Milanese analysts found Eric's supervisions inspiring and illuminating and wanted to be able to keep and share their valuable experience by giving it a written form. The moving and grateful tribute that Franco De Masi pays to Eric, which appears as an introduction to the clinical seminars, shows how central Brenman's seminars were in the development of many Milanese colleagues.

The Italian edition of the book contained all of Eric Brenman's published papers, and five clinical seminars. Eric has added an unpublished paper to the English version, 'The recovery of the good object relationship: the conflict with the superego', which gives this book its title and gathers together some of his most significant theoretical views. Some of the papers have been previously published in the *International Journal of Psychoanalysis* and will be familiar to the English reader. Collected together, the papers give a much more organic sense of the development of Eric Brenman's clinical and theoretical thinking, of the various themes which he has addressed in his long psychoanalytical career, allowing for a better understanding of his distinctive voice amongst post-Kleinian analysts.

For the English edition we have retained three of the clinical seminars in their entirety as they are very relevant to contemporary psychoanalytical debate: the trans-generational transmission of trauma, the analysis of borderline pathology, and the psychoanalytical approach to severely deprived patients.

Although the clinical seminars, as one would expect, are discursive in style, and do not claim to have the conceptual rigour of a paper, they convey very effectively Eric's qualities as a supervisor, and show supervision as a process, 'work in progress', where ideas take shape in a creative exchange and where conceptualization is always firmly rooted in clinical practice. Those who know Eric as a teacher will be able to recognize his clinical astuteness as well as his maieutic, facilitating, non-prescriptive style of supervision, which, in this case, also had to take into account a different psychoanalytical culture. The seminars also show his balanced approach to the clinical material, and the absence of reassuring, all-knowing certainties, something which also permeates his clinical work. When he helps the analyst to formulate his interventions, Eric is always mindful of the patient's struggle to cope with the vicissitudes of life (in light of the emotional equipment he possesses), but also of the powerful, distorting and destructive forces which interfere with this struggle. The task of the analyst is to widen the patient's horizons, restricted by forces which attack truth and human understanding and aim to perpetuate a narrow mental picture in both members of the analytical couple, and to provide a suitable space for a different kind of development.

I decided not to edit the seminars too much and I am aware that some repetition is unavoidable. Giving the full transcript, however, I thought, would be useful for thinking about the process of supervision itself, which is a topic of great interest to many of us today. The seminars also highlight many issues which are relevant to the present debate about psychoanalytical technique: the interplay between the here and now of the transference and the history, the nature of the patient's internal and external objects and their capacity to equip the patient to face psychic pain and the reality of life, the patient's ability to receive interpretations about destructiveness when there isn't a sufficiently solid internalized connection with a good object, the analyst as an object who can truly bear with the patient what is felt to be unbearable and who is constantly monitoring how the patient assesses his capacity to do so, to name but a few.

Readers familiar with other Kleinian writers will be able to compare Brenman's technique, as it emerges from the supervisions, to that of other Kleinian analysts and see the differences.

The publication, perhaps overdue, of this book allows us to hear this distinctive voice in the present psychoanalytical discourse. In his paper on 'The value of reconstruction in adult psychoanalysis', Brenman talks about what shapes our identity as analysts. He writes that we all have to work through oedipal and pre-oedipal anxieties related to our analytical parents (Freud and our teachers), so that our past objects are not murdered, but also so that we are not limited by defensive restrictions, which could be seen as the killing of new analytical knowledge. It seems to me that Eric does just this: he is sufficiently connected with his good original analytical objects to venture into new and different psychoanalytical explorations.

I will try to describe what seem to me the most significant of these new explorations.

The first, I think, is Brenman's development of the notion of analytical containment. His frame of reference includes Freud, Melanie Klein and Bion, and Rosenfeld's description of containment as an active process. He fully embraces what he describes as Bion's shift to the human relationship. The centrality of the 'human relationship' in the analytical relationship is an ever-present concern, and, it seems to me, essential in shaping Eric's theoretical thinking and technique. Analytic technique is seen as something which does not transcend the reality of human relationships but is an instrument to heighten awareness. It is the emphasis on the human relationship between the analyst and the patient which is a *sine qua non*, if the analyst wants to help the patient in the move from the omnipotence of the paranoid-schizoid position to the human reality of the depressive position. There is an interrelatedness and an acknowledgement of reciprocity between analyst and patient, and both analyst and patient need to recognize the value, and the meaning, that they have for one another. If the analyst has to help his patient in facing what is unbearable, the patient needs to have an experience of an analytical object truly capable of facing what is unbearable. The analyst has to go through his depressive position, at a personal level and especially when he has to deal with his feelings of hopelessness and worthlessness in the analysis, and when the patient questions him as a truly 'good object'. The patient observes the analyst in his entirety and great attention has to be paid to how the analyst is introjected in the patient's inner world, distinguishing what is projection from what is correct perception. Brenman warns us against the risks of presenting ourselves, in a narcissistic way, as perfect containers, setting in motion (as he describes in his paper 'The narcissism of the analyst') 'a superhuman immaculate model, which promotes a further narcissistic identification by the patient', confirming his hopelessness about achieving true and limited human understanding. In his paper 'Matters of life and death – real and assumed' Eric Brenman looks at how containment develops within the conflict between life and death instincts, between love and destructiveness. He also reconnects us to the very significant role (sometimes perhaps not sufficiently borne in mind) given by Melanie Klein, in most of her writings, to the survival of the good object and its importance in mitigating hate and destructiveness, and to the process of reparation.

Brenman attributes a central role to the mother's capacity to help the infant to give up the primitive defences of the paranoid-schizoid position and to negotiate the reality of the depressive position. Freud's theory about life and death instincts is articulated by Brenman into a human dimension, in the unfolding of the early relationship between the mother and her baby. He thinks that the mother acts as a protective shield (as described by Freud in 'Instincts and their vicissitudes') against excessive stimuli and, because of this, she contributes, to some degree, to the construction of the ideal breast (which the baby turns to in order to avoid persecution), and shares in the omnipotent delusion of the paranoid-schizoid position, which insulates from the truth of dependency and the threat of catastrophe. This process, to begin with, is necessary for survival and it deflects the death instinct. Gradually the mother helps the infant to give up the primitive system of defences within the development of a loving human relationship, and what was once believed to be life saving (omnipotence, projection of the death instinct, insulation and delusion) becomes 'falsehood as the human truth born out of depressive position love becomes more realized'. A good object is ultimately the result of what happens between the mother and the baby in the working through of the depressive position, and it is the recovery of this good object relationship which is the central task of every analysis. The analyst, like a good enough mother, should then be mindful both of the hold of primitive defences and of the value of human understanding, enabling the patient to cope with the vicissitudes of life. Brenman widens the concept of containment, articulating it both in an instinct and an object relational perspective. In this framework, great developmental importance is given to the absence of an object which provides this kind of containment and leaves the person to go back, fighting for his life, as it were, to the paranoid–schizoid position.

Brenman also adds his voice to the discussion about the clinical usefulness of the death instinct. I think his emphasis on the crucial role of the mother/infant relationship and the mother's capacity to negotiate primitive anxieties is somewhat different from the best-known Kleinian papers on the subject, such as those of Hanna Segal and Michael Feldman, and, because of this, it enriches this debate.

Another significant theoretical contribution (with interesting implications for technique) is the importance of the role of the superego, namely the primitive ruthless superego, in shaping the conflict between love and destructiveness and in determining its outcome. Brenman's ideas on the superego are presented in organic form in his paper 'The recovery of the good object relationship: the conflict with the superego', published here for the first time, but are referred to in many of his other papers. He sees, like Freud and Abraham, the melancholic superego as the prototype of this kind of superego, but he sees it in operation in many other pathological states, and, in fact, as an important part, although not necessarily always visible, of the normal landscape of internal objects. It is one of the earliest organizations in the psyche, and can be moderated by loving human understanding. The superego he describes is related to Melanie Klein's primitive superego, to Strachey's views on the superego in his paper on the mutative interpretation, to Bion's 'ego destructive superego' and to O'Shaughnessy's 'abnormal form of superego' and to Rosenfeld's ideas about destructive narcissism. With a deceptively simple, but compelling, conceptualization, Brenman thinks that this kind of superego takes over when the process of internalizing a good object has failed. The ever-present conflict between ordinary human object relationships and this god-like superego plays an integral part in the move between paranoid-schizoid and depressive position. The superego which attacks the very value of human understanding is like a fundamentalist god which demands total devotion. The story of Oedipus and his internal and external objects is revisited in a very original 'reconstructive' manner, as a narrative dominated by the allegiance to this god-like superego and the lack of human understanding. One of the tasks of analysis of a patient who does not have a good internalized object and whose internal world is dominated by this form of superego is to offer the patient an experience of a new understanding object, which moderates the power of the superego.

How far the good object can modify the destructiveness of the superego, and how effective the superego is in overruling the good object, is the crucial struggle in analysis. Brenman maintains that only a patient with some access to a good object relationship can make use of an interpretation about his destructiveness in a way that can truly help him in his struggle with love and hate. He thinks that without a sufficient attachment to a good object, an interpretation about the patient's destructiveness, in severely depressed and/or narcissistic patients or patients stuck in a sado-masochistic impasse, is experienced as a reproach from another inflexible superego which demands that the patient should be ideal and free of hatred.

A further contribution which Brenman makes to the current psycho-analytical debate is in the area of history and reconstruction.

From his papers and from the supervisions, one gets the sense that history and reconstructions play a bigger part than in the writings of other Kleinian analysts. In his paper on 'The value of reconstruction' Brenman states that it is not enough in clinical practice, as opposed to theory, to analyse truth and resistance, if the patient does not have an object who can bear with him what is felt to be unbearable, not only in the present, but also in the past, an object that will go with the patient in an exploration.

Analysis does not answer the questions about history, but provides the security to explore them. The relationship with the analyst is a new relationship which allows a different kind of exploration of the patient's history. The analyst is not a historian but behaves like Virgil accompanying the patient on his journey, 'going with' the patient in his exploration.

Brenman also believes that reconstruction has a fundamental role in allowing a full process of mourning and reparation.

Finally just a few brief words about Eric's writing style. His clinical descriptions are vivid, compassionate, rich in emotions: patients come alive as whole human beings. When he thinks theoretically he tries to capture and describe complexity rather than aiming at simplified, tidy certitudes. You get a liberating sense of looking at ample emotional and intellectual landscapes, which can accommodate many ideas, rather than at a narrowly focused picture: sometimes, because of this, there is a certain laborious, wandering, 'philosophical' quality about his writing style. But then analysis is a laborious process, where trying to make sense is always mixed with uncertainty and not knowing. Not infrequently, he ventures out of the consulting room to make connections with the wider world of human endeavours, like literature, art, philosophy, and this gives his writing invaluable breadth and depth and restores psychoanalysis as a humanistic science, where cross-fertilization with other disciplines is encouraged and valued.

Eric Brenman, so aware of the disasters that emotional fundamentalism creates in our patients, warns us against the dangers of fundamentalism, in all its aspects, in our profession, against the risks of elevating psycho-analytical 'truths' to the level of ideological masters which narrow our field of vision. He promotes a humanistic, 'depressive position' kind of analysis, where the recovery of good object relationships becomes an analytical aim: we are asked to think of analysis as a strenuous, uneven effort towards a truly reparative process, a journey where hope and limitations, success and failure, understanding and non-understanding are constant companions.

Preface

Eric Brenman

All studies begin with an enquiry – getting to know – attempting to understand. The understanding needs to go through a further examination of the validity of the discovery and its usefulness. Later this poses further questions – a never-ending quest.

Freud at one stage of his life regarded himself as a conquistador, who attempted to discover the riddle of the sphinx, untrammelled by the desire to help people. To be a detached observer may have the advantage of getting nearer to the truth in some ways, and the human factor may distort the accuracy of the observations. Knowing the constitutional make up of human beings is basically important. In the clinical practice of psychoanalysis we inevitably meet the variable human predicaments that play a vital part in the outcome.

Whilst Freud originally regarded the transference only as a hindrance to knowing, as we know, later, his understanding of the transference became an invaluable clinical tool opening new human truths Freud further encountered how difficult it is to meet and experience psychic truth. Unlike other studies, the process of psychoanalysis aiming at the discovery of the truth about ourselves is a mixed blessing, by no means always welcome. In fact this may be experienced as so overwhelming as to disrupt psychic equilibrium. Defences against knowing and experiencing become important factors of consideration. At the same time, being helped to cope forms the basis for providing the equipment for further creative developments and a human relationship which at its best can lead to knowing, valuing and caring for each other.

The acquisition of the strength to bear knowing and experiencing, and knowing how much one can bear, has become an ever important factor. Freud in his paper on 'Mourning and melancholia' and right up to his last

clinical paper on 'Analysis terminable and interminable' concerned himself
with this problem. Out of this, based on the work of Klein, Winnicott,
Bion and numerous others, grew the study of the good object relationship, which enables and allows for fulfilment in bearing human good and
bad experience and the fruits of obtaining knowledge. Bion's work on containing, in which the mother contains the knowledge that enables her to
contain the baby's needs, and subsequently helps the baby to acquire this
capacity, has now become a cornerstone in psychoanalysis.

In education, the concept of equipping a person to cope with the realities
of life is central; psychoanalysis extends this to another reality, dealing with
the experience of knowing more of the reality of the internal world.

This book is mainly concerned with how particular individuals deal
with these issues and how the analyst may approach this task. Many of the
papers are about this subject. The Italian version of the book started life
with a request from the Milan Psychoanalytic Society to publish tapes of
the seminars which I conducted with them over a period of some twenty-
five years.

I had originally been invited to introduce them to new developments
in psychoanalysis, particularly the work of Melanie Klein. I was faced with
the task of having to select what I thought might be helpful, taking into
account the building blocks which they were using. I considered that it
was important to know their foundation stones, which were different from
mine, and to supply food for thought that might help them to assimilate
new ways of understanding. I did not want them to give up those elements,
which held them together, then to be left with no means of support. I
considered that if that were to happen, they might feel driven either to
reject, or to completely identify with, new forms of understanding. They
would then lose their identity – that is, who they were and where they
came from.

The Italian book was published with much more detail about the early
seminars; the analysts wished to add some of my previously published
papers. In this new English edition, the detail of the seminars has been
severely cut and just gives a flavour of the teaching which took place. A
lot of water has flowed under the bridge since then; these seminars now
seem somewhat simplistic and repetitive, but the ideas were new to them at
the time.

I had learned from my experience with them what all analysts have to
experience in their clinical work – that there is a primary task of understanding what the patient feels, who the patient is and where the patient
comes from; how the patient builds up a capacity to experience more and
more about life and the self, without losing his/her own identity.

For this reason I chose to use as a model Sophocles' play, *Oedipus Rex*, which of course was the inspiration for Freud's discovery of the Oedipus complex, with which I knew they would all be familiar. *Oedipus Rex* deals with the drama and the circumstances involved in the development of a unique individual, the task with which we are confronted in teaching and in everyday psychoanalysis.

Freud constructed a theory of the universal murderous rivalry which starts early in life, within the father, mother, son triad. Whilst this theory has stood the test of time, we are aware that however universal the Oedipus complex is, it does not always have the same tragic consequences of the play. Other factors come into play.

What helps to modify these forces and what exacerbates the murderous rivalry is of enormous importance, and, as Klein emphasised in her work, much depends on earlier experience; Freud and numerous later workers also explored this issue. I am also using this play as a model as it so closely matches clinical experience and I hope that it may illustrate some major factors about knowing and experiencing and coping with these vicissitudes.

The basic background of the play is that the gods have ordained that Oedipus will kill his father and marry his mother and that no human intervention will be of any avail. One may take this as an expression of the force of the primitive nature of mankind who worship this omnipotent power. In this scenario the ultimate judge is not a forgiving, loving, reparative god, but an omnipotent god which ordains; there is nothing that can influence the outcome.

No man is an island; everything takes place within an object relationship. In the play, the relationship is one within which priority is given to the singular omnipotent God who discounts other beings and demands exclusive worship. Nevertheless the statement of the gods (that human intervention cannot take place) suggests that human intervention is a significant power as a counter-force even though this has to be crushed.

Freud (in 'Instincts and their vicissitudes') wrote that hate is the older of the emotions. Melanie Klein's view stresses both the enormous power of hatred determined to have its way, and the equally strong power of love. In Freud's reference to the Oedipus play we have a play about fundamentalism. Freud selected the basic primitive process; this seems to me to be absolutely true and is a view which is totally followed by Klein. When Oedipus realises what he has done, in spite of the understanding of the chorus, he is never to be forgiven; he is to suffer for the rest of his life.

It is interesting to note that Melanie Klein, in her incursions into Greek drama, chooses the trilogy of Aeschylus which deals with these primitive processes in the pursuit of the Trojan wars. Agamemnon sacrifices his daughter Iphigenia for favourable winds; his wife Clytemnestra ultimately kills him (when he returns from Troy) for such an unforgivable murder. Their son Orestes then kills his mother for killing the father and it seems that this tragedy will continue like an endless feud.

Melanie Klein recounts here the meeting of the gods who are there to decide whether Orestes should be forgiven or not. Half of the gods say – forgive; and the other half say – don't forgive. The goddess Athena, in order to break the terrible cycle of killing, gives the casting vote in favour of forgiveness. Here Klein stresses the delicate balance between forgiveness and punishment, and the ultimate choice of human intervention of loving understanding over the powerful primitive processes.

Freud realised how important this was (in 'Mourning and melancholia'); retaining the love of the good object enabled a mourner to overcome depression, as opposed to the melancholic who had no good object available to his consciousness, Freud was also concerned (in 'Analysis terminable and interminable') with identifying the factors which enable good elements to survive; he did indeed think that this had something to do with what he called a feminine process; in my view he left this legacy to be further explored.

Melanie Klein spent much of her life writing about the good object, which enabled one to cope with the very violent primitive processes; she explored to the nth degree destructive cruelty, but was nonetheless always concerned with the basic good object and its survival. The good object relationship is essential in order to cope with the powerful primitive forces; the appropriate valuing of the 'good breast' relationship that takes precedence over primitive gratification – in essence the humanisation process.

All the papers which follow are concerned with this theme – namely, what enables a good object relationship to modify these primitive processes, and what militates against this. The purpose of this book and indeed the purpose of the clinical practice of psychoanalysis rest on the efficacy of human intervention. Most of us regard the provision of a good object/breast/mother, bearing what is unbearable to the infant and empathising with the predicament of that infant and providing appropriate nourishment and help to deal with that experience and develop knowledge, as essential for growth. This bond that develops, the bond of valuing and being concerned with each other, can be strong enough to cope with internal and external events, and is the bedrock of human meaningfulness. The combined love and concern of both parties and its development give ground for faith and appreciation in living – one is not alone and human endeavour is the main source of finding meaning and being meaningful.

The aim of this book is in line with the aim of those analysts who consider that the recapturing of the early good object relationship is essential to acquire the strength to meet the vicissitudes of life.

Acknowledgements

This book is the outcome of a long labour during the course of which there have been many helpmates, of whom I shall single out only a few; my psychoanalytic training began with Hanna Segal, to whom I am indebted for much more than this book; her strong commitment to psychoanalytic enquiry was an inspiration. I am also grateful to my supervisors, in particular the late Herbert Rosenfeld, and subsequently my many enriching discusssions with Wilfred Bion.

More recently, I have already thanked Franco De Masi, Paola Capozzi, Dino Lanzara and Roberto Basile for their part in the Italian book, out of which this project grew. I am again hugely grateful to Franco for encouraging me and others to undertake this English edition. I would like to thank the Melanie Klein Trust for supporting the translations from Italian, and Philip Slotkin for his very able translations.

Gigliola Fornari Spoto has undertaken the editorial task and I am grateful for her considerable effort and her much valued help, particularly as this came at a time when she had many other pressing concerns. And the General Editor, Dana Birksted-Breen, too, who has been untiringly helpful in a most thoughtful and creative way.

I was pleased that the British Museum allowed us to use the Rembrandt drawing of 'The child being taught to walk' for the cover, and thanks to the IJPA (Chapters 2, 3, 5 and 6), EPF (Chapter 1), Karnac (Chapter 7) and Centro Milanese di Psicoanalisi Cesare Musatti (Chapters 9, 10 and 11) for permission to publish. At Routledge, Claire Lipscomb and Kate Hawes have been hugely obliging and helpful.

Closer to home, Daniel Pick has always encouraged me and been ever willing to provide generous help. Above all, this book would not have been brought together without the tolerance and support in countless different ways – scientifically and personally – of my wife, Irma Brenman Pick, and this book is dedicated to her.

1

The narcissism of the analyst: its effect in clinical practice

In the play *The Bacchae* of Euripides, the citizens of Thebes pride themselves on their rational and intellectual life. The god, Dionysus, presents himself and demands recognition: the repudiation of Dionysus leads to the tragic consequence of the enactment of the most extreme form of narcissistic cannibalism.

Freud, in 'Analysis terminable and interminable', one of his last papers, questioned the efficacy of psychoanalysis. He indicated that the power of primitive forces and defences is so strong that we may be too narcissistic in our belief that understanding can change mankind all that much. It is one thing to describe psychic processes, another to effect change in clinical practice.

Freud had already realised that insight and intellectual understanding were not enough. He recognised the power of transference love and advocated the adoption of the neutral position. In time, the transference became a clinical tool.

Today we use the understanding of transference and countertransference in an increasingly complex way and know that the experiences we have are not only those that the patient puts into us, but these experiences interact with the analyst's personality and pathology. The narcissism of the analyst is no exception.

In 'Instincts and their vicissitudes' Freud contended that narcissism and hate were the earliest impulses and were later modified by love. If we accept this view and include Freud's belief that all forces are common to us all, the analyst has to reckon with love, hatred, and the pursuit of truth as constantly interacting in himself, with subsequent distortions of truth, not

1

least by narcissism. To eat from the Tree of Knowledge carries with it the danger of attempting to become God.

The analytic setting is arranged as the best means we know of pursuing psychic truth, yet we arrange fees and times for our benefit as well as the patient's. We pursue knowledge, partly for our own interest, and we are pleased if our patients do well and develop. We obtain satisfaction from the patient's development, and whether voiced or not, the patient knows this. Indeed, to deny this would be to refute the patient's contribution to our lives; narcissism in the extreme, akin to a mother conveying to the baby that she was not pleased it was born and gained no joy, pride or gratification from motherhood. Thus, the adoption of the neutral position is a complex problem and requires intricate interpretation.

I wish to approach this problem from a few aspects of what we know about narcissism and to question its operation in the analyst.

Freud, in his 'Two principles of mental functioning', stated that the giving up of the pleasure principle for the reality principle was helped by the love of the educators. This enhances a quest for love with all its narcissistic overtones, not only in the child or patient, but the analyst's pleasure in this development can stimulate excessive narcissistic activity.

I assume that the desire for fusion and coalescence is both a defence against separateness and a deep narcissistic yearning. I believe the analyst and the patient can be party to this and can become encapsulated in a so-called analysis to obviate the facts of life. The analysis *may* proceed to both their satisfaction, with little achievement.

If we consider the narcissistic cannibalistic processes described by Abraham and later developed by Klein, whereby the good and desirable elements of the object are ruthlessly incorporated by the infant with simultaneous projection into the object of the bad elements, we must ask ourselves how much this *may* be unconsciously perpetrated by the analyst. This process, akin to destructive narcissism as described by Rosenfeld, *can* lend itself to the negation of the worthwhileness of the patient, with the analyst behaving as if he were the ideal breast rather than a person who *may* have something useful to *say*. It *can* also lead to a desensitisation of what it is like to be in the patient's position, and of the analyst's role as a transference object.

Even empathy, generally considered to be a *sine qua non* of clinical practice, and the basis for human concern, carries with it an element of sharing that is essential, yet if the analyst does not also distance himself from the patient this can lead to excessive narcissistic identification. Empathy cannot, and in my view, should not, operate without some element of the patient being 'my child'. The patient needs to experience some degree of belonging, and yet distance and separateness are essential for growth. However, the 'my child, my patient' factor can also lead to the patient being the representative of the analyst's narcissism, with overestimation of the patient or hatred of the patient for letting the analyst down.

There *was* a time when projective identification *was* largely considered to operate as one-way traffic, and only the pervading moods the analyst picked up were considered important. The patient is highly sensitive to the real as well as the imagined mood and attitude of the analyst and is continually concerned about the true feelings of the analyst. Analytic technique does not transcend the reality of human relationships – it is an instrument to heighten awareness.

The very skills of analysis can lend themselves to narcissistic indulgence. There is the danger of an ill patient, whose main problem is containing and needing to be contained, being served with excessively intricate interpretations which satisfy the narcissism of the analyst at the expense of the patient being forced to bear the unbearable. Even in a 'relatively well' patient, I had the experience of elaborating my interpretations in one session, following which she dreamed: 'My husband brought home masses of vegetables which were more than anyone could *eat*, and I was expected not only to cook them, but eat them, flowers and all.' Although consciously not complaining, it emerged that she had experienced the previous session as excessively elaborately decorative and indigestible. Issues are never simple and, in this example, envious elements and a desire to titillate my narcissism were operative as well as a justifiable complaint.

Yet no love is meaningful without the donor having some self-interest. The love a mother gives *can* only be measured against giving up some self-interest. The interaction between self-interest and concern needs to be balanced, lest there be adverse consequences either way.

The analyst not only relates to the patient and the patient's relationships, but to his own relationships to himself, his inner world, psychoanalysis and his own analyst. This limits his capacity for new experiences, yet he needs some roots without being immobilised. I have often wondered what analysts did with their countertransference before it was officially sanctioned. Did they have such a narcissistic identification with analysis and their ego ideal, with a consequent narcissistic harsh superego that restricted them? Conversely, can we now so overestimate the importance of our own reactions that valuable material is neglected?

In clinical practice the pursuit of truth goes hand in glove with the ego strength to bear it. This strength is derived from supporting relationships, internal and external, given by limited human beings. This poses the question, how much can an analyst be deeply involved and tolerate anxieties in a session? I think there is always a danger of detaching oneself too much in a narcissistic way and posturing as a perfect container and so setting in motion a super-human immaculate model. This can lead to a further narcissistic identification by the patient with consequent character falseness, possible breakdown and dangerous acting out. Yet it seems right to struggle to contain as much as we can.

We know of Abraham's struggle to comprehend Freud's view that the self-reproaches of the melancholic were attacks on his object. This was particularly difficult for Abraham as at the time he was depressed over his own father's death and was initially unable to be aware of the reproaches against the father in himself. Yet he overcame the resistances related to the wound to his own self-esteem to make a great breakthrough in the understanding of manic depression.

In the course of psychoanalysis various contributors have added enormously to our knowledge. They have pursued what is meaningful in a courageous, if not heroic, way, but pursuit of one kind of meaning may lead to the crushing of other meaningful issues. This is in the nature of growth; it is, in my view, impossible to discover new meaning without an element of a Eureka narcissistic glow with which we fall in love, and later we have to go back to the drawing board to review our narcissistic idealisation. Freud set us a great example in his repeated revision of theories.

It seems that narcissism is a dirty word – the enemy of object love, which it so often is, with split parts of the personality hating and rejecting each other as in the Greek tragedy of *the Bacchae*. Yet in what we choose to call normality, narcissism and object love live side by side, not only in conflict but in some degree of harmony.

It is a moot point whether one can totally separate narcissistic fusion from a sense of belonging and sharing. There is a fine distinction between the borders of cannibalistic incorporation and normal acquisition of enquiry and discovery. Where normal pride ends and omnipotence begins may be difficult to discern and, in my view, deprivation of the experience of being considered as significant is one element in intensifying omnipotence. There must be a balance between empathy and living a life of one's own. This is itself a source of debate and too much analytic preoccupation with the problem, as opposed to getting on with life, is a narcissistic disease in itself.

The particular way I have chosen to look at the problem is that of two people, analyst and patient, giving appropriate and inappropriate meaning to each other. When we talk of attacks on meaning and linking, what could be more conducive to this than two people who attack each other's meaning? This must precede attacks on parental intercourse linking.

Possibly the most challenging of all narcissistic problems for the analyst is the state of affairs where the analyst is made to feel meaningless and his belief in analysis a futile delusion. How the analyst copes with this is of the utmost importance, for if he cannot face this and differentiate the good and worthwhile from the unworthwhile, he does not meet the depressive position himself and therefore cannot give the patient a sufficiently strengthening introject to help the patient meet the depressive position. As we well know, there are patients who are exceptionally skilful in producing this state of mind in the analyst and who attempt to make us act out by reassurance, psychological and physical. They may force the analyst to feel despair – the analyst may act out his experience of rejection by writing the patient off, or adopt an over-rigid position, which blocks fresh experience.

The clinical examples which follow concentrate on the way the analyst's narcissism and belief in himself are both attacked and over-stimulated to the point of seduction.

Clinical example 1

The patient, a handsome American homosexual, aged 50, came to analysis complaining of depression. From what I could reconstruct of his parents and siblings, I considered his family background was unhealthy. Previously he had had long periods of various kinds of analysis.

One of his first communications was that I would insist on attempting to cure his homosexuality, which he was adamant about preserving. It was conveyed that I was arrogantly narcissistic in considering it to be psychogenic in origin, and I would be attacking what was meaningful to him. This contention applied not only to homosexuality, but to other areas as well. His homosexuality took two forms:

1 The adulation of sadistic ruthless men who buggered him; he was afraid that the power of these impulses would lead him to pick up a murderer; the sexual choice of a ruthless narcissist.
2 The worship of, and wish to coalesce with, beautiful god-like youths who were thought to be perfect. He took a delight in procuring them and triumphing over fellow homosexuals. A complex narcissistic process.

In his sexual choices he identified with sadistic destructive narcissists who reduced him to nothing; he idealised the empty 'perfect' youth. Yet in his personal relationships, these were the very people with whom he was constantly at war.

In his personal life, both historical and current, he was preoccupied with the hatred of bullies who humiliated him and made him feel – in his own words – a 'nothing'. He was chronically preoccupied with hating such people and plotting their downfall. Likewise, he hated omnipotent, narcissistic people who were empty, behaved like tin gods and expected to be worshipped. Both themes were very much alive in the transference.

Early on in our relationship, his omnipotent, contemptuous, scathing behaviour, conducted in an elegant, sophisticated, intelligent, cultured and, to him, charming way, gave me the impression that if he buggered me about, he expected that I would be captivated by his brilliance – an attempt to get me to occupy a perverse role in which I was supposed to enjoy the buggering and worship his eloquent perfection.

His knowledge and erudition on matters of culture at times put me in the position of a captive audience. He tried to inveigle me into collusive attacks on Philistines and to lure me into a perverse attack on human endeavour and breast-like qualities, while regarding him as the ideal object. His efforts to engage me in this narcissistic 'game' had such seductive qualities that I had constantly to be aware of these processes. The power of his oratory was such that I had seriously to consider whether the analysis I offered, or the values I held, were of any significance, as matched against his communications. Indeed, at times I had to remind myself how ill he was and have a consultation with myself to counteract the impression that to offer interpretations was a narcissistic overestimation of my work. The problem was to show these forces in operation without negating what was truly worthwhile in him, lest I did to him what he did to me.

The humour and guile of his conduct can perhaps be illustrated by this opening to a session:

> 'I was reading Keats last night. By the way, Brenman, Keats is a well-known English poet.'

I found this seductively humorous. He paired me with him and simultaneously narcissistically negated any culture in me; but to take it up without collecting a number of associations would be viewed by him as egocentric touchiness on my part. Above all, it was designed to make analysis itself a pretentious occupation.

Any skill I tried to employ to show him what was going on was considered by him a narcissistic display. Indeed, when one's own meaningfulness is negated, one has to be cautious of such enactment. I found that restricting myself to essential interpretations and showing him how persecuted he was by similar attacks on himself by his colleagues was the gateway to shifting the emphasis on to the reality of human relationships. Above all, containing the narcissistic attacks and stimulation gave him a different experience from that of his own inner world.

Weekend separations brought about deterioration; I considered that to show him this would be interpreted by him as my narcissism. I interpreted both the break and his expected contention that I gave undue significance to myself and my analysis by making such a reference. His reply was 'Not bad, Brenman. 4 out of 10. But don't be discouraged. Try harder. You may get 5 out of 10. I can't promise, but it is always good to try.' Whatever other processes were in operation, he put me in the position of almost being significant; with perseverance I might become acceptable.

In my view, he was making me feel what it was like to be humiliated with just enough significance to go on functioning without a hopeless depression (his symptom). The interpretation by itself is relatively easy, but not to react at all would convey that not only his attacks, but his predicament, meant nothing to me. He needed me to interpret in such a way that he knew that I understood the pain, would not be vengeful, that I could endure it and establish a different relationship.

He once saw me at the opera *Fidelio* and said 'I saw you at the opera. As you know, *Fidelio* has only three arias worth hearing, so you must have a great interest in music just to go for the three arias.'

Work on the infinite nuances which had been taken up so much in the past enabled me to confine myself to his allusion to my pretensions and ignorance and my total lack of capacity to enjoy life as a *whole* and how it was crippled by my narcissistic preoccupations. I interpreted this picture of me and reminded him of his presence at the opera.

The following night he dreamed. He prefaced the dream by telling me that Graham Greene had analysis, which was no use to him, and told me the dream in which he went underground, later under the sea, and there found a man tied to a lavatory seat, who was dead and had been there for a long time, and that man was himself and he became afraid.

He gave numerous associations – rare for him – and I shall give only two.

1 A girl friend who gave up her life, tied to a sadist.
2 How he hated the Kaiser on a TV programme, who, on the death of his father, could only be delighted and say: 'Father is dead, now I am Emperor of Germany.'

I had to consider whether, as in the past, he was contending that this analysis was useless, and I was the sadist he was tied to, or the dead, anal figure. In contrast to past experience I felt he was predominantly talking of himself and his inner world, and the patient himself now realised how the human good alive part of himself had been dead for a long time and he hated the narcissistic part of himself wedded to sadism and regal triumph. (The fear was of a persecuting superego.)

The main point I wish to make is that the development that took place was in my view only possible through the interpretation of the narcissism of the analyst as a transference figure, and by projections, and also in reality. He negated my significance and tested my capacity to function and care and not engage in vicious counterattacks.

After working this through it became clear how much his whole life was dominated by his feeling that he was made to feel a 'nothing', and all his intellectual skills were directed to making his objects feel that they were nothing. He could not come alive properly if he had no meaning, and neither could my analysis, subjected to the same fate. Only one person could be meaningful at a time. Consequently, no real intercourse between two people, *both* having meaning, could take place. This was his major symptom – and I believe this to be the basis of many, if not all, problems of perversion.

I cannot deal here with the pain related to the bringing alive of the true infantile part of himself and the guilt about the part he played in its destruction; obviously this was very important.

In this case, the hatred of the narcissistic parents, who reacted to the patient's own narcissism by counter-hatred rather than achieving something better, was crucial. Attempts were repeatedly made to recreate this as a repetition compulsion in which the *modus vivendi* was one party making the other feel the more narcissistic and loveless. I was subjected to enormous stimulation to relive this pattern, and to doubt my real parental attributes.

Clinical example 2

The patient, a woman of 38, with four children, was in the process of divorce. She was apparently co-operative, appreciative, with a good capacity for love. She responded well to interpretations, but with idealisation of me, interpretation of which was resisted. She interspersed this, almost invariably following breaks, with smashing everything up, when, in her own words, the devil took her over and proved I did not care for her. This was shown to be related to the realisation that she was not unique to me.

She was the middle sister of three. According to the patient, the mother 'switched off' and the patient and the younger sister, together with the mother, idealised the father. The patient herself was switched off to her despair about her mother, defended against by excessive idealisation of the father, producing a difficult transference problem, stimulating my narcissistic role as the father and including the mother transference. Her elder sister was said to be a protestor who demanded things for herself and was sent away to boarding school and later became psychotic. The patient felt she was the 'good girl' who swept garden paths and was related to the father in mutual idealisation. So I had evidence to think that this would be repeated in the transference, which did take place with attempts to stimulate my narcissism and create this mutual idealisation. At times the analysis was too comfortable to be healthy.

Following a complex dream, it became clear that she was terrified I might meet her outside the analysis and see her as she really was. Hence, I had good reason to believe that she felt a narcissistic collusion was in operation and we would be disillusioned about each other.

Her psychotic sister, Joan, was a very important figure; in so many ways she was very much admired and was felt to be the only genuine member of the family. This was, however, dangerous, as Joan smashed up her sanity and was sent away. Sometimes the patient felt she was 'all Joan', sometimes, 'no Joan at all'. There were many dreams in which the patient was identified with Joan.

The patient admired the way I coped. The picture emerged that her internal father coped by using techniques that avoided real personal involvement; in the transference there was often something lacking in the parent–infant relationship. It was too comfortable. On one occasion I was told well in advance that she intended to miss a Friday session for apparently valid family reasons. There was clear evidence from dreams that the sister Joan part of herself would react violently to the prolonged weekend break. She returned on the Monday, claimed she coped well with the break, and brought the following dream: 'I was queueing up for food, was offered chicken, but I did not want chicken. I wanted other food. And I was charged too much and had a furious row with the vendor.'

This raises many questions, but I will confine myself to the role of the analyst's narcissism. Am I feeding her with chicken-heartedness and undermining her belief in her capacity to cope – an accusation she had made before the break? Does this refer to me as a transference figure, the mother that chickens out by switching off to her needs, and/or the father that chickens out by techniques that bypass issues – my analytic technique? Am I too narcissistic in stressing the importance of each session – or am I narcissistic in overestimating our work together that enables her to cope? Had I failed to be firm enough about the missed session and unconsciously colluded to send her away as her parents did to sister Joan? Was this an improvement that she could have a row about the price she paid for confronting conflicts, including paying fees for the missed session?

The issues were manifold, but not to include doubts, imagined and real, about my analysis would be the most narcissistic practice.

★

The debate brings into play not only the patient's welfare, but the analyst's narcissism over the question of being right or wrong, too weak or too forceful, too trusting or doubting, optimistic or pessimistic, too indulgent or too rejecting – the problem we all face in the decision about the termination of an analysis. As with the infant–mother relation, the patient learns from the way the analyst responds to needs, anxieties and attacks. No mother or analyst can practise immaculate conception and attempts to do so negate the facts of life.

We react inside ourselves – at best being a good enough container. As a mother needs a father, we need access to internal resources, psychoanalytic knowledge and the help of our colleagues to examine the interaction of our involvements and learn from our experience.

Not to take account of this does, in my view, result in the excesses that I described in the first part of my paper and, like the citizens of Thebes, we ignore our narcissism at our patients' and our own peril.

References

Bion, W. (1957) The differentiation of psychotic from non psychotic personalities. *International Journal of Psycho-Analysis*, 38: 266.

Freud, S. (1911) Formulations on the two principles of mental functioning. SE 12.

—— (1914) On narcissism. SE 14.

—— (1915) Instincts and their vicissitudes. SE 14.

—— (1937) Analysis terminable and interminable. SE 23.

Klein, M. (1946) Notes on some schizoid mechanisms. *International Journal of Psycho-Analysis* 27: 99.

—— (1955) On identification. *The Writings of Melanie Klein*, Vol. 3. London: Hogarth Press.

Rosenfeld, H. (1971) Destructive narcissism: investigation of aggressive aspects of narcissism. *International Journal of Psycho-Analysis* 32: 169.

Segal, H. (1956) 'Ophelia': depression in schizophrenia. *International Journal of Psycho-Analysis* 37: 339.

Winnicott, D. (1960) The theory of the parent–infant relationship. *International Journal of Psycho-Analysis* 41: 585.

2

The value of reconstruction in adult psychoanalysis

It is inherent in man to seek knowledge, to enquire and discover. It seems important for him to pursue enquiry about his origins, to find his roots; he needs roots and objects, he cannot function alone. To my mind, knowing his background provides him with a sense of continuity and meaning. Only if he feels he belongs can he achieve his own identity. Reconstruction is of value as a means of rediscovering roots, past objects and lost parts of the self.

In man's ambivalence, however, he has a love–hate relationship with the knowledge of the truth, as he does with all relationships, and he may shape the truth, past and present, at the service of his wishes, loves, hates and defences.

History can be doctored for infinite reasons, and those that attempt to reconstruct the past are subject to these vicissitudes; this applies to analyst and analysand. Less important truths may obscure more important ones: who ultimately can determine the priority of specific truths?

Freud in 1937, late in his career, gave this example of reconstruction:

Up to your nth year you regarded yourself as the sole possessor of your mother, then came another baby and brought grave disillusionment. Your mother left you for some time and even after her reappearance she was never devoted to you exclusively. Your feelings towards your mother became ambivalent, your father gained a new importance for you. . . .

Earlier psychoanalytical theories had stressed the relationship with the father as central and reconstructions were made accordingly.

In addition we know that Freud constructed a sexual trauma theory and, when he realized his error, constructed a theory of infantile sexual instincts and fantasies. It seems to me therefore that the issue of responsibility is, and always has been, an important dynamic in psychoanalysis. For various reasons the analyst may construct theories implying either that the patient's parents or that the patient's nature is responsible. These basic assumptions may govern the nature of reconstruction (Freud, 1899, 1905).

We are now aware of complex interactions between child and parent and likewise between analyst and patient. The patient may not only transfer his fantasies on to the analyst, but may attempt to persuade the analyst to hold certain views or even attempt or succeed in making the analyst act out. These powerful interactions between patient and analyst may distort the truth.

With the use of greater skills in handling the countertransference, we now use the experience of being persuaded to hold certain views as an important analytic dynamic and use it to communicate this process to the patient. Distortion of the truth in the construction of the part played by environment or instincts occurs at the deepest levels and may be influenced by the biases and pathology of both analyst and patient. The reshaping of the truth may be not only the current practice of the patient, but a repetition of the past.

It may be the way the patient manipulated his parents, or he may be attempting to make the analyst experience what it is like to be fashioned by a parent. He may identify with such a parent and reverse roles in revenge. In depth the patient may be communicating a belief, both his and his parents', that the truth is unbearable and that distortion of the truth is the sole means of surviving and preventing a catastrophe.

Freud considered that in analysing the transference, the repetition compulsion could be changed to recollection; the patient could be enabled to differentiate the past from the present. He also said that the neurotic suffers from recollections so that the past has the power to dominate the present, however differentiated it may be. I shall return to this theme later.

The main emphasis of my paper is that in clinical practice, in contrast to theory, it is not enough to analyse the truth and resistances if the patient does not have an object who will bear with him what is felt to be unbearable, not only in the present, but also in the past; an object who will 'go with' the patient in exploration. Analysis does not answer historical questions but provides the security to explore them.

It can be argued that if the past is relived in the transference and the patient enabled to face the truth in his current life, he is equipped with an object (the introjected analyst) which strengthens his ego. Although I believe this to be essential, I do not believe it to be sufficient. To face guilt and make reparation to past objects, to mourn what is lost and irreparable, to come to terms with the limitations of past objects, as well as the self and the analyst, is important work and requires reconstructions. Also, of course, the recapturing of good aspects of past objects and the past self is invaluable in rebuilding.

If one regards analysis as a means of discovering truth, both current and in the past, then the foundations, the constructions on which this is built, are of fundamental importance. It is to this area that I am addressing myself – to the analysis of those object relationships, internal and external, that assist, hinder or distort the exploration of the truth. It is the analysis of the transference that is central in this work.

I also take the view that even when strength has been built up, in times of crises the patient loses some of his new acquisitions and regresses to the *ancien régime*. I consider this to be the case not only because of reactions leading to the loss of the internalized analyst, but also because of the powerful bonds of the past, from which I believe there is never complete emancipation, whatever new introjects may take place.

In embarking on my first clinical example, in view of my statements about historical distortion, I am bound to say that the limited information I give is partly constructed from what the patient has told me and that I am selecting what I believe to be relevant.

The patient is an unmarried man, an only child, now aged 25, with obsessional restrictions and impaired intuition. His scientific training was used to limit his personal experience.

According to the patient, his background was very restricted. He was idealized by his mother and played the role of the ideal son. His father was described as withdrawn, 'switched off' and unsuccessful. His uncle, a successful rich lawyer restricted to the letter of the law rather than the spirit, was said to have been admired by the mother as much as the father was despised and was presented as a commendable model to the patient.

At a time when the patient had made reasonable progress in the analysis, he met at a party someone he assumed to be a colleague of mine. He invested this person with brilliance and enormous understanding.

He presented the following dreams, and was not sure which was the first dream and which was the second – an interesting feature.

In the first dream presented he is in a beautiful building with large rooms, all unfurnished. In the central hall there is a magnificent dome made of many windows which can be individually opened. His sense of wonder changes to overwhelming terror and he wishes to run out of the building for fear of going mad.

I note that I am not furnished with direct associations, and I find myself associating to my assumed colleague as someone in the patient's mind able to illuminate with brilliance.

13

In the second dream he is in a luxurious building with rich wall-to-wall carpets and the walls are completely curtained as if the whole room is carpeted. All the rooms are narrow and small.

He associated this part of the dream to his rich uncle's house (though, in the uncle's actual house the physical size of the rooms was large). He told me he used to laugh in a superior way at his uncle for leading this rich restricted life with no real experiences, but also envied his wealth and success. He believed that to a large extent he had constructed his life on his uncle's pattern.

I considered that he was showing me choices available to him.

1 A life of potential beauty and multiple illuminations, carrying with it, however, the fear of going mad, because it was not furnished, structured with helpful objects.
2 A highly organized cosseted defence with material success, which was narrowly restricted but safe, using the values and defences of his mother, and uncle, as well as his own, and protecting him from disturbing envy of a fuller capacity to live.

At that moment he was quite unconscious of his need for helpful objects to explore life. He met an assumed colleague thought to be brilliant, dreamed of entering this beautiful building, and there was no evidence of the admired person or any other figure in the dream. He was all alone and the venture broke down.

Whatever was considered admirable was omnipotently entered and taken over, whether the rich uncle or the brilliant illuminating person. This was a pattern well known to us. For example, when he attended a public lecture I gave, he endowed me with brilliance in order to fuse with me, and triumph over others viewed as limited, and then had an enormous struggle not to rush out of the lecture hall in panic.

Work on these problems of omnipotent intrusion and contempt for limitation led him to be more in touch with his need for helpful objects to explore life and his own impulses including greed and envy.

This led him to explore me to see what I was made of, my strengths, capacities and limitations. Feeling assisted by me in these explorations, he began to experience me as helpful and his truth-seeking self strengthened. Finding an object that assists in enquiry leads the patient to review his earlier objects.

It was after considerable analytic work on these issues that he furnished me with the association that the beautiful building was a historic house he knew well and this furthered his interest in his own history. The dome was also associated to the breast.

It is a matter of clinical judgement to consider at that moment whether history is used as a defence against current discomfort or whether a review of history would expand and enrich the understanding of the present. Or in the language of the patient's dream, analysis may restrict itself in the safe confines of the present, or go mad or wild in the belief that infinite windows can be opened on history without the secure foundation of the current understanding in the transference.

Throughout the analysis of these issues the patient needs the experience of an understanding current object (the analyst) who goes with him to explore the dilemma of restriction (claustrophobia) or terror of new experience (agoraphobia).

From repeated transference and countertransference experiences, it seemed that the patient held the view that I admired his omnipotence as a proud mother wishing to identify with him. At other times I was made to feel a nonentity. I was subjected to living in this culture in which I either 'joined in' or was to be rejected. In this culture real work and achievement were dismissed as unimportant and omnipotence stole the credit.

The patient was responsible for constructing such a culture in the 'here and now' and analysis of this structure was my task. What was being relived was an interaction with internal objects built up in the past, and this needed to be reviewed and integrated. There were derivatives in the social culture in which he grew up, built initially on the earlier history in which his own omnipotence interacted with a mother who was in many ways a good caring historic breast, but also seemed to have fed his omnipotence with her Messianic worship of him and contempt for his father.

Considered in the context of these earlier and later relationships, the patient's current nature becomes more understandable to him. He does not have to feel either omnipotently responsible, or the helpless victim of his culture.

The second patient I wish to present is an unmarried woman, aged 28, who sought help in a state of suicidal depression, helplessness and total inability to work. She is the daughter of successful academic parents who married late in life. Her parents maintained a keen academic interest in psycho-analysis and were alleged to have 'analysed' the patient with 'sweet reason' as far back as she could remember.

From childhood she had undergone different analyses over many years. There was a history of succeeding academically and then dropping out at the last moment (final examinations). She changed career studies a few times and repeated the pattern. She was almost married on a number of occasions and broke off at the eleventh hour. The potential careers of the patient were felt to be not her own choices but those of her parents.

15

She formed a precarious intense attachment to me in her desperation, but became more remote when crisis was not pressing and she felt she could survive. She chose to embark on a course of study, yet had doubts as to whether it really was her own decision, and it seemed that she was not able to trust in her choice as representing her own wishes.

In many ways I could see her as a 'false self', 'as if' character who could not graduate and go out into the real world: someone who could become engaged but not married and committed to a real relationship, someone who could be academic but not live.

From early on in the analysis, when I interpreted to her what I believed to be her feelings, she would interrupt, analyse herself and demonstrate that she knew that her feelings were irrational and that she had to educate herself as to what was sensible and logical, so that no real experience of what she was feeling was allowed to develop. She 'got in' first in anticipation of what she thought was expected, wishing to show what a good analysand she was. In other words, the patient was making constructions designed to avoid meeting her real feelings and experiences. This suggested that perhaps she was reliving in the analysis a lifestyle in which 'educators' had made constructions to obviate feeling. She was propitiating and pleasing them, unconscious of her need for someone to be concerned about her feelings. This repeated pattern was followed by dreams of violent protest and it was a long time before I could show her the link in any way that she experienced as meaningful.

The complexities of this problem may be illustrated in the following dream. She lived in a house, though the exact whereabouts were not clear. The top area was occupied by a couple who claimed they lived there. She felt it to be her own apartment but she was not sure. The couple were very reasonable and understanding and even offered her the use of the accommodation, so that she began to feel she was probably in error and that they were the rightful owners and not herself.

The debate as to who was the rightful owner of her mind and my mind, and what came from where, was the subject of the analysis.

At this stage any reference to the past being reenacted in the present is, to say the least, useless. One may construct that a dialogue ensues with internal objects who, far from helping her to know herself and her rightful place, confuse her with ostensible kindness, such that the patient doubts her own judgement. This links with an experience in the transference of feeling 'analysed' by me with sweet reason. The issue is further complicated when the patient takes over the analysis with her own 'sweet reason' and does not allow me to contribute. Who is doing what to whom becomes a difficult problem.

16

Above all, I felt prevented from establishing a meaningful relationship. What I found most valuable was the use of this countertransference experience. I felt I was walking on eggshells, that any strong intervention which broke this pattern might produce collapse. I began to feel that what was governing the analysis was a sense of enormous frailty.

The patient occupied my mind with her 'sweet reason' analysis and I formed the impression that I was supposed to admire it and abandon my own views. I also felt that if I intervened I would disrupt her security and catastrophic breakdown might follow. She conducted herself in a way that prevented me from having intercourse with my own views so that I experienced that there was no accommodation for me as an individual. I could not come alive and express myself; I felt a wish to say 'shut up and listen to me', yet to do so would be disastrous. I seemed obliged to become a model of frail sweet reason.

If I did not give expression to myself, it felt that the analysis would be a disaster and I would lose my self-respect. Yet if I did give expression to my feelings, the analysis would also be a disaster and again I would lose my self-respect. It seemed we were in a *folie à deux* – two reasonable people keeping each other going and avoiding personal experience and feelings, with no individuality or real accommodation for living, as described in her dream.

I found myself making more extra-transference interpretations than usual, but it seemed to be the only means of reaching her. I formed the opinion that what was being relived was a parent/infant relationship which strongly conveyed that on no account were we to interact with real feeling since we both appeared to be too frail to do so.

Dreams occurred in which there were upturned boats with flaming red bottoms, but analysis of being turned upside down in flaming rage in either of us proved to be of only academic interest to the patient.

I formed the view that if we could not interact in the sessions then action would be likely to take place outside our relationship – acting out.

I also considered that the excessive extra-transference interpretations I made were a kind of acting out, action outside our relationship, and that this pattern was of long standing – a repetition of the past. It seemed that this non-relationship was considered by the patient to be superior to emotional interaction and that she feared that either or both of us would lose face if we responded with feeling. This necessitated the analysis of her belief that omniscience was superior to experiencing life.

By the time considerable work had been done on this problem and I felt that some strength had been gained, she reported that one of her tutors had exploded in rage with her. It appeared that she had argued her case with sweet reason and turned his boat upside down and he saw flaming red. She produced this account partly as though I was supposed to share her view of her tutor's unreasonableness and partly, I felt, with relief. I showed her how she provoked this reaction in the tutor, her sense of superiority and triumph in making him lose control, her fear of retribution, with the relief that this was now experienced as less dangerous; I considered that she needed to enact this outside because she believed that I was too frail to experience the emotions produced in the tutor. She believed my containment to be my avoidance of experience based on my frailty, a view she had of her parents. Though this was not the first time I had given such an interpretation, the fact that this had been enacted and survived seemed an important experience for her.

It seems to me that perhaps acting out often has this component: a relationship with a parent experienced as not interacting with genuine emotions. The introjection of an identification with such a parent makes expression of true feelings catastrophic. In this case frailty was disguised by acting as if the emotions of interaction could be totally contained, and the patient experienced what I considered to be my containment as my living this lie of a successful academic, just as she described her parents.

For a considerable time we worked at the problem of bringing the acting out back into the transference. When the analysis became more alive and she was able to experience more of her own feelings she rewarded me with material about a proposed acting out. She in fact sought to buy a book which she believed her parents would advocate but contrived to buy the wrong book wrapped in a thin envelope. Her aim was to return to the shop, insist she was deceived, be fobbed off with contrived reason and then sue the vendor for violating the Trade Descriptions Act.

Her prosecution was designed ruthlessly to expose the informants, myself and her parents, in the name of justice. She would prove that she had been provided in the past and present with the wrong education wrapped in a thin cover. Thus, she could be totally innocent, the frail victim of villainy; a masochistic device to conceal sadism. Patients so often become or create the very parents they hate. This issue, with all its projective and introjective identifications, requires careful analysis as a prime consideration.

The sado-masochistic fixation of clinging and hating, with a corresponding relentless superego, is a feature long known in psychoanalysis. It cannot be modified without detailed analysis and the experience of a new understanding object that goes with the patient, enabling a more loving and creative relation to develop. Reconstruction can uncover both constructive and unconstructive interactions with past objects. The bringing alive of past creative interactions and integrating these with creative constructions in the analysis and giving up the past grievances of negative relationships is the analytic work and life work – the value of reconstruction.

What is past environment and what is innate is always a complex problem in reconstructions and I would like now to look at this question by venturing some further reconstructions of the Oedipus myth. I am starting from the assumption that Oedipus failed to resolve his Oedipus complex (Klein, 1928).

We are told that Laius, father of Oedipus, was informed by the omnipotent gods that his son would kill him and marry his mother. Laius, with this belief, assumed that no human interaction could prevent the killing, that omnipotence is stronger than humanity. He abandoned his son to die.

We accept, following Freud, that the son's murderousness against his father and wish to marry the mother is a correct interpretation of Oedipus' propensities; one construction. It begs the question as to the behaviour of the father – is it a myth created by his son or a report of a real and severe infantile trauma, in which case we would understand Oedipus' need for revenge differently.

When Oedipus was rescued by the shepherd, he was brought up by the King of Corinth as if he were the King's son. We are told then that there are two fathers or two aspects of the father; one felt to care and attend to the needs of the oedipal child, another who sent him away, but there is no mention of the need for a caring mother. Considered from the point of view of what equipment Oedipus had to meet his Oedipus complex, it is difficult to imagine that any analyst would believe that he was furnished with a good enough environment or objects to deal with his problems at the start of life.

Freud used the Oedipus myth to give us profound insights into the sexual and aggressive nature of the child – an epoch-making construction of a genius. Later workers have added further dimensions to our understanding of the pre-oedipal factors that govern or modify earlier primitive instincts and processes.

We can construct a trauma theory that Oedipus was the victim of circumstances, or an instinct theory that he was totally responsible for his crime. In my view, the interaction between nature and nurture is of prime importance.

We could further argue that the later good experiences of Oedipus brought up by the King of Corinth were not enough to avert the tragedy. Likewise, however good an analyst may be, he may be powerless against the forces of the past. If we are to be more than a Greek chorus, then effective interventions are required. Psychoanalysis is based on the belief that the patient can be helped by knowledge and analysis of his own propensities. He also needs to know what modifies these propensities and what exacerbates them, in the present, and how this operated in the past – the analyst may thus wish to know the history of the patient. However, such knowledge is not properly usable except through the analysis of the repetition compulsion in the transference. In the case of the oedipal patient, the analyst has to bear the unbearable that Oedipus could not meet, and only after working this through can the patient have the strength to explore the past with the analyst, not as a historian, but as a Virgil – supporting the patient in his exploration. In this way we hope to help the patient to see himself and his parents without plucking out his eyes.

I have also tried to show that the analyst has experiences in the counter-transference which enable him to feel what the patient is going through and perhaps has gone through, and the nature of the transference objects available to confront issues. However good the analyst is, and however well he is internalized, the past objects and experiences, good and bad, are vitally necessary and need to be integrated with the analytic experience.

The compulsion of Oedipus to go back to the scene of the crime is operative in us all. Particularly at crises, patients regress to their previous patterns and object relationships. This is partly due to the breakdown of the internal analytic relationship, the reasons for which are manifold. Nonetheless, resolution is never complete and the bond of the past is powerful.

In the case of the female patient I described, after considerable improvement, she contemplated, prematurely in my view, ending analysis a year hence. She dreamed as follows.

She was taking a journey, walking in a new country reciting Latin verbs (the good pupil of the past with a dead language), and was in a state of depersonalization, looking at a mountain (breast) covered in snow (associated with coldness, drugs producing depersonalization, and the drugging parents who negated her individuality).

In such instances it is necessary not only to consider a current dismissal of analysis but also the fact that the moment the patient is confronted with fresh anxieties he, to some extent, goes back to the status quo ante.

I believe that acceptance of this as a fact of life may better equip the patient to meet these issues in the future so that some elements of self-analysis may continue, in which the patient can use such reconstructions as an implement in future self-understanding.

Perhaps like Oedipus, we all meet at the cross-roads confrontation with our parental figures embodied in Freud and our own analysts and teachers.

We need in our work with our patients, and in our construction of theories, constantly to review and reconstruct our own oedipal and pre-oedipal impulses, yearnings and grievances in order to prevent the murder of past objects and their contributions and not to be limited by defensive restrictions – the murder of new knowledge. We hope to recapture creative interactions and recreate new developments.

References

Freud, S. (1899) Screen memories. SE 3.
—— (1905) Three essays on the theory of sexuality. SE 7.
—— (1937) Construction in analysis. SE 23.
Klein, M. (1928) Early stages of the Oedipus complex. In *Contributions to Psycho-Analysis*. London: Hogarth/Institute of Psychoanalysis, 1948.

3

Separation:
a clinical problem

The problem of separation has long concerned the analyst who may observe marked changes in patients following weekend, holiday and day to day breaks. The analyst may also observe reactions to silences in the session, the quality of separateness and togetherness, normal and pathological, manifest in the daily work with the patient.

A relatively healthy patient faced with separation is ordinarily able to bear a certain amount of anxiety, frustration, greed, envy, jealousy and hatred. Such a patient has an internal picture of an analyst who is mindful of him, yet able to have mutually enjoyable intercourse with others. He experiences the analyst as someone concerned about the patient's life outside the analysis. This is not too distorted by excessive intrusion and pathological projective identification.

If the core of a good enough relationship between the patient and his objects is sufficiently established, then the analyst is in a position gainfully to show the consequences of separation. The analyst can show how the real creative relationship becomes disrupted during separation by feelings of jealousy, envy, frustration, etc. The analyst needs to preserve what has been achieved and analyse the pain, grief, and the destructive and defensive devices employed by the patient which destroy the meaningful achievements of the relationship. Thus the analyst can help to reestablish the good achieving aspects of the relationship and provide the patient with the opportunity to see what the destructive and defensive elements have done during separation. The patient then can mourn the loss, face the guilt about damage, and work at the reparative reconstruction of the truth. To achieve this the patient needs to be relatively healthy. Sometimes, however, the severity of the illness militates against this understanding, either more or less, or virtually *in toto*. It is to this problem that I am addressing myself.

The problem becomes more taxing when the analyst witnesses repeated reactions to separation which remain unrecognized by the patient.

The patient may act out: he may indulge in loveless sexuality, stuff himself with food, drink, hatred, criticisms and grievances to comfort himself. He may become excessively intrusive or, by virtue of projection, feel excessively intruded into by others. He may be occupied with continuous activity to avoid the experience of separation, plan moving house, dream of idyllic relationships or attempt to establish fusion and coalescence with objects. He may contrive menaces that need constant attention, occupy himself with paranoid activity, physical fitness, hypochondriasis and various kinds of masturbation. Separation is not consciously recognized. In order not to experience separation, compulsive attachments take place with various objects – exciting, hateful, idyllic, etc. – which require constant pathological attachment to avoid realization of what is missing.

The variety of defensive occupations is limitless. Such disturbing activities, which may merit attention in their own right, may be used to occupy analyst and patient in order to obscure the fact of the prime importance of separation. These devices ensure that there is no space (no separateness) in which to be aware of the issue of separation. The analyst may be aware that separation has catastrophic consequences. We are all familiar with the experience of witnessing the effects of separation and the difficulty of making this knowledge meaningful to the patient.

The clinical area I shall concentrate on is that of depressive illness – melancholia; and I would like to refresh our minds with some of the clinical observations of Freud (1917) and Abraham (1924).

The picture is one in which the patient feels hopelessly depressed, useless and futile. He feels judged by a superego with which he is in agreement: he is worthless, a thief and fraud, he has lived a lie and stolen undeserved approbation. The patient believes there are no redeeming features; he is unworthy of love and deserves to suffer and to be excommunicated.

Freud and Abraham were able to show at different times that the patient treated his objects in exactly the same way as his superego treated him. They further demonstrated that in the transference the analyst was treated with omnipotent contempt. Far from the patient being humble, commensurate with his description of himself as valueless, the analyst was in fact treated as a useless pretentious person not worthy of value or love; a meaningless person to be tortured and excommunicated. As the patient judges so is he judged. One may take the view that the patient was so judged by, say, his early objects and he now vengefully judges these objects. I shall not enter into the controversial issue as to which comes first. The clinical picture is one in which the patient and his internal objects are locked in this mutual escalating interaction – a pattern linked with sado-masochism and aggression based on oral cannibalism.

Freud pointed out that these patients are fixated to this type of object relationship and do not seek a better object: they are enmeshed in clinging and hating. That is to say, they are separated from a better object which, as far as their perception is concerned, does not exist.

Abraham was able to show that during the session these patients treat their object as if they own it (equating the object with faeces). For that reason they do not experience the proper loss of a love object. Because the object is owned, separation is regarded as the failure of the analyst to fulfil his obligations – he is a deserter, who neglects his duties and indulges in disgusting sensuous pleasures. Were the analyst to supply constant service, this would be taken for granted and only the deficiencies would be noted, as a cause for justifiable reproach – the patient would be separated from a sharing understanding relationship.

This pattern corresponds to the nature of the harsh superego. This supreme judge sees only moral faults, has no appreciation of the good aspects of the person and shows no consideration for the difficult cir-cumstances that lead to imperfections. The harsh superego expects total service, moral rectitude and absolute goodness as a matter of course and is justified in cruel punishment and banishment in the face of failure. It owns the patient like an omnipotent god requiring total surrender, obedience and worship. The patient treats his analyst in the same way.

During separation from a good enough human object the patient is not alone, he is in constant relationship with a torturing superego. If, in the transference, that superego analyst is all the patient has, then he is well advised to separate from it. But if he does he fears an absolute void inhabited by primitive persecutors: that is HELL. He cannot live with the analyst and cannot live without him.

Later workers, especially those of the Kleinian school, have shown that the primitive harsh superego is linked with a powerful narcissistic organ-ization which does everything in its power to prevent patient and analyst from having access to a good enough human object, rendering human understanding weak, frightened and contemptible. The forces at work attempt to SEPARATE both patient and analyst from relating in a way appreciative of normal love and creative human endeavour. Like all madness, its aim is to enter into sanity and take over. It separates access to sane judgement by its seductive ingenuity in persuading the subject that the humility of truth needs no allegiance. Guilt and concern, factors that stand up against such violations, are swept aside in contempt. As in the propaganda of war, truth is the first casualty.

24

Identification with this madness leads to the employment of defences that combine manic triumph and paranoia and separate the subject from human relationships. These defences are well known in the social history of man at war. In this situation the perpetrator is separated from the knowledge of true human values and the awareness of guilt over their destruction.

This gross activity is recognizable to the analyst. Nevertheless, subtle and less perceptible manic and paranoid defences may escape detection and may be used to avoid the awareness of the painful aspects of separation from a good human relationship. Similarly, other defences such as idealization, akin to mania, in which the analyst is invested with all the virtues that the patient identifies with, can be observed in their gross manifestations, but may be used in subtler ways to separate both analyst and patient from the truth and the awareness of its mutilation.

A vital and most telling feature shown by Freud was that in mourning the mourner knows what he has lost; in melancholia he must have lost a love object but the patient's perception is such that he does not know what he has lost: a factor of enormous clinical importance. I think we can add with confidence that these omnipotent destructive patients did not know the value of what they were getting from Freud and Abraham. This feature was explored by Melanie Klein (1957) where she demonstrated that the patient's attacks can result in a perception of the object as completely bad, and in her work on the destructive components of envy.

To summarize:

1 It takes some health and a good relationship in which to understand separation and to work through pain, loss and the preservation of good internalization.
2 In varying degrees, numbers of disturbed patients do not have sufficiently established helpful objects and parts of the self available. They cling and hate sado-masochistically and are separated from creative help. They are trapped in a vicious cycle.
3 They get inside their objects and are either fused with an ideal illusion or engaged in destructive intrusion and by projection feel invaded by persecutors.
4 In melancholia the patient believes there is no worthwhile goodness and is in the grip of a superego that makes him feel useless and worthless and that there is no good in others: he is separated from hope. Goodness is obviated and he believes it is a delusion, like a character in a Beckett play. In such cases the painful and bad elements are not necessarily issues of dispute in the analysis; it is the goodness in others and in themselves

which is denuded and they are separated from access to help and hope. In normal mourning melancholic elements are present but a person can draw from the goodness of loving supporters, their own love, and good memories, to initiate recovery. The melancholic is separated from such help and clings to grievances, as that is all he has.

5 These patients are separated from good help in the actual session and substitute idealization, fusion, grievance and excitation. They are cut off from a creative personal relationship and the 'psychoanalytic interpretation' is felt as devoid of the human endeavour that creates understanding. Thus there is no shared responsibility; one party is felt to be totally responsible and totally blameworthy. There is no valued creative relationship as a product of intercourse, in which the patient can feel that he and his analyst have something shared which needs preserving and developing.

The possibility of mutual satisfaction in development is missing. I wish to explore how the patient becomes separated from a helpful relationship and how he might recapture this. I shall try to illustrate some of the problems of interpreting separation anxiety clinically by reference to a patient who suffered from bouts of melancholia.

My patient is a presentable attractive Englishman aged 31. He was a day boy at a well-known public school and achieved well at a prestigious university. He is the only child of ambitious parents. They had lost considerable family wealth during the war, and his father was determined and successful at reestablishing the family wealth and social prestige. Both parents died of a tropical disease while abroad on a business trip when the patient was 25 years old.

The patient's initial account of his parents was that they were ambitious, authoritative and affectionless. According to the patient, his parents' major attention was devoted to ensuring that the patient would never be in a position in which he was poor and would feel himself to be a nonentity; instead he would be wealthy, successful and significant. The parents' contribution to the patient was to ensure success and there was little personal affection: the father was the important figure and the mother the willing servant, an ally in securing the family's place in society. This relentless picture was modified in the analysis but unconsciously governed the patient's thinking and is to some extent still present. The patient reported that if he failed in any way at school, the family were plunged into gloom and vituperative condemnation and rejection of him. The patient's account implied that he was separated from loving, concerned, helpful parents. I observed that he did not yearn for love and help but railed against his alleged deprivation and bad treatment and was strongly attached to such grievances. In the course of his analysis fonder memories were recovered.

The patient had episodes of minor breakdown at school when he was depressed, could not work, was considered a failure and was very nearly asked to leave his preparatory school on occasions. During these episodes he indulged in compulsive masturbation and compulsively went to the cinema.

His achievements at university were in a field of study in opposition to his parents' wish for him to become a businessman or enter into an establishment profession. His intellectual work, in which he achieved considerable success, included a detailed study of the destructive nature of authoritarian systems and a search for alternative solutions.

His first engagement broke down because his fiancée could not tolerate what she believed to be his omnipotent authoritative devaluation of her, and she left him. His first analysis also broke down. He suffered from severe depressive episodes with severe symptoms but managed to escape hospitalization or the breakdown of his career. Episodes of manic omnipotent triumph did not produce clinical breakdown but profuse intellectual activity which was well regarded in some quarters. The destructive manic elements were enacted in his relationship with women. There had been no proper mourning of his parents' death.

His analysis with me showed the character elements, as described by Freud and Abraham, operating at the earliest level of dependency, as described by Melanie Klein.

The material I am presenting is that of his return after a holiday break, in the third year of analysis. Prior to the break some positive and co-operative experiences and memories had been achieved. He returned conveying his reluctance in coming back to analysis after what he described at the time as a pleasurable holiday, though later it was found to be not so pleasurable. He gave me the impression that I would not be pleased to hear the good news about his holiday experiences and that I would wish to claim excessive significance for myself and would undervalue his achievements and pleasure. Mainly he conveyed it was a burden to come back to me.

He then reported two dreams. In the first dream he was climbing a mountain and gradually he discovered his wife was on his shoulders impeding his progress. He was furious that she had arrived there without asking and, in effect, without his knowing.

He then told me the second dream in which his wife claimed to have been raped, but in the dream he believed that she had seduced a man, and had made the false claim of rape; she wanted a penis inside her and refused to admit it. He was so furious that he hit her, not, as far as he could tell, out of jealousy, but because she would not admit her desire.

As I understood the dream, her need was sexualized and she claimed intrusion and he KNEW this was a lie. The responsibility for the cruel rapacious possessiveness was projected on to his wife who was accused of projecting these practices on to a third party.

I had reason to believe from his attitude to me on his return that he experienced me as having insinuated myself as a weight round his neck and that I was a heavy liability to carry. Furthermore, my view in relation to the second dream was that he felt I would put my oar in and insist that he missed me and wanted me. I considered that he believed I would rape his mind with my omnipotent interpretations and belittle him.

After interpreting along these lines he associated that his first dream reminded him of a time when he had taken a girlfriend up a mountain to show her the beauties of the view and he had got lost and had become very anxious. It was she who comforted him and helped him down. This seemed to be an invitation to me to show him that he was 'high' and wished to give me a marvellous view of himself and that I should comfort him and lead him down to terra firma. I had much material for interpretation. I interpreted the combination of his plea to be comforted and led down to earth, coupled with his claim that I would force myself upon him to insist on my importance. This I linked with past experiences in which he had described occasions when he had wanted to be comforted, but had accused the person comforting him of imposing.

He went on to describe his relationship with an academic friend in which he did not know if he talked too much or whether the friend was picking his brains for his own ends. That relationship was uncomfortable because he could not judge. I considered that part of him experienced the analysis as academic, devoid of personal feelings. I interpreted his dilemma with me and his need to know the nature of our relationship. He could not judge whether I was using him or whether he was talking and demanding too much, and I would find him burdensome. I pointed out that a state of affairs existed as in the dream – that it was difficult to come out into the open about desires or a need to be carried or helped.

He told me a further dream, dreamed during the holiday, which he now remembered. He was discussing interesting psychoanalytic issues with three distinguished and internationally known analysts. I was in another room and the door was closed. I was sitting quietly and made no attempt to intrude.

He gave no associations (no reference to International Conferences, about which he had no reason to be aware). The contention seemed to be that in the dream I was not banging on the door asking to be let in. It seemed that I was self-contained and could bear the experience of his being in such important company. It was obvious that he was 'where it was all happening', and I was excluded.

The most compelling feeling was that I was too contained to a point of indifference and displayed no feeling of exclusion, no jealousy and no curiosity. His only comment was that I was so composed – implying 'too composed' – thus living a lie. The lie being my denial of separation anxiety, my refusal to admit his meaning, and my omnipotent denial of jealousy and rage. He was thus analysed by an analyst parent who could not acknowledge separation problems in himself. I interpreted this experience of my indifference and my refusal to admit to feelings of exclusion and a wish to come in. I wondered in my own mind if the dream was elaborated now to draw attention to my relative inactivity in the session at this point.

He then told me that in the past when his mother had returned from journeys and had asked his father if he missed her, his father would brush the question aside as if insulted, and walk off. I interpreted that he believed, and he believed that I believed, that the admission of ordinary human missing of a person in a relationship was a loss of face and had to be dismissed, as the delusion of complete self-sufficiency was considered more important than human beings valuing each other – omnipotence contemptuous of human truth.

I also showed him that if the issue of 'loss of face' was so important either to him or to me, there was a dependency of an extreme order of omnipotent liars, who claimed total self-sufficiency, and he was thus separated from any experience of a truthful caring person who had the courage to admit ordinary human need. He had brushed this question aside, and did not know what he had lost, and was cut off from the good work and relationship built up before the holiday break.

It is my contention that only after this issue has been met and explored in detail can fruitful analysis of sado-masochism take place. That is to say, that while there was clear evidence of sado-masochism, say in the rape dream or his rejection of me and triumph over me in his intercourse with important analysts in the third dream, what was missing at that moment was the experience of a human caring relationship in which a mind was used for helpful and creative understanding. I believe that where this issue governs, interpretation of sado-masochism by itself is experienced by the patient as a meeting of cruel omnipotence with counter-omnipotence.

It is my contention that if the depressive feels that he has no personal meaning, he believes that omnipotence is the only means available to him. Likewise, if he gives no human meaning to his objects, only their punitive ruthlessness can be felt to be operative. A depressive has no faith in goodness. Goodness cannot be recaptured if a ruthless superego only shows how bad he is. For that is how the analyst is experienced by the patient and the patient cannot have an experience of a different analyst until he is helped to rediscover what he has lost.

In successful mourning, when the object is lost, the mourner initially feels desolate, bereft, hates the lost object for dying and feels in some way responsible. But by the process of mourning he recalls the good relationship he once had, cherishes that relationship, and cherishes the memory inside himself. He says goodbye to the external object and builds a memory to the past creative aspects of the relationship which assists in rebuilding new relationships, with people and work. He allows new experiences to nourish him and he mates with them.

This capacity to mourn separation and loss does not arise *de novo*. It has been built up before in a relationship with a mother who has dealt reasonably successfully with feeding after separation from the womb, and coped with the problem of frustration, greed and anxiety and negotiated these problems in a gainful way, enabling new developments to take place. The same process takes place at every weaning, including assisting the infant to bear the knowledge of the father's presence and the problems presented by new babies. Thus, these separations from the wished-for ideal and more fulfilling intimacies can be borne by problem solving, with a mother who assists the infant/child's creative mind in mourning and establishing new creations. The successful dealing with these problems promotes new development and the joy of creativity. The predominance of hatred and unrelieved unbearable anxiety, linked with insufficient help or the over-indulgence that negates the necessity of confronting these issues, weakens the capacity to mourn.

As I have said, the capacity to mourn and love does not arrive *de novo*, but has a history. I think this is what Abraham was concerned with when he wrote about the 'free period' in melancholia.

This patient demonstrated his ways of dealing with such issues in the actual session.

1 He could behave as if I did not exist and I had to bear the experience of exclusion and separation.
2 At times he could not bear any gap between a communication he made to me and my response. He demanded immediate engagement by me to obviate this experience, and would feel terribly neglected if there was the slightest space.
3 He contrived my attention in numerous issues to avoid our separateness.

4 He tried to inveigle me into a ménage à trois – himself, me and an object called 'psycho-analysis' in which we were to be continuously engaged 'talking shop' so that we would never get to know each other, a practice akin to that which had occupied him during the holiday separation and was illustrated in his 'holiday' dreams.

5 Problems which arose in our relationship could be 'cut out' and replaced by engagement with other business. This feature had occurred in past separations where he had cut out the knowledge of his fiancée, indulging in a brief affair and obliterating awareness that he was engaged. He likewise felt that I cut him out of my mind to such an extent that no part of him existed for me when I was engaged in other relationships.

6 Two consecutive sessions might follow in which either:

    a he behaved as if the previous session had not existed;

    b or, he continued straight on in the following session, from where he had left off in the previous one, as though the separation had not taken place.

I cannot discuss all the processes at work, but hope I have drawn attention to some of these elements in the three dreams – for example:

1 In the mountain climb dream he does not experience separation, but instead he is burdened by a wife who adheres to him.

2 In the second dream he is outraged by a wife who won't admit her need: by this means he avoids recognition of his needs, and denies responsibility for the cruel rapacious possessiveness.

3 In the third dream he does not experience separation, as he is with three important analysts and I am the left out person, and he watches my attempt to deal with the problem. In this dream he sees me as denying the pain of separation and living a lie.

It can be seen that the patient denied his own separation anxiety and was occupied with the way others allegedly denied separation and loss. He arranged to project separation problems into others and accused them of insinuating themselves into him, arranging alleged incidents of rape or displaying phoney self-containment. In the session he viewed me as using these devices. At the same time he watched with diligent observation to see how I dealt with separation from him both during absences and in the session itself. It seemed to me that he had no access to a model of a parent who could honestly confront separation and keep the good aspects of him alive – that is to say, he viewed his objects as not being able to achieve the depressive position.

The mother, parent, or analyst who cannot experience loss is thus separated from the knowledge of a good object that is needed. The mother is experienced as being both separated from the knowledge of the valuable aspects of her own baby, and cut off from contact with the baby part of herself which would enable her to empathize with her baby. This results in the feeling that the patient is nursed by an analyst mother who does not know what is needed and missing. At worst the patient may have the experience of a mother who might know what is missing, and the pain caused by loss, and who cruelly denies help to her own baby.

For this reason it is of vital importance that the analyst interprets the lost good parts of the relationship in detail, to provide an experience of a parent who can bear knowing what is lost and has faith in bearing this experience and recapturing lost good elements. The patient watches to test the analyst, in a climate of hopeful expectation, punctuated by doubt, vengeance, envy and omnipotent contempt. In short, the demonstration by the analyst of dealing with loss and separation must be provided when the sado-masochism and omnipotence are interpreted. Therapeutic change comes about through a 'change of heart' when the good part can bear knowing what is lost for whatever reasons.

The pain of deprivation in the past through absence of provisions, and through the destruction of objects, is the most crucial feature of any analysis, and the success of the outcome depends on how well this is met and worked through. Time does not allow me to explore what is ultimately the main problem. However the foundations for being able to work through the pain, and depression and guilt over the responsibility of destruction, can only be established if the analyst keeps his own contact with separation anxiety and withstands the pain of maintaining this course when bombarded with rejection, contempt and reproach, and is able to analyse and link these attacks with the experience of separation.

Melanie Klein, writing 'On the sense of loneliness' (1963), states:

> A harsh superego can never be felt to forgive destructive impulses; in fact, it demands that they should not exist. Although the superego is built up largely from a split-off part of the ego on to which impulses are projected, it is also inevitably influenced by the introjection of the personalities of the actual parents and of their relation to the child. The harsher the superego, the greater will be loneliness, because its severe demands increase depressive and paranoid anxieties.

Severely depressive patients are lonely and do not know they are lonely – as Klein states, 'they yearn for an unattainable perfect state'.

I would like to add that in my patient, because the good enough relations and feelings were 'cut out', so the demand for perfection was always dominant. The establishment of a mother who can love in spite of the loss of perfection and mourn its loss, who can bear loss and forgive destructiveness, is an essential experience. The need for an analyst who, in Bion's terms, speaks the language of achievement rather than the language of blame is a *sine qua non*.

To recover those good aspects of the parents, objects, analyst and the self that are lost is essential work in analysis. This can only be achieved if the analyst's orientation is based on showing the importance of these elements – for without their presence and operation there is little to modify the omnipotent destructiveness, the harsh superego, or to provide a viable alternative to idealization. The analyst needs to show what the patient is separated from, when the patient is not conscious of this factor.

The analyst needs to provide the strength to withstand the omnipotent contempt, and resist the power of the repetition compulsion, where the analyst is 'blue-printed' to act out the sadistic moralizing, or the masochistic pseudo-tolerance, or to supply an ideal delusional provision to obviate problems.

The analyst's emphasis on what the patient is separated from, and the analyst's capacity for continued contact with the 'good enough' human endeavour, enable the problem of separation, in and out of the session, to be tackled in a meaningful way.

References

Abraham, K. (1924) Notes on the psychogenesis of melancholia. In *Selected Papers of Karl Abraham*. London: Hogarth Press, 1927, pp. 453–464.

Freud, S. (1917) Mourning and melancholia. SE 14.

Klein, M. (1935) A contribution to the psychogenesis of manic-depressive states. In *Contributions to Psychoanalysis*. London: Hogarth Press, 1948, pp. 282–338.

—— (1957) Envy and gratitude. In *Envy and Gratitude and Other Works*. London: Hogarth Press, 1975, pp. 176–235.

—— (1963) On the sense of loneliness. In *Envy and Gratitude and Other Works*. London: Hogarth Press, 1975, pp. 300–313.

4

Matters of life and death –
real and assumed

This is an attempt to present in a brief paper views that have been germinating over a long period: the ideas are based on the work of Freud, Klein and Bion.

I would like, from the outset, to state that it is my belief that the impact of the life and death instincts on the human mind are so powerful and overwhelming, and require such defences to cope with these forces, that our capacity to understand them is limited and distorted. I also believe that the provision of human object relationships makes it *more* possible to understand these forces, to contain and be aware of them and thus to enable the achievement of some awareness of the truth about life and death instincts. At the same time, these object relationships are themselves subject to the forces of life and death and thus distortions of understanding take place, initiated both by the power of the impact of the infant on the mother and of the mother on the infant. This applies also of course to subsequent relationships. I hope in the course of the paper to be able to throw some light on both these problems – the limits of understanding, the need for a relationship to improve understanding, and how that relationship can be influenced, and indeed, corrupted, by defences coping with life and death instincts.

I shall start with a condensed view of Freud's work, partly for historical interest and partly because I find his structural formulations a necessary foundation on which to build my thinking. Freud did in fact link his structural views with an object relationship theory, and, as we know, Melanie Klein made the object relationship central to her thesis.

It seems to me useful to consider the scientific climate at the time when Freud presented his views on the death instinct. I find it difficult to read 'Beyond the pleasure principle' without feeling that Freud considered his

34

ideas on the life and death instincts to be enormously important. Although he prefaced his views by saying that 'it is a far fetched speculation', I believe that Freud had little doubt about the universal biological and psychodynamic significance of his work.

Some ten years later, when writing 'Civilisation and its discontents', Freud wrote on his theory of life and death instincts:

> To begin with, it was only tentatively that I put forward the views I developed, but in the course of time they have gained such a hold on me that I can no longer think in any other way. To my mind they are more serviceable from the theoretical standpoint than any other possible one; they provide that simplification, without either ignoring or doing violence to the facts for which we strive in our scientific work.
>
> (SE, 1930, 21: 119)

Freud considered that these theories in no way invalidated other theories and that they were of primary importance and basic to the understanding of mankind. Melanie Klein and her co-workers believed these views to be of clinical importance.

The opposition to the death instinct theory and the contention that it was unscientific and unpsychoanalytic produced many so-called psychoanalytic explanations of Freud's alleged aberration. The favourite of these was the contention that Freud's theory was a consequence of his reaction to the death from influenza of his daughter Sophie. In fact, when Freud wrote 'Beyond the pleasure principle' in autumn 1919, Sophie was in perfect health. Freud, anticipating the adverse response to his views, asked Max Eitingon to certify that 'Beyond the pleasure principle' was written when Sophie was in good health.

Freud had associated the aggressive impulses with self-preservative instincts or ego instincts in 1915 in 'Instincts and their vicissitudes', in which he dealt with the polarity of love and hate. In 'Beyond the pleasure principle' he gave the aggressive impulse independent status as the primal death instinct, divorcing it from both libidinal and self-preservative (ego) instincts.

In 'Beyond the pleasure principle' Freud explored the role of the pleasure principle and questioned whether it occupied the role of primacy. His account of the cotton reel game led him to the view that there was in operation a tendency beyond the pleasure principle, more primitive and independent of it. I believe that the 'cotton reel game' is open to alternative interpretation. Freud went on to develop, to my mind, a work of great genius in which he explored his views on the role of the life and death instincts.

35

These views were revolutionary. In essence, the repetition compulsion was cited as a compulsion for an organism to return to the inorganic state – the earlier state – an involution. Later in the paper he implied another compulsion: a compulsive evolution in which life is repeated with its new developments – a compulsion for evolution and a compulsion for involution.

On the issue of the repetition compulsion to return to the inorganic state, Freud wrote: 'It seems that an instinct is an urge, inherent in organic life to restore an earlier state of things which the living entity has been obliged to abandon under the pressure of external disturbing forces.' One forms the impression that living entities are 'willy-nilly' forced into life only to return to the inorganic state. Freud later states: 'There is no exception, everything dies for internal reasons – becomes inorganic once again.' Freud further states: 'The aim of all life is death.' He considered this to be the universal rule; only the sex instincts could preserve life by reproduction. Although this theory refers to the individual entity being programmed for inevitable death and reproduction ensuring the creation of new life, Freud does not take up the interaction between these themes as part of his scientific theory on dynamic motivation.

On the operation of life and death instincts, Freud writes: 'The germ cells (sexual) work against the death of living substance and succeed in winning potential immortality, though that may mean only lengthening the road to death.' He writes: 'the most impressive proof of organic compulsion to repeat life is the phenomenon of hereditary and the facts of embryology'. He goes on to say: 'We see how the germ of a living animal is obliged in the course of its development to recapitulate (even if only in a transient and abbreviated fashion) the structures of all forms from which it sprung instead of proceeding by the shortest path to its final shape.' In Freud's account of embryological development, he notes that old systems do make way for the new. In this statement Freud implies quite the opposite of a narcissistic process by the implication of the significance of new development.

To sum up so far:

1 We are programmed to go through an evolution where life proceeds and develops (barring intervention).
2 We are programmed for involution leading to death – nothing can prevent this.
3 We are programmed to go through evolution in embryological development where earlier forms die, give way and promote new creations.

4 The new replaces the old and also dies.
5 Sexual reproduction ensures the repetition so that individuals die but are capable of new creations.

The question I raise and to which I shall return is: are there psychodynamic parallels which are important to take into account in our theory and practice?

We can speculate about the dynamics of producing such a theory and we can also speculate about the dynamics of opposition to such a theory. I have decided not to explore this issue in this paper, but I would welcome discussion.

To proceed with the next section of my paper. As a preliminary remark, I would stress that I do not understand Freud's views on the death instinct to signify merely a return of the organism to the inanimate. He makes ample reference to the destructive component of the death instinct operating from the beginning of life with the most fruitful statements and implications. Although Freud does not spell out the impact of the life and death instincts on the early ego, his implications are far-reaching. It is this area that this section will attempt to explore – that is, the role of life and death instincts in the DEVELOPMENT OF THE INDIVIDUAL.

Freud went a lot further than his speculation about life and death as universal biological phenomena. He introduced his views concerning the role of life and death instincts in the individual at first by discussing the unicellular organism. He pointed out that the living cell had a protective insulating 'crust' that protected it from stimulation of the powerful energies from the outside. This cell wall formed a protective shield which allowed some life-giving communication to pass through, but not the full force of outside energies. Otherwise, the cell would be KILLED. That is, the protective shield of DEAD MATTER filtered communication and protected life from the certain death which would follow were it more exposed.

Freud further postulated that in multicellular organisms some cells die and by so doing protect vital cells in the organism. He said that some cells sacrifice themselves for the sake of others.

My interest in this phenomenon, which led me to re-read 'Beyond the pleasure principle', was stimulated by an interest in the notion of the function of the skin. Biologically, the skin negotiates between inside and outside. In order to form a skin, the outer layers of which are made up of cells that have DIED, enough dead cells have to be laid down to protect the individual from damage. But if there are too many dead cells, this prevents the communication of light, nutrition and sensory experience required in appropriate 'doses' to promote life. In addition we know that appropriate heat loss, sweating, etc., is essential for life. Too much insulation or too little will lead to death. As I understand this, if we are too 'thin skinned' we die, and if we are too 'thick skinned' (scleroderma) we die. I use the connotation of 'thick skinned' and 'thin skinned' deliberately, to evoke questions of psychodynamic equivalents. What I am leading up to, of course, is the nature of psychological defences, their role as a necessity for survival and their destruction of psychic life.

This process runs throughout the biology of the individual body – for example, white blood cells sacrifice their life to combat ever-present infection; if we have too few, we die from deficiency; if too many, we die of leukaemia.

The balance of life and death forces determines the nature of development in the individual. Both forces – life and death – are essential for the development of life of the individual. Defences are necessary for survival and an excess produces deadliness.

Freud took the great imaginative leap of suggesting that this formulation could be applied to the understanding of the mental apparatus. Whilst he did not use the analogy of skin, I feel this to be implied. He postulated that the cerebral cortex, derived from the ectodermal layer in embryological development, also had this protective function. Insulation against excessive stimulation operated and protected the psyche from overwhelming stimuli in order to allow enough stimulation to take place and promote functioning and life. Freud went further – he postulated that excitation coming from WITHIN was also excessive (too much for the psyche to cope with) and was dealt with by projection. Once projected, these stimuli were insulated from returning by a further protective shield to prevent overwhelming stimulation. It seems to me that this concept is analogous to Melanie Klein's view of the paranoid-schizoid position. The death instinct is projected outwards and the return of the death instinct which threatens annihilation is defended against by an insulating layer. This notion implies that the threat of murderous persecution is warded off. In Melanie Klein's concept, as I understand it, the paranoid-schizoid position supposes projection of the death instinct outwards and its return threatens persecution and fragmentation. Freud's concept of the deadening protective shield gives a further dimension to the term schizoid – a feature one observes in excessively schizoid personalities.

For me a most interesting question is: is the 'protective shield' of semi-dead cells a result of the partial killing off of parts of the organism? The parallel questions as regards psychic life would be: do psychological defences partly KILL our perceptual apparatus and is this a necessary DEFENCE in development? This killing of awareness in *part* is necessary for survival; if

38

excessive, it results in mental and emotional deficiency that destroys psychic life.

I will pause here to recapitulate these notions. If this formulation is reasonably correct or useful, it can be summarised as follows:

1 Exposure to outside stimuli is too much to be tolerated.
2 The impulses from within – in this case the death instinct (this applies to all instincts) – are too much to tolerate.
3 Projection is necessary for survival (I will deal later with projection as a communication).
4 Insulation protects us from outside stimulation and the return of the projected death instinct.
5 The very insulation we employ ensures that we limit our KNOWING as knowing can only be tolerated up to a certain point. (I will deal later with the replacement of knowledge by delusion.) Fuller knowing is only possible to experience later in development, and only with the assistance of a human relationship which provides help and enquiry and insight.

Before I proceed to the main issue of this paper – the role of object relationships in dealing with life and death instincts – there are two other issues on which I will briefly comment.

The first issue is to raise questions about the insulating layer that protects the psyche from overwhelming and destructive experience. If what Freud says is true, and it does seem so to me, part of our perceptual apparatus is deadened as a defence. We then have to consider that the killing of awareness, and thus deadening of capacity to be aware, is partly necessary to allow further life experience to take place. It is not only the psychotic who attacks the perceptual apparatus as a means of coping with unbearable experience; to some degree this applies to us all. Thus, the later experiencing and learning, of that which seems to be nearer to truth, has to encounter both the destruction of truth and the destruction of our perceptual capacity. I will not explore this in detail but refer in some measure to this issue later on. It corresponds to Bion's views on +K and −K.

This raises the question of the nature of all defences employed by the psyche. Whilst external reality may or may not be changed by defences, the perception of reality is changed. All defences create a delusion or illusion and cannot operate without corruption and mutilation of the perceptual apparatus. I do not know whether this was Bion's view, but the views I put forward derive from his writing. Later in the paper I will refer to the operation of this process in the context of an object relationship.

The second issue that seems to be important is to examine what we mean by sexuality. In Freud's view, it is sexuality that carries the life instinct. In this context sexuality means the creation of new life – he did not mean merely sensuous pleasure. Furthermore, the creation of sexuality does not stop at sexual intercourse, it is an ongoing process that produces new life that the mother and father continue to relate to. In short, like all processes, it is a cycle, not a single event.

The concept of sexuality arriving on the scene later in development is referred to by Freud in 'Beyond the pleasure principle'. He writes:

> Even though it is certain that sexuality and the distinction between the sexes did not exist when life began, the possibility remains that the instincts which were later to be described as sexual may have been in operation from the very first, and it may not be true that it was only at a later time that they started upon their work of opposing the activities of the Ego instincts.

Freud was referring to the beginning of life in the process of evolution. However, as he thought that there were the earlier precursors of sexuality in evolution in the development of the individual, it can be argued that early sexuality operates at the beginning of life. The nature of that 'sexuality' and its operation was not defined. I shall refer to my views on this issue later in the paper.

The role of object relationships in dealing with life and death instincts

In Freud's speculations about the life and death instincts he did not explore the role of early object relationships. The views I put forward are based on the work of Melanie Klein and her co-workers. In this view the instincts of life and death operate from the beginning, as Freud postulated. Melanie Klein believed that there is a perceptual apparatus capable of experience, an ego (however rudimentary) from the beginning of life, and that this ego is capable of some perception of an object which is introjected. The operation of projection into the object leads to re-introjection of the projections. These (if all goes well) are modified by good experience so that an increasing awareness of self and object can be an ongoing development.

Furthermore, in this view, a form of sexuality operates from the beginning in a variety of ways. There is an equation of nipple–mouth with penis–vagina and container–contained. The mother receives projections and the creative life-giving process is her creative endeavour in mating with the projections to enable nourishment and new development to take place.

As I understand it, there is an intercourse between the mother and baby, physical and psychical, that results in a new creation, the relationship. This relationship creates something new and unique that promotes survival, a new understanding and development. This new creation has its own life and capacity to engage in further creative matings – the transferring of internal object relationships capable of repetition, modification and new developments.

The first area to which I will refer, is the way in which, I believe, the early object relationship between mother and infant corresponds to Freud's theory of life and death instincts and the protective shield. A reasonably intuitive mother (and analyst) attempts to promote growth in the infant by exercising judgement as to how much stimulation and experience are appropriate, dosing the infant accordingly. The mother holds, protects, shields and provides adequate experience. She prevents catastrophic exposure but provides what is felt to be helpful. The mother provides this, not only to deal with external stimulation, but to cope with internal demands; forging the infant's capacity to experience more and more is part of the mother's task. How the mother acquires this intuition and her confidence in that intuition are beyond the scope of this paper.

As no relationship can provide perfect help, there is a residuum of unnegotiated impulses which leads to the formation of defences produced in the infant.

The mother, providing a physical and psychological breast (or equivalent) and a human mind container, picks up projections and provides what is required. This relationship is not passive, but is a to and fro intercourse. Freud postulated that all instincts strive for complete satisfaction; this, I believe, is undoubtedly true. The desire for nourishment, sensual and libidinal satisfaction to the nth degree takes place with aggressive assertion. The infant projects the death instinct and the mother looks after the fear of death and of persecutors.

In the course of this interaction there is a rudimentary concept that the infant is relating to an idealised object with which he fuses and which he feels he owns. This is of course an omnipotent delusion which aims at optimum gratification as well as the projection of catastrophically danger- ous death instinct components into a persecutory breast. The combination of omnipotent projection and splitting is used in the service of survival.

The reliving of the yearning for the 'ideal state' recurs in life – a common example being the state of falling in love and in such a state the experience is in varying degrees perceived as a matter of life and death. The capacity to work through this illusion depends on what equipment the lovers carry with them to create a more real relationship.

The particular area I have chosen to focus on is the omnipotent delusion in the paranoid-schizoid position – a delusion which insulates the infant from the truth of dependency and threat of catastrophe; by the construction of the idealised breast, the baby experiences complete satisfaction and fulfilment. This powerful constellation not only deflects the death instinct outwards but contains the belief that the threat can be eliminated and an ideal state achieved. I believe that, to some extent, the mother shares this delusion.

If we ask the question, how does the mother help the baby to some degree to give up this primitive position and move to reality, then I think a good deal depends on the mother's capacity to negotiate this issue.

The mother uses her empathic capacity to identify with the baby and then moves from a state of 'being in love' with the baby to maturity. The mother's capacity for empathy enables her to 'tune into' the baby's state of mind. The baby's limited capacity to tolerate true experience depends a great deal on the mother's capacity to encounter anxiety. The mother herself has limited tolerance of perception. The mother's capacity to tolerate the truth depends in turn on the quality of her 'sexual' relationship with her objects and their equivalents in relation to internal objects. If this goes well, then the mother is assisted in helping the baby to form an intercourse in which a more realistic relationship develops. Thus, the primitive way of coping with issues of life and death becomes partly transformed and the value of a loving object relationship modifies the earlier system. The mother's joy in this 'intercourse' promotes a new mode of life with faith and hope. On the other hand, the mother's fear, hatred and hopelessness in this encounter militates against this and reinforces belief in the primitive defences as the only means available to ensure survival.

The point I am making is, what was once a truth (omnipotence, projection of death instincts, insulation and delusion) as a means of saving life, becomes a falsehood as the human truth born out of a 'depressive position, love' becomes more realised. The interpretation of what is and what is not a life and death issue depends on this movement.

To illustrate the complexity of this problem, we might attempt to examine what happens if the realistic (depressive position) relationship breaks down. To put the question more correctly: 'What happens when a precariously established realistic relationship breaks down?'

For example, we might look at a case of drug addiction. Here we may find that the ongoing precarious realistically loving relationship breaks down and the person turns to drugs. The drug in turn produces consequences. The awareness of external and internal reality is attacked by use of the drug, and a deadening of perception of reality takes place. Together with attacks on perception, the realisation of the value of a human relationship dealing with truth is also destroyed. The old system of killing perception, the creation of an idealised fusion and the obviation of persecutors is resurrected. The addict destroys true perception at a conscious level. The addict achieves delusional coalescence but, above all, kills the realisation of the value of a realistically human object which could be his salvation. By reverting to the *ancien régime* he believes he is 'dying for a fix' to bring him alive. This is a truth as far as the addict's perception is concerned, but, in fact, becomes the death of him.

Milder addictions, 'dying for a drink' or smoke, etc., do not become catastrophic if the return to the more valued mature human relationship predominates. One does not of course need a pharmacological drug to produce this effect. A delusion, especially if it is shared, can effect the same results. For example, a manic or paranoid defence may show the same mechanism – possession of all the good, projection of the bad – but can only exist if the perceptual apparatus capable of perceiving a more truthful version is sufficiently deadened, and with it the murder of the value of a more truthful human relationship (depressive position). As we know, the more perverse the relationships that are established that support the murder of truth and the feeding of a delusion, the more food for corruption nourishes the madness.

The point I make again is that what was once a truth (omnipotence, projection, insulation and delusion) as a means of saving life, becomes a lie.

The acquisition of nourishment that promotes life

The acquiring of nourishment physical and psychical to develop life contains creative (sexual) and primitive elements. The imbibing of milk and psychological help enables the development of new life in the baby: and the appreciative incorporation by the infant and the appreciative fulfilment of the mother establishes an ongoing mutually creative relationship. In introjection, that which is taken in mates creatively to promote further life and creative development – an earlier form of sexuality.

The operation of the primitive elements of cannibalism as described by Freud, Abraham and Klein contains devouring components that in various degrees kill and eat. The psychic equivalents are omnipotence and omniscience. In other words, the 'good breast' is not only loved, but devoured

43

and destroyed, and although interaction between mother and infant can increase or decrease propensities that facilitate the love of life or its murder, it is the belief of Melanie Klein and Freud and Abraham that both these positive and negative drives are innate.

The coming together of the primitive cannibalism and the love of life and of its providers, if successfully negotiated, helps to establish the depressive position. In this position there is regret at damage done and reparation ensues. This heightens awareness of the value of life and the pain of loss. The nature of successful mourning is in itself a creative (sexual) act in which the lost object is installed in memory and the relationship with this internal object results in internal creative intercourse. Those areas which fail to establish integration are dealt with by splitting and projection, so that side by side with integration the primitive forces operate.

The projected split-off primitive elements are not only feared but revered. It is my belief that the earlier patterns, in which the primitive ways of dealing with life, death and survival are yearned for, may be given priority. The corruption that takes place to give these elements a justifiable morality (partly to obviate guilt) leads not only to worship of such processes: they are deemed necessary for survival as in the worship of primitive 'gods' which demand human sacrifice. They are felt to be the source of life and the delusional belief in them is given precedence. The projection and idealisation lead to the need to propitiate these 'gods' and make human truths an inferior construction: this corrupts human moral values.

I would like to illustrate some of these features with a brief clinical example, in a not too ill patient – a married man in his thirties, a community lawyer suffering from bouts of depression of a moderately severe form.

He is in his third year of analysis. He arrives in the consulting room, 'plonks' himself on the couch (I think with a feeling of relief) and says: 'Everything is too much, I feel like fading out.' He tells me he just wants me to be there and say nothing, and conveys that it is 'all too much' and that I (the analyst) will only add to his burden if I speak. He reiterates that it is best if I am quiet and he is left alone.

He then gives me a horrendous account of having had to cope with two delinquent clients who are a terrible trouble. The frightening culmination of his story is that at one point during his interview one of the clients locked the door and then stood over him with an air of such menace that he felt that if he made one wrong move he could be murdered. He was petrified with fear but managed somehow to cope with the situation.

I had little reason to doubt his story but of course could not judge the degree of threat of murder that actually confronted him.

44

What I felt reasonably sure about was that whatever murderous intervention he might fear from me, he consciously felt reasonably secure with me. I could not judge whether he feared that I would deny his experience, exacerbate his anxiety and open up dreads that he felt best left alone.

After a short period of silence he added: 'What can you do with these people [the two clients]? They are so deprived of basic support and don't even know it. How can anyone begin to deal with them?'

The patient's ability to bring together his wish to blot everything out (and to see my intervention as an additional threat), and to perceive the need for basic support (and the tragedy of persons who do not know they need help), makes interpretation possible and brings relief. His wish for insight and help was stronger at that time than his desire to obviate awareness. Unlike a more ill patient, he does not greatly destroy my value and the contribution I can make, at least at a more conscious level.

Later in the session he tells me about having dinner the previous evening with a distinguished lawyer – a friend of his father. This lawyer spoke with erudition and finesse, quoting from French and German, which my patient could not follow. My patient felt so shabby and inadequate, ignorant and useless, that he wished the floor would open and swallow him up and he lost all confidence in himself. This hopeless feeling predominated in spite of my patient knowing that this distinguished lawyer suffered from depressive breakdowns in which he had revealed himself as an omnipotent pretender on many occasions. It was only on the way home that his wife, reminding him of this, helped him to recover his composure. Even though this distinguished lawyer was known to be an expert underminer, my patient fell under his spell and became an adulating victim. I will not go into the reasons why my patient was so vulnerable and to what extent he saw me as the undermining lawyer, or what devices he used to make me feel undermined in my capacity to contribute to our dialogue. What I wish to emphasise is that the patient's capacity to engage in his work was undermined, not only by the horrendous issues in his deprived clients, but also by his internal object that did not work with him to encounter issues, but made him feel that what equipment he had available for use was deplorably mundane and valueless. In other words, he was slavishly enmeshed with an idealised object (partly himself) and the helpful intercourse between good parts of himself and me was undermined.

His belief that he suffered from inadequacy and depletion was a defence against awareness of envy of true human creativity. Melanie Klein believed envy was part of the death instinct. The patient's envy of his object's ascribed self-sufficiency screened his awareness of an object's capacity to develop a mating, creative (sexual) relationship.

I introduce this small (oversimplified) vignette to link with another issue pertaining to life and death issues. That is, the very human objects (originally the breast and its psychic equivalents) are on the one hand used to encounter the issues of life and promote growth, and on the other hand, attacked and cannibalistically devoured and robbed of their value.

I will approach this issue obliquely. If we look at our patients dominated by a harsh superego which judges them for their wrongs and deficiencies and has the effect of making them feel totally worthless and bad, with no redeeming features, and question the reasons for the submission to and worship of such a superego, we are obliged to ask some questions. Why does this superego not ask for reparation, but virtually demand 'human sacrifice'? Why is such a superego worshipped as a supreme judge? What right has this judge to make such exorbitant super-human demands? Why are such primitive 'gods' given such a status and why do persons propitiate these 'gods' as if they are the source of life and death and annihilation will ensue if such a judge is not fully satisfied?

I am only able to see this as the split-off infantile cannibalism that not only demands total satisfaction and omnipotent worship but feels justified in exacting horrendous punishment if the wishes are not fulfilled. That is to say that there is a cannibalistic impulse suffused with envious greed that perverts the truth, evades modification by the depressive position, believes in 'divine right' and is split off, denied and worshipped.

King Lear, of course, was forthright in his demands when he gave up his kingdom. He required total worship and banished the good enough daughter. Such overt practice, usually the prerogative of kings and spoiled children, is not on the whole overt except in leaders who are given special status. The corruption of truth, which is necessary to vindicate such demands, leads to the death of others.

All such practices are, in my view, anti-sexual in the broadest sense. It is only the intercourse of different persons who recognise they need each other in order to create, that can modify this primitive process. Sexist, racist, elitist patterns are designed to establish the primitive processes that were once a matter of survival, but if not modified by the truth of 'mutual sexuality', become the murderer of truth and persons.

Corruption of the truth about issues of life and death is what we are confronted with in our daily work. The ramifications are extensive and I make only a limited reference in this paper. I think it is fitting to note how much sexuality as an enjoyed creative act has been the subject of vilification. It is also worth noting that sexuality governed by violence, sadism and the negation of human creativity may become elevated and considered to be essential. The sexual deviant will so often turn to dehumanised sensuous pleasure as a salvation, felt as essential to life, with a corresponding impoverishment of the knowledge of what is more meaningful and creative.

The most important area – the combination of 'catastrophe and denial' and its oscillation, which is the predicament of the baby coping with issues of life and death – can replace thinking about the real issues of life and death. We know as analysts that whilst omnipotence and primitive destruction can be executed by a single person, constructive (sexual) achievement requires the intercourse of the creative forms in two persons building together. I think Freud is right when he says that only the sexual instinct ensures life and creativity. Even the interaction between primitive and human (depressive position) is creative. Hanna Segal, in her paper on 'Aesthetics', shows that this intercourse produces creative art as opposed to sterile, 'idealised art'.

I have attempted to give some views on what helps and hinders the movement to realistic creative human truth. I have also given some views on the breakdown of creative relationships leading to the resurrection of primitive patterns of dealing with life and death issues.

I have not had time to speak in any detail of factors that corrupt human truth. I would like to emphasise again that the breakdown of human creative intercourse, starting from the beginning of life, not only leads to the regression to primitive 'thinking', but that the primitive way of dealing with life and death issues brings with it an insulating layer of killed perceptions so that insight cannot be used and the primitive patterns are reinforced. It is this process of the deadening of the awareness of the destructive nature of the death instinct, which is anti-life, and its projection and denial which attribute the death instinct to outside forces, that engages us in our daily work.

References

Bion, W.R. *Elements of Psycho-analysis*. London: Tavistock Press, 1963.
—— *Transformations*. London: Tavistock Press, 1965.
Freud, S. Instincts and their vicissitudes (1915) SE 14: III.
—— Beyond the pleasure principle (1920) SE 18: 3.
—— Civilisation and its discontents (1930) SE 21: 59.
Klein, M. *Contributions to Psycho-analysis 1921–1945*. London: Hogarth Press, 1948.
—— *Envy and Gratitude*. New York: Basic Books, 1957.
Segal, H. 'A psycho-analytical contribution to aesthetics', *International Journal of Psycho-Analysis* 32 (1952).
Sulloway, F. *Freud: Biologist of the Mind*. London: Andre Deutsch, 1979.

5

Cruelty and narrowmindedness

In normal development love modifies cruelty; in order to perpetuate cruelty, steps have to be taken to prevent human love from operating. My contention is that in order to maintain the practice of cruelty, a singular narrowmindedness of purpose is put into operation. This has the function of squeezing out humanity and preventing human understanding from modifying the cruelty. The consequence of this process produces a cruelty which is 'inhuman'.

If we consider the Oedipus myth from the angle of the role played by the gods, we can follow this process. The god Apollo had ordained that Oedipus would kill his father Laius and marry his mother Jocasta. No mortal, that is, human, intervention could be proof against the gods' prediction. Here we see the omnipotent narrowminded persistence: nothing can stand in the way of the omnipotent gods' determination.

Laius' only hope was that Oedipus would not survive. Here we see counter-cruelty presented as the only solution. Oedipus was delivered to a shepherd with orders to abandon him on a mountain; but human compassion, the antidote to cruelty, intervened, as the shepherd had not the heart to do this and entrusted the child to a Corinthian shepherd. But this humanity was of no avail.

As a result of cruel destiny, Oedipus killed his father on his journey to escape patricide, emphasizing again the impotence of human understanding. After marrying Jocasta, Oedipus had to root out his father's murderer, and pursued this course with persistent vigour, excluding all human counsel. The tragic revelation led to his plucking out his eyes, and his abandonment to cruel exile.

What this myth shows, over and above the accepted interpretation, is that the powerful omnipotent gods are determined to triumph over human compassion and understanding, and this in itself prompts counter-cruelty. The revelation of guilt likewise leads to the relentless cruel judgement of loveless exile, with the deprivation of human comfort; equivalent to the cruelty of the superego. Some human comfort was, however, derived from his daughter Antigone.

It seems to me that this myth shows another interesting feature; the omnipotent cruel and relentless gods are actually worshipped and revered and given a higher status than human love; I think that it is because they are in fact 'loved' (as well as feared) more than humanity that such catastrophes take place.

When love and hate clash, either we feel guilt and make reparation, or we are persecuted by guilt. To avoid either consequence, we can pervert the truth, draw strength from a good object and feel free to practise cruelty in the name of goodness. It is as though we omnipotently hijack human righteousness and conduct cruelty in the name of justice.

We now take for granted that omnipotent behaviour belongs to the nature of man. History affords us many examples of this: the Hitler regime, idealized omnipotent national conquest, revolutions and their subsequent regimes. This perversion is well illustrated by the Spanish Inquisition, which took the Christian ethic of tolerance, understanding and brotherly love, and tortured ruthlessly in the name of Christianity.

In Greek tragedy the chorus sees the tragedy in a broader spectrum, but only hopelessly observes while the Tragic Hero is locked in the narrow confines of his destiny. The analyst witnesses, as the chorus does, but hopes that intervention of understanding can modify the process. In my clinical examples I refer to patients who are persistently cruel and who persist with their grievances in a cruel way and, by projection, experience the interpretations of the analyst as having the identical qualities of cruelty. I also wish to show the narrowing of perception (narrowmindedness) that facilitates this process, and with it the avoidance of psychotic catastrophe.

First clinical example

The patient, a Jewish woman of 42, born in Eastern Europe, presented with belligerent complaints of suffering. She had had two previous attempts at analysis. She complained of intolerable suffering. She was in agony of spirit, depressed in a tortured way. She had unbearable backache which was unresponsive to medical treatment, agonizing headaches, stabbing pains in her eyes, with an inability to concentrate, inability to see clearly, and difficulty in focusing her eyes for any long period.

49

I learned in the course of treatment that she had tormented her husband, humiliated and derided him, left him for long periods, having affairs with his knowledge; she neglected her child, and was cruel and spiteful to her acquaintances. She believed, however, that she was the victim of cruel fate, and she felt cruelly treated by almost everyone.

Her previous analysis, which lasted one year, was spent screaming at her analyst, reproaching her, and complaining of inhuman treatment.

By the time she came to me for treatment, her husband had divorced her. She spent the first period of analysis screaming at me and complaining.

In the analysis I felt trapped in a cruel siege, unable to interpret meaningfully as she went on and on with her grievances, which she documented with the relish of a collector of antiques.

She accused me of being a cold, merciless Anglo-Saxon, and complained that I forced her to yield to my analytic theory, with complete disregard for her human plight.

The combination of cruel attacks on me and, by projection, the guilt of cruelty that was alleged to be mine, showed her particular need to have someone who could both tolerate being the victim of cruelty and bear the guilty responsibility for these attacks.

For example, she dreamed that she parked a lorry at a parking meter. The lorry, however, was too big and took up too many spaces. She was approached by a traffic-warden who questioned her. She immediately rammed the lorry into a telephone kiosk and smashed it up.

She associated the traffic-warden with the small-mindedness of a petty official, later attributed to me. Apart from many other meanings in her dream, the rage which smashed up all forms of communication (the telephone) was her reaction to what she perceived as my small-minded omnipotent officialdom; her perception of me was as one who could only moralize, only see where she was doing 'wrong' (a harsh superego). She felt I could not see her need to park the lorry; to find a resting place or home. She felt I could have no sympathy with her requirements for more space, more time, more sessions, or with her plight.

Therefore, living in such a cruel and narrowminded reproachful environment, all she could do was to smash up our means of communication: the analysis.

It is of interest to note that she herself had no conscious knowledge of her need to 'park' herself and be given a 'home' by me. She saw me as behaving like a Tin God, but was not aware of her need for me.

She obtained some relief from my interpretation. I was also able to show her some of her own behaviour; that she was acutely 'switched on' to my faults, showing the acumen of a specialist. She was 'switched off' to

50

any goodness and helpfulness which might be in me, to her own dependent needs, and to the fact that she really behaved in this way.

This patient was uprooted from her home by the Nazis at the age of 14, and her parents were taken to a concentration camp where they subsequently perished. This tragedy played a vital part in her development. However, it did not seem to me that the picture of me as a traffic-warden corresponded to the brutality of the Nazis, but rather to the officiousness of the projected child part of herself.

I learned in the course of subsequent sessions that she had uprooted – left her husband and child to go abroad for her artistic pursuits, with little regard for their needs, or indeed, her own.

Gradually I was able to study the dossier she had built up about me. I was depicted as complacent and smug, and she seemed determined to put an end to my peace of mind. She maintained that I practised analysis solely in order to make money and in order to believe I knew everything about life. She tried to make me feel that my whole belief in psychoanalysis was based on a lie motivated by my greedy omniscience. Above all, she wanted to know if I could face this false life I had built up; face the illusion and the guilt and have to give it up with nothing to fall back on. She even begrudged the fact that I could practise as a doctor if I realized psychoanalysis was a delusion; I was to be left with nothing at all.

These attacks on me were her attempt to destroy my goodness and creativity, but above all, I felt at the time that she conveyed to me an ordeal that she felt I would not have the courage to face. I knew what I was supposed to experience, and that she had to face this in herself; she wanted the experience of someone who could share such a predicament and give her the strength to face this in her life. Her cruel fate was to realize that she had built her life on a lie, and that she had nothing left. The lie was for her quite specific. She was a woman of talent who had created works of art depicting deep human qualities, but her personal life was devoid of these qualities. She felt alone, unloved, and persecuted by a reproachful superego.

The capacity to tolerate these projections, and my sharing her task in facing the way she had built up her life, gave her some security. She gradually was able to see this as an internal problem which tormented her whenever she had to make a decision. For example, when she had to buy kitchen units, she felt that if she bought a large unit she would be tortured with the thought that she had spent too much money. On the other hand, if she bought a small unit, she was tortured with thoughts of being mean and stupid and thereby spoiling the whole character of the kitchen. Both thoughts were cruel and relentless, and she felt exhausted.

In actual fact, whatever decision she made would not be all that bad in reality. However, each 'voice' in the argument had this cruel quality. If she spent extra money she was reproached for producing a state of utter bankruptcy, and she would regret it for the rest of her life; she would be excommunicated and forced to live in guilt. Equally, if she was careful with money her whole mean character would be exposed and disgraced so that she would again be derided and reproached for spoiling the whole house.

The quality in all this cruelty, her behaviour to me, her picture of my behaviour to her, and the elements in the internal conflict, all had the same unbearable consequence – that she would be excommunicated, left alone, unlovable, with the reproach that she had ruined everything irreparably, and there would be no chance of forgiveness or opportunity for reparation. To my mind it was characterized by another quality; there was no 'rest of her life' available to carry on with. The whole of life was narrowed to these elements, and there was nothing else. Every issue was one of life-and-death. It followed closely the pattern of fanatic puritanism, in which any one sin leads to eternal damnation.

Gradually some elements of a good understanding analyst began to develop, relieving the cruelty. But I wish to show what happened to this understanding.

During a session she experienced feeling understood, and she felt that I empathized with her predicament; she obtained great relief from her physical pain. By the next session (after a weekend break), her memory of the good session was lost.

She did, however, produce a dream: she was a student at the university hostel in Kiev, where there was a special area provided for her to rest and find shelter, and she was nursed by a couple who understood her as an individual.

She associated: that it was odd of her to find comfort in the capital of Ukraine, which she considered was the capital of pogroms against the Jews. She felt it perverse and strange to give such qualities to such people, who did not deserve this.

She came to realize:

1 That she had destroyed the good memory of an understanding session; equated with love.
2 That the good humanity was given to omnipotent racists who practised cruelty, but whose cruelty was denied; instead they were idealized as so comforting.

In this she re-enacted her past history, when she had despised her parents, identified herself with fair-haired, blue-eyed Aryans, and likened herself to them, in spite of their arrogant contempt of her Jewish qualities.

So it could be seen that she identified herself with cruel omnipotent gods, perverting the good aspects of her parents and my analysis. She bestowed the attributes of human understanding and love on to the tormentors with whom the omnipotent part of herself identified.

She did come to realize that in her belief that she was the champion of humanity (that was the way she practised cruelty) she stole the humanity from her parents and me, and she was the perpetrator of cruelty. It was she who practised the Inquisition in her analysis, in the name of righteousness, with fanatic persistence, and even contrived to suffer in its cause.

Later on, she dreamed of going to a station with a time-bomb in her belly. This she associated with an explosive outburst with her ex-husband when he was boarding a train, accusing him of infidelity. This she 'timed' to justify her outrage and squeeze out of her mind that she had left him for three months for an affair. By narrowing her mind to his possible infidelity she occluded her guilt and could produce the explosion for this isolated incident. This coincided with my approaching holidays.

The same night, she dreamed of an Amazon woman, who was evil but did not know what she had done. This woman's head was cruelly smashed again and again, and the onlookers thought this was just. Among the onlookers was the figure of Justice, but instead of being blindfolded, this figure of Justice had daggers in her eyes.

She associated that she had wanted to paint a picture of Amazon life. If she created a picture of other people's cruelty she could justifiably attack it in a relentless way. But in order to do this, the vision of Justice was not made impartial by blindfolding; instead the eyes were filled with daggers. Here she could both 'look daggers' and have her perceptions attacked by daggers. (One is reminded of the fate of Oedipus.)

The daggers in the eyes of the figure of Justice she associated to the stabbing pain in her eyes, and her inability to concentrate and have any breadth of vision. The analysis of this relieved the pains in her eyes but confronted her with guilt, and she could now see the injustice of her attacks that had been so righteously upheld.

The analysis of the guilt is of course essential; the experiencing of it is made difficult by the narrowminded unforgiving torture of the super-ego.

She could defend herself against this by a desire to devote her life to what she believed to be an all-righteous cause, by fighting for Israel.

The rationalization of self-centred omnipotent narrowmindedness, and the defence against guilt, were perpetuated in the name of survival. Consequently all issues were felt as struggles of life-and-death, and so became unbearable. She thus so narrowed her perception that she was constantly in the position of the baby whose only horizon was the nipple, and it was right and natural to focus her life on satisfying her needs, and to demand that I too focus my mind on the satisfaction of her needs.

The great tragedy of her life was that at the age of 14 she had had to leave her country with her brother and sister to escape extermination by the Nazis and so survive. Her parents stayed behind and were murdered. So her survival was felt to be at the expense of her parents' lives, and she felt she should have shared their fate. The guilt over this never left her, and she felt reparation was impossible. It was not only the burden of guilt that prevented the enjoyment of life, but she began to see there was a 'kill-joy' part of herself in operation. (In fact, this was the cause of a good deal of guilt.)

She realized there was a part of herself that behaved in a particularly cruel way. If I did not satisfy her completely and make her feel special and unique, she killed my analysis and my work in a vicious annihilation. When I pointed this out to her she claimed that I condemned her to feeling guilty and tortured as unlovable for the rest of her life.

The fact that I tolerated this, contained it, continued to try to understand and help her, brought her no joy. She could not see that she was killing joy and comfort; only the pain she suffered. She screamed and shouted at the pain that she felt I inflicted on her.

When she saw that it was the good parents in me she destroyed in her self-absorption, she obtained dramatic relief and eventually could appreciate me and feel sorry. She could then experience guilt, together with a more understanding superego, and have more strength and hope to deal with it.

This was in contrast to her actual past, where I have reason to believe that her mother submitted to her attacks, with the patient introjecting a hopelessly destroyed and reproachful mother.

Developments in the analysis

In an earlier account of this patient, I described how she was locked in the narrow confines of cruelty and cut off from a 'home'. Gradually some concept of a home was built in the analysis, which enabled humanity to counteract cruelty. Following the dream about 'Kiev' we saw the beginning

54

of her realization of her need for a home for the needy baby part of herself, and her recognition that she stole from her parents and myself and gave our good attributes to the cruel 'ideal Aryans' with whom she identified.

We also discovered that she had her own ways of trying to provide herself with a home. She could establish a comforting home if she was in a blurred state of mind, with no distinction between herself and her object. She got a feeling of 'belonging' in intense physical sexual union. She also had a feeling of security in her manic paranoid episodes when all the goodness was felt to be inside her. But none of these experiences could nourish her and assist in growth. All these processes destroyed the really helpful separate breast-mother-analyst.

The analysis of these issues enabled her to recognize the paramount importance of her search for a home for the needy parts of herself. She came to value the psychological home I gave her and the home given to her by friends; she began to admire people who provided homes and those who could admit their need for homes.

She described vividly to me how she met a Russian Jew who managed to leave the Soviet Union and was in transit to Israel. This man had sacrificed an important prestigious position in his field of work. He assumed, for her, heroic proportions and she yearned to be united with such a man, who could keep a concept of home alive in him, risk prison in his country, and finally achieve his home in Israel.

She spoke with genuine admiration about the fact that this Russian Jew had given up his worldly success for more human aspirations. After meeting this man, however, she had a dream in which she was fishing in the River Thames. She caught something at the end of her line but she could not pull in her catch, however hard she tried. Eventually she followed the line and it was attached to a metal box which was embedded in rock. The box had written on it 'Bank X' and inside 'Café Y'.

(I use 'X' and 'Y' to disguise identity.) Bank 'X' was associated with her ex-husband's bank and the time when money seemed inexhaustible. Café 'Y' was associated with a café where she used to meet her artistic friends who would 'run the world' in a superior fashion from their coffee tables. The Thames was associated with the publishers of artistic books which she hoped would publish her art.

She soon realized that in spite of the preface to the dream of the sacrifice of worldly success for a 'human home', her yearning for money and success was firmly embedded and rock-like. This dream does contain an element of her search for 'omnipotent gods' (Café 'Y'), but it did not seem to me sinister and cruel in nature. The overall picture is her search for money and success, which had some realistic basis. She was not nursed in a 'cruel perverse home' as she was in the dream about Kiev. She was fishing for money and success and there was a struggle between the different parts of herself. She struggled with her ambivalence, instead of reverting to a perverse solution to obviate this.

But what I consider the most striking development was the way she reacted to the realization of what she was doing in the dream. She did not have to 'pluck out her eyes', narrow her perception, justify herself or feel mercilessly reproached. She could look at this part of herself, give it a home, and realize it was her task to struggle with these elements. I believe this was the result of my having a 'home' to these parts of her as well as the needy parts, and the subsequent introjection of my 'psychological home'. This enabled the analysis to proceed in a way in which insight could be used constructively rather than being regarded as the cruel reproach of a moralizing superego.

On her own reflection, she recognized the power of these forces and thought about the way she behaved with her son, being rejecting if he were not highly successful. She felt genuine guilt and seemed determined to give him a proper home whatever he achieved or did not achieve.

A most significant part of her development was the giving of a home to the memory of her mother. She had described her mother, perhaps not inaccurately, as always anxious, always complaining about her father and nagging her if she, the patient, was not 'just so', and not at all interested in the patient's work or enjoyment. She stood somewhere between a broken-down mother and a demanding figure. Now she could see her mother as depressed and unhappy but always striving; a woman who gained satisfaction from making a good physical home for the family, who always fed and clothed her well and did what she could in 'her way'. It was a sad picture in many ways, but there was one feature that left its mark – this was her mother's struggling and carrying on in spite of adversity and depression. It was this quality of her mother that the patient felt sustained her (the patient) in her journey across Europe and Turkey when she left her native land at the age of 14.

It was through the realization of what I endured in giving her a 'psychological home' that she gave a home to the memory of her real mother, drew strength from this and felt free to avail herself of new loving experiences without feeling she abandoned her mother. She could now begin to live in a more generous world which reduced her hatred and helped her to deal with her aggression, and mitigated the vicious circle of her previous cruel and narrow world.

Second clinical example

In the first example, I described how the patient narrowed her perception as the means of survival. In the second clinical example the penis took the place of the nipple and was the focal point in the patient's world.

This patient was a homosexual male aged 30. It first seemed that his narrowmindedness was localized in sensuous satisfaction, but it soon became apparent that the penis stood for very much more. His whole life revolved around worshipping penises. He had sexual adventures in public lavatories many times a day, mainly of fellatio or being the passive partner in anal intercourse. He would go into eulogies about these penises – they were straight, upright, noble, etc. The fact that these penises belonged to men who sometimes robbed him of money or assaulted him did not lead to any modification of his views. Any strength he obtained from me was denied and attributed to these penises.

For example, he would be relieved of some misery in a session, proceed to lose all the understanding I gave him, and turn to these 'magnificent' penises for relief, only to be plunged into depression, once again. This pattern was repeated again and again. In essence the buggery was always cruel and was used to triumph over the good internal object, linked in the analysis with my understanding.

In the countertransference he produced a feeling of helplessness in me and a feeling that there was nothing I could do against the powerful omnipotence of the religion of phallic worship. He tried to force me to believe in his system and to get me to admit my impotent envy of his exciting exploits.

When this picture of a phallic world began to break down, and he experienced depression, he would eulogize depressive writers and try to make me believe that only those who saw the futility of human life were the true giants of the human mind; and the others, like me, were pathetic cowards. Again, there were persistent, narrow, cruel attacks against life itself. What became clear was the omnipotent cruelty, which made creativity and joy as nothing by comparison with his depression.

When he moved to heterosexuality he mercilessly focused his mind on all the defects of his girlfriend and tormented her for her deficiencies with an arrogant belief in his god-like superiority. He was identified with the ideal object and felt entitled to torment the actual girl for her failings.

After laborious analysis he began to come closer to the realization of his cruelty and to approach some feelings of guilt.

His ace card in acting out was to come one day to the session in a distraught state, earlier than his appointment, and go into the waiting room. Soon after arriving, he left my house knowing I could hear him leave, and paraded outside my house, knowing I could see him from my window. He knew I would not call him in, so when he did come to the door, missing about five minutes of his session, he was now armed with righteous reproach. Here was he, the patient, distraught with suffering, and I, the analyst, extremely cruel, worshipping my analytic technique and putting it above humanity and suffering. I would never deviate to help him, so he could now establish that the cruelty was mine.

Throughout the whole pattern of this cruelty, the narcissistic pre-occupation that he was right, he knew the real truth, he loved the really worthy objects, was persistently maintained. Ultimately he alone walked with 'humanity' and I had none.

I have little doubt about his basic envy of humanity and creativity, but the point I wish to emphasize is the way he narrowed his perception to 'his world' and kept out any fuller understanding. His analysis was not like this all the time, of course, but it is the strength of this feature and its power that I wish to emphasize. This pattern was resurrected at every crisis.

Whatever the perversion and narrow preoccupation may be, I think that it is ultimately goodness, humanity and truth that are so sorely coveted. It also shows in this case the painfulness of guilt in realizing what he had done; he had to frame me for this sin, and was prepared to suffer to vindicate himself.

Theoretical considerations

Freud (1917), in 'Mourning and melancholia', described how the melan-cholic would both torture his object and cling to it, refusing to establish a new object relationship. Abraham (1924) made the observation that in the cruelty of melancholia these patients treated the object as if they owned it. Both Freud and Abraham emphasized the regression to narcissism, with no differentiation between self and object.

As I understand Melanie Klein's concept of the depressive position (1934), a development takes place in which the infant begins to realize the separateness of himself and the object. As I see it, he is therefore confronted with inferiority and envy of the mother, a realization of the human non-ideal mother, whom he does not own; and therefore has to confront frustration, guilt, and the anxiety of losing this mother.

In order to remain in the narcissistic position, attacks are made on this awareness, which include attacks on the internal object. These attacks destroy the awareness of the human mother and the patient is therefore left in a cruel, loveless world.

To put this another way: perception develops from the nipple to the breast, to the body, face, and ultimately the mother's mind and love, producing a picture of 'Mummy'. This can be introjected and given a 'home' inside the infant's mind and feed the infant's capacity to love. It is the obliteration of the concept of the whole human mother that narrows the picture of the world to a cruel loveless place.

Furthermore, the attacks on the real mother for not being the 'ideal breast' (which satisfies through narcissistic identification the demand to have the ideal, and be the ideal) lead to the incorporation of a super-ego which demands that the infant has to satisfy it for the rest of his life. Therefore he lives in a cruel, exacting, narrow world, which feeds his fear and hatred, and he is forced to worship this system, subordinate himself and identify with it, partly out of fear, and partly because it contains his own vengeful omnipotence. This superego–ego ideal dominates his life. That which Freud and Abraham described as the patient clinging to his object and treating his object as if he owns it, now becomes, through introjection, a patient possessed by a cruel superego which will not let him be free.

He is therefore confined to his narrow loveless narcissistic demands, governed by narrow loveless narcissistic gods. Added to this, the infant casts out and abandons the real human mother to cruel exile, and introjects a mother that does the same to him, and therefore gives him no home. In addition, the narcissistic part of the personality exiles the needy real baby part of himself. A home is therefore only given to gods and the god-like narcissistic part of the self, leading to a 'false self' and living a lie.

This problem is complicated still further as the infant may have been denied a good home in the first place. He may have had a mother who rejected the baby part of him, could not stand his anxieties, and failed in this sense to provide a home for this baby. His anxious needy self may have been psychologically cast out and abandoned in cruel exile. He may have had a mother who could only tolerate an 'ideal baby' and rejected the real baby, or he may have had a mother who over-indulged him and satisfied his omnipotent cravings. In either case, he lusts for vengeance and the re-creation of the 'ideal world'.

By the time the patient arrives for analysis we are therefore faced with a complex problem. But it seems to me the clinical task is to enable the patient to make use of a fuller, understanding, loving world which is the only experience that can rescue him.

I have attempted to show in this paper how such patients try to confine the analyst's understanding to the justification of their grievances under the guise of moral justice, and squeeze out or prevent any fuller love from modifying this situation. In doing so, they cast themselves into exile, devoid of love, at the mercy of the primitive superego.

The sum total of this narcissistic organization ensures that the patient does not find a good home in which to grow up, enjoy life and have the experience of human sharing.

With a 'good home', problems of cruelty are humanized by interaction with parents. I cannot help speculating: 'Would Oedipus have behaved as he did had he been brought up at home?' His tragedy was that he started life in exile and finished in exile.

The converse of the cruel vicious circle is mutual shared concern; the mother giving a home for the baby inside her mind, and the baby giving a home for the real mother inside his mind.

Conclusion

The normal process that leads to seeing the mother as a separate person who feels pain, joy and gives creatively is, in cases of cruelty, viciously squeezed out of perception, leading to a narrow mind.

The narrowing of perception restricts the imagery of the whole object to the role of a nipple that the patient owns, and so restricts conscious love and conscious guilt.

Demands are put on this object to be ideal and consider the patient ideal, or be vengefully punished.

Goodness is hijacked and perverted to the side of cruelty to give it strength and avoid catastrophe. This perversion is worshipped as a religion and the analyst is required to convert to this worship, and 'God help you if you don't'. The introjection of this leads to a cruel superego and establishes a hopeless vicious circle of cruelty and slavish devotion to a cruel, perverse, moralizing god. The real mother is cast out and abandoned and the real needy 'baby part' is likewise cast into exile.

An unfavourable early and analytic environment may: support the omnipotent delusion; enact counter-cruelty; provide its own omnipotent cruelty as a model for identification; collapse or die. All may have disastrous consequences.

The role of the analyst is to widen the patient's perception against militant attacks designed to keep both his and the patient's minds narrowed, and to supply the right environment by his careful analysis. The fuller understanding of the analyst must be matched against the narrowmind-edness, as this fuller understanding is the means of modifying cruelty and allowing goodness, strength to deal with hatred, and forgiveness to intervene.

By this means a 'home' is given to new good experiences; this enables the good aspects of the original 'home' to be rehoused inside the patient's mind. An exiled mother comes home, becomes an ally in the work of goodness and the task of mitigating cruelty is strengthened and shared.

References

Abraham, K. (1924) A short study of the development of the libido, viewed in the light of mental disorders. In *Selected Papers on Psychoanalysis*. London: Hogarth Press, 1942, pp. 418–501.

Freud, S. (1917) Mourning and melancholia. SE 14.

Klein, M. (1934) A contribution to the psychogenesis of manic-depressive states. In *Contributions to Psychoanalysis*. London: Hogarth Press, 1975.

6

Hysteria

We generally regard as health, a capacity to meet the realities of life (external and internal), and that this capacity is capable of growth. In illness, excessive defences are employed as a way of dealing with the vicissitudes of life, stunting development and increasing the fears of negotiating reality. In this paper, I explore a psychic organization which we tend to call hysteria. I hope to show how the 'hysteric' feels held together by his defences and faulty object relationships and simultaneously mutilates and is terrified of reality.

At first I thought I had very little use for the concept of hysteria and regarded it as an obsolete diagnosis which was part of the history of psychiatry and psychoanalysis, yet at the same time I felt I could not ignore it, as something like hysterical features occurred so frequently and so pervasively in clinical work. I think that many features which are regarded as hysteric have now been refined and understood in more detailed ways – such as the studies of narcissism. Freud himself had a great deal to say on the subject in his early writings (1893–1895) but seemed to depart from the theme as more knowledge was acquired about psychopathology.

I wondered if the diagnosis of 'hysteria' was meaningful and when I discussed this with colleagues, I found many who shared this view. A few colleagues said they did not know what hysteria was but they knew an hysteric when they met one. This view is not without its value because it indicates that there is a concept of a 'hysterical character' who affects one in a way that produces antipathy, and I hope to show reasons for this in the course of the paper.

I also looked at the problem from the point of view of hysteria as a defence against psychosis and thought it might be valid to talk of an 'hysterical defence'. At the same time, in clinical work I have come across extremely 'mad' behaviour and found that I was saying to myself 'this is not psychotic, this is hysterical'. I believe I was part wrong and part right. Hysteria is so plastic and presents itself in any and every disease and it is such an umbrella term that it covers 'a multitude of sins'.

All the features I describe in this paper can be seen in other diseases but I think there is a particular pattern in the hysterical character which, if understood, can be clinically useful, whatever diagnostic label one may ultimately prefer to use.

If we consider those conditions generally accepted as hysterical, we find the following. In the case of the phobic there is a threatening persecutory symptom; in conversion hysteria, a crippling symptom. In both cases, the symptoms are either viewed in terms of potential catastrophe or have already produced a crippling partial catastrophe whilst the remainder of the personality appears to be in ostensibly good order. In fact we know that this split may be so persuasive that physicians often attempt treatment of the symptom and ignore the personality. The combination seems to be that of catastrophe and denial. In the *belle indifférence* this defensive dissociation is carried to the extreme.

In my view the hysterical character, with its features of splitting and projection, shows the same combination of catastrophe and denial, that is, the patient is persecuted by objects about whom he has a list of catastrophic atrocity stories, whilst the rest of the personality remains ostensibly in good order.

This split of catastrophe and denial is widespread in psychopathology. I would like now to consider what it is that differentiates hysteria from other conditions, in particular psychosis. It is my belief that the hysteric is able to make an apparent relationship with live external objects. Such an external object, a person, is used to hold the hysteric together and to prevent more serious breakdown into depression or disintegration – schizophrenia.

Freud's (now) famous statement that the hysteric requires to give up the symptoms to share the general unhappiness of mankind is undoubtedly true. But I believe that this cannot be achieved without a mature helpmate, and this is precisely what does not seem to be available to the hysteric, or sought after as desirable. On the contrary, he tries to convert the object into supporting him/her to be a successful hysteric. Being a prima donna is viewed as superior to meeting reality. In a similar process the obsessional makes his ritual superior, and the manic makes his triumph superior to human understanding. They do not know what they need or what they have lost. Instead, what is available, for whatever reasons, is what I call the hysterogenic mother. So when, in Kleinian terms, what is required is support for a move from the paranoid-schizoid position of idealization, to the depressive position of working through the pain of reality, guilt and achieving some reparation, the hysterogenic mother instead appears to support the false reassurance of idealization as superior to realism.

By virtue of this denial of the problems, the hysterogenic mother simultaneously protects the child from having to face the pain and anxiety, yet exacerbates the anxieties by conveying that it would be overwhelmingly catastrophic to have to face them.

The basic theme of this paper is that the use of the external object relationship, which appears as a relationship to a whole object, is essentially narcissistic, and that an ostensibly whole object is used as a part object to prevent breakdown. It is also my view that the hysteric's use of the external object involves an attack on his own psychic reality. It is this practice that is my focus. The practice is not exclusive to hysteria, it occurs in fetishism, perversion and, indeed, all psychopathology. What I think is specific to those cases we call hysteria is the particular way they set about attempting to use this, by using live, ostensibly whole, external objects who are also subject to having their psychic reality attacked.

The hysteric has access to many methods whereby he uses his object to negate psychic truth. In particular, he employs persuasion and ostensible proof to negate truth together with identification with a phantasy object.

I shall consider this problem from the point of view of the negation of psychic reality (his own or others') and later from the point of view of its defensive use: in other words as a way of life and as a defence.

How does the hysteric use his object to negate psychic truth?

The persuasive propaganda in hysteria is so organized to give proof that a certain condition is true. This is true in mania, paranoia and depression. Nevertheless, it is especially striking in hysteria and it is woven into the fabric of reality with such skill that it is often extremely deceiving.

We are familiar with processes such as:

1 I am frigid, therefore I can deny sexuality. Or it can be – I have lots of orgasms, therefore there is no sexual problem.
2 I am the victim of aggression – each of my three husbands beat me.
3 I have been seduced or raped – the victim of sexuality and aggression.

The accomplished hysterics suffer as evidence, work their fingers to the bone, give up marriages to look after mothers and always provide proof.

They can have proof of maltreatment, or false arrest, provoke others to be awful and present themselves as free of vices. They can work on their analyst to 'prove' there is nothing wrong with them – it is their spouse, mother, etc. They can even arrange mutual idealization to prove perfection.

I would like to refer to the Don Juan syndrome to show the negation of psychic reality. Freud (1893–1895) considered that in hysteria there is a stalemate tug-of-war between sexuality and repression. The Don Juan manages to achieve a pseudosexuality at the service of his narcissistic conquest. He uses external objects to persuade them of his supremacy and lives through his imagined picture of himself inside his objects.

I believe this process is used not only for sexual triumph and prowess but also to triumph over the 'breast' – helpful analyst – to become the wise, understanding, all-loving breast himself. I would like to illustrate something of this persuasiveness in a patient of mine who combined hysteric phobic symptoms with an hysterical character.

Mr X was a married man with no children. He first presented with crippling pains in his chest which he felt were 'like a vice gripping him'. He was so overwhelmed with anxiety that he feared he would go mad. He insisted on my starting treatment straight away and threatened a breakdown if I did not do so. I did not acquiesce in his demands but told him that I could either try to find someone who could start analysis sooner, or that he could get in touch with me if he felt his pain and anxieties were too much. When he did telephone me later on, he told me that he felt so much better that he thought analysis was unnecessary. Nevertheless, he started his analysis at the agreed time.

He was a successful businessman who, helped by his wife, had built up a thriving company. His parents were poor but managed to help him achieve a university education.

His behaviour with me was arrogant and pompous. He had episodes of violent pains and panics which were resolvable in the sessions. He tried to manipulate me to give him the precise times he wanted with no consideration for other patients or me. He grudged paying fees which he could well afford, and wanted me to work for no money to prove that I cared for him. He presented himself as special in contradictory ways: devoted, caring, full of sexual prowess, sacrificial, ruthless and so on. He tried to control me and to get me to conduct the analysis 'his way'. For months he attempted to persuade me to abandon my technique to prove that I really cared for him and that I was not phobically dominated by my technique which he claimed I was terrified of abandoning. On one occasion an urgent message for the patient was telephoned to my house and I conveyed it to him and thus broke my technique. He was apparently very grateful and thanked me, and considered this a triumph for my humanity over technique. A flood of dreams followed of which I shall report three.

The Russian Navy had lured the German Navy into a sense of false security by a friendly peace pact. When the German Navy came into the harbour, they were annihilated.

A repeated dream about the film 'Death in Venice'. His version was that of a professor seduced by a beautiful boy ending in the professor's death.

A dream in which he came to the private part of my house for a session and wanted to go to the lavatory. I insisted on going with him and there was no light in the lavatory. I explained (an obvious lie) that the electricity supply was out of order but there was an electric heater in the lavatory to disprove this. I smiled at him in a peculiar way which, on association, reminded him of a secondhand car salesman who once tried to sell him a car which looked lovely and was supposed to be marvellous but had a faulty engine.

Now let us look at this material. Mr X is a patient who has been engaged in persuading me to abandon my technique to prove that I really cared for him. Although he was apparently pleased to be given the message by me, we see in the first dream that I am represented by the German Navy (he thinks Brenman is a German name), lured and seduced into a sense of false security by a friendly peace pact. The outcome is that I am viewed as having capitulated to his machinations which results in my annihilation. This theme is repeated in the second dream.

In the third dream, I am portrayed as the seducer pretending to accompany him and offer love, but instead depriving him of the light – the truth. I reminded him of and became for him a secondhand (it is secondhand because it contains his projections) car salesman who is trying to sell him a skin-deep (shiny car) façade, an ostensibly marvellous solution, which, however, houses a faulty engine: a combination of physical perfection and omnipotence with ultimate lack of performance and impotence. He claims that he was led into the lavatory by me, that is, my ostensible kindness is a 'shitty' trick. Yet he put me in the lavatory, in the 'shit'.

We see he has created for me a double-bind situation. He urges and seduces me to be kind (he feels it is his initiation). When I give him the message I am annihilated as corrupt. If, on the other hand, I had not given him the message (which was the cancellation of an appointment in a town in Europe six hundred miles away – if he had not been given the message he would have taken a fruitless plane journey), then he would have grounds to pillory me as cruel and rigid and would, indeed, have a 'justifiable grievance'. My giving him the message was at one level experienced as robbing him of his justifiable grievance. This double-bind situation was one that plagued him internally; for example, in the conduct of his business affairs. If he was generous, an internal voice made him feel he was triumphed over and he was a 'sucker'. If he was ruthless, an inner voice reproached him for his greed and ruthlessness. This made it impossible for him to resolve a conflict, and if he was stuck in the conflict, he felt despised and weak. There was, of course, no sense of balance. There was no object available bearing ambivalence and balance – a feature I will refer to later.

The narcissistic organization is of paramount importance. The pretence of being loving and friendly is not designed to achieve a loving relationship, but to be the falsely adored object of love and to triumph over so-called loving objects who are then despised and annihilated.

This, in my view, also illuminates a point of technical importance in the treatment of such cases. By virtue of projection, the patient believes everything the analyst says is designed to convert him to believe in the analyst's lie of being loving, good and omnipotent. I have found this factor extremely useful. Before analysis of this episode, all my interpretations were felt by him to be my persuasion at the service of my narcissism.

The point I wish to make as regards the hysterical character is this: the old-fashioned hysteric converted the conflict into somatic symptoms – but also attempted to persuade the physician into the false belief that the rest of the personality was normal. I believe that in the hysterical character, the analyst is the target of conversion to agree with the patient's machinations.

If we take another look at the dreams, we see another point. It is difficult to work out who is the Russian Navy and who is the German Navy – who is the professor and who is the seducing boy: who seduces whom? There is such a mix-up as to who is identified with what, and the plasticity and changeability because of this mixed-up identification is my next point of reference.

Identification

Identification has always been regarded as a feature of hysteria. The problem really is 'what is the nature of identification?'

In the Dora case, Freud (1905, pp. 40–42) instanced that Dora developed a cough like Mrs K who was her sexual rival. He also cited an epidemic of fainting in a girls' school in which one girl received a love letter and fainted and the other girls, also wishing to receive love letters, fainted as well (1908).

In his paper on bisexuality, Freud described a patient who, in an 'hysterical seizure', tried to take off her clothes with one hand whilst making an effort to keep them on by grasping them with the other hand. Freud considered she was identifying herself simultaneously with a man raping a woman and with a woman being attacked. I have treated patients who have tried to convince me, having already convinced themselves, of both their purity and sexiness.

I believe that multiple identification always takes place in hysteria. The identification is not based on sympathetic identification – empathy. There is no real introjective identification of sharing or of someone sharing with them. Instead there are projective identifications, usually of a 'whole object kind', not with a real object but with a phantasy object. The understanding of the object they identify with is minimal and used only for wishful thinking. This process is promiscuous and can change with chameleon-like ease – like Walter Mitty. Hysterics live vicariously through others. What one also notices is the minimal importance of the 'real self', to my mind commensurate with the negation of psychic reality and the excessive use of external whole live objects or, better still, whole live-cum-fantasy objects – a fantasy, yet linked with a real person.

In the male patient I described, I would like to show something of these multiple identifications. He was unfaithful to his wife and had an affair with one of his female employees. He raged against his wife because she objected to this, and hysterically screamed that he should be absolutely free. He claimed that he respected freedom and gave an itinerary of examples for proof, including permission for his wife to have as many affairs as she wished, whilst he felt sure this would not happen. At that moment he identified himself with the champions of freedom – the new generation – and believed in this absolutely.

When he discovered that his mistress was unfaithful to him he was outraged, saying 'how could she do this to me?' He had sacrificed everything for her and was utterly devoted. He sought revenge by wanting, not only to sack her, but to ensure that no one would ever employ her. He held himself up as a model of faithful devotion and completely identified himself with this picture. Here we can see the capricious, plastic identification with ideals rather than real people.

Some time later when he was improving, he rearranged his business affairs to give more pay and a greater share to his junior partners. He realized that he was assailed by a struggle with contradictory views. On the one hand he felt that everything should be given to the business, the profits should be reinvested and he and the partners should sacrifice their salaries. He realized he was the business – both the baby who had to have everything and the mother who supplied the food. At the same time he hated the business that made such demands on him, and thought that he should get everything out of the business and not look after it at all and it should supply him with everything.

He realized that in the conflict he was both the ideal breast who should be everything, and the ideal baby who should have everything. He was caught in the conflict of wanting to satisfy both completely, with no capacity to give and take. He linked this with what he considered to be the character of his mother. I shall refer to this point later. These features show a violent greedy dependency as follows.

I wish now to refer to the problem of greedy dependency and link it with the features of proof, passion and identification which I have described.

This patient, who would often revile the analysis as useless and ruining him financially and spoke of my wasting his time, nevertheless wanted sessions to go on all day and at weekends and also tried to make me change my technique, quoting from psychiatric literature to prove his point.

In the early days of his analysis, it was a useless dependency because, not accrediting me with worth, and not having appreciation, he never took in a helpful experience which supported his inside. I was subjected to the fate of his wife who emotionally carried him, helped him build up the business, and was told she was an enormous financial liability. He identified with the breast while his wife and I were identified with parasitic pretentious babies.

He dreamed of crossing a vast expanse of water on his back, unaided. In the course of the session I learned of his story of an hysterical woman who had persuaded two Buddhist monks to carry her across a stream. (It is worth noting how asexual the helpers have to be.) He managed in the course of the session to admit that he did get some help from me and his wife and his parents, and was carried by people; he did not float himself.

During the next session he dreamed of being in a walled garden with two figures who later were associated with these two monks. In the session he reverted to my uselessness and unhelpfulness. When I reminded him of his experience of being helped, I learned the rest of the story about the monks.

There was a wise older monk and a novice who, after they had carried the hysterical woman, continued with their walk. One hour later the novice monk said: 'That was a cheek, that woman getting us to carry her.' To which the wise senior monk replied: 'That was an hour ago.' He implied that the novice monk (me) was making an hysterical fuss, full of hysterical grievances, and here was the wise senior monk (the patient) carrying on with the journey to wisdom. The patient depicts one object making an interminable fuss and never getting on with life and another object that forgets, as if events had not happened. In my view, this lack of balance is another manifestation of the catastrophe–denial combination.

I believe that in these multiple identifications, a greedy dependency is practised with simultaneous identification with the breast as the source of wisdom, support and the victim of exploitation. In this case a further identification is made in which the patient is the mature, senior, wise priest who can cope with it all and get on with the important issues in life.

In this dependency, hysterics try to change reality by making mother/ parent/analyst believe the patient's version of the truth. Their aim is to change the picture of 'what they are – what they do, plus what you are and what you do' and they have proof, theories, evidence, etc., and chop and change identities in order to destroy the intuitive knowledge of what is real and true. They do this to the analyst and themselves with the consequence I shall describe later.

This differs from psychotic paranoia in that the craving for love (really narcissistic love) is obviously there, or near to the surface. They behave in a way indicative of: 'I'll make you love me if I have to break every bone in your body' or, more accurately, 'I'll make you adore me by driving you mad and changing your reality sense.' This is coupled with the belief that one can be a 'successful hysteric', and if they cannot use mutual idealization as a defence, they employ the method I describe.

The identification is shallow: like their object choices and their lives – skin deep. It is with a fantasy and not a real object, hence this greed does not provide psychic nourishment and psychic growth is stunted.

They attack true knowledge and enquiry and though they yearn for evidence of love, they do not really look for it, only the infant's delusion of narcissistic love. The tragedy is that they do not make themselves available for love in the form of help. This is to say, there is no healthy narcissism, the love is demanded for the omnipotent false self.

So far I have tried to show how the truth – psychic reality – is attacked and attempts are made to change it. The consequence is to have no real supporting objects to nourish the true self-dependent part of the person- ality. The patients introject damaged and persecutory objects from which they have to defend themselves. Also, therefore, they contain unmodified primitive impulses and a primitive harsh superego. As a result of this *modus vivendi* they then have to defend themselves against psychic catastrophe.

I would now like to look at the relationship between hysteria and melancholia. The hysteric attempts to get rid of guilt as he gets rid of anxiety, by arranging for an external object to carry the guilt and provide 'proof' of his contentions. He does not take the final revenge on his objects as he needs them, and so tortures them by making them feel guilty.

Now this is a feature described by Freud (1917) and Abraham (1924) in the psychopathology of melancholia; both writers realized the arrogance and omnipotence of the melancholic. In melancholia the patients get the analyst to carry them, take responsibility, and reward them my making them feel failures, guilty and responsible for potential suicide. It could be argued that these are hysterical aspects of depression. I do not want to press this point, but would like to refer to the relationship between hysteria and depression in which one could postulate an hysterical defence against depression.

The melancholic often ushers in his illness with 'delusions' of self-reproach – he is a cheat, morally worthless, lives a lie. Freud considered that the self-accusation carried a great deal of truth and that it was unscientific to deny these assertions. From this it could be argued that, prior to the melancholic breakdown, these kinds of patients did lead a false life and were a kind of 'successful hysteric' using other people to collude with the denial of truth; the melancholia is the moment of truth – unbearable to face owing to the harsh superego. This would be particularly so when the live object that was used is now dead or gone and the patient is alone at the mercy of the superego. Thus one can postulate two processes.

1 The hysterical lie breaks down and the patient is plunged into depression.
2 That in order to avoid the hopeless agony of depression, there is the use of hysterical devices of projection of guilt and responsibility in order to be saved.

This double process throws light on the difficult problem of suicide and the risk of suicide. For I believe if the hysterical defence breaks down and the hysteric gets near to melancholia, there is danger of suicide. On the other hand, the hysteric uses the threat of suicide to make others carry guilt and look after him. As threats of suicide may contain both these elements, it is sometimes difficult to assess the risk. I think understanding this problem of the relationship between melancholia and hysteria can be helpful.

More about the hysterical defences

I have touched on the relationships of hysteria and depression. The question I am asking is: 'What would happen if the hysteric did not use hysterical mechanisms?' Would he break down and be plunged into psychosis? Can we say that hysteria defends against psychosis any more than any other disease? I do not believe this; however, the point at issue, as I see it, is over the use of supporting objects – a live person who keeps the hysteric going and holds him together.

A patient with hysterical features had this dream at the time of feeling a victim of aggression and feeling innocent of aggression herself.

She was in her flat which was occupied by Irish patients who were lying in bed in a helpless state. She was indignant that they were there and wanted them to leave. She started opening the door in an effort to get rid of them but, as she half opened the door, outside there were howling dangerous cats and dogs. If she let them in, it would be extremely dangerous, even endangering her life.

She associated to the IRA who wanted to take over Northern Ireland and were, therefore, not so innocent, in fact were lethally dangerous. It was soon recognized that this was herself – ill – a helpless invalid who punished others by making them feel responsible and guilty for the way they treated her. If, however, she got rid of this part of herself, look what dangerous uncontrollable aspects of her personality would be let in.

Furthermore, the Irish patients required nursing and looking after, which they demanded as a right – so they were looked after and cared for and could occupy the whole life of the nursing mother and doctor. (Hysterics do get people to nurse and look after them.)

As I see it, she defended herself against uncontrollable fear and over-whelming demands (cats and dogs) by being an invalid and therefore avoiding threatening, dangerous catastrophe; but, in the defence, in becoming the invalid, she experienced parts of herself as the IRA who intended to take over the country. By her very illness and helplessness, she hoped to achieve complete possessive domination without having to confront the means she used. In my view, this suggests hysteria is a defence against overwhelming anxiety and is also a *modus vivendi*.

A further aspect of the dream was that she noticed, in a corner, her mother washing her hair. This was associated with hysterical aspects of her mother who would, according to the patient, in fact flamboyantly wash her own hair in order to make the family feel she was saving money for them while they spent money and lived well.

This raises another problem. The person who could possibly help her to deal with this problem was having the same hysterical characteristics as herself. This leads to another question – what kind of object does the hysteric have to help them deal with problems? I will refer to this later but would like to take it up now in some part:

1 The mother does not apply herself to the problem of how to help, but leaves the patient unaided.

2   In the very 'washing it right out of her hair' she dissociates herself from the problem and gets rid of it.

3   The patient is also the mother who washes things out of her hair to get rid of trouble and feel virtuous, either by the patient's projection or modelling on the mother. Hence the issue will be repeated and washed out again and again.

4   In addition, the patient washed away the good and helpful aspects of the mother and was left with the hysterical aspects of the mother as the internal mother. The recovery of the good aspects of her mother later helped her to get stronger.

The combination of denial and catastrophe

In phobias, the area of phobia is constantly threatening catastrophe and the rest of the personality is assumed to be healthy by denial and contrivance. The same combination is true of conversion hysteria with a crippling symptom. It is also true in the character of the hysteric who is always 'too good to be true' and whose object is unbearably atrocious. This combination is not specific to hysteria and belongs to underlying splitting processes.

A book has been published by an American journalist whose son committed suicide. The boy had seen eight psychiatrists, four of whom had said there was nothing wrong with him and four had said he was so ill that he needed to go to a mental hospital.

It seems that the hysteric has the capacity to make people believe there is nothing wrong with him or sometimes can provoke the reaction 'There is nothing wrong – just pull your socks up and stop moaning and being sorry for yourself.' Equally they create havoc and desperate anxiety in their objects. What they are not good at is getting a balanced view of the state of affairs or assisting the physician to get a balanced view.

Now what is the method in this madness? It seems to me that there is a 'pull' if not a yearning for these extreme states. There is also a fear that integration will produce guilt and madness. Freud wrote of the wishful-thinking fantasy as a basis of hysteria. I am interested in predeterminants at an earlier level. Are there earlier conflicts – precursors of conflict between wishful thinking and repression?

Melanie Klein (1946), in 'Notes on some schizoid mechanisms', referred to the problem at the earliest level of the infant at the breast. I quote:

> In hallucinatory gratification . . . two interrelated processes take place: the omnipotent conjuring up of the ideal object and situation, and the equally important annihilation of the bad persecutory object and the

painful situation. These processes are based on splitting both the object and the ego.

(p. 102)

She shows the conflict between wishful thinking in its primitive form and the threat of persecutory catastrophe. In the same paper, Klein goes on to say:

> With an unassimilated idealized object there goes a feeling that the ego has no life and no values of its own. I would suggest that the conditions of flight to the unassimilated idealized object [I think later daydreams] necessitate further splitting processes within the ego. For parts of the ego attempt to unite with the ideal object, while other parts strive to deal with the internal persecutors. . . . If states of splitting and therefore of disintegration, which the ego is unable to overcome, occur too frequently and go on for too long, then in my view they must be regarded as a sign of schizophrenic illness. . . .

(p. 103)

The problem as I see it is: how does the hysteric avoid psychotic catastrophe? I have touched on the relationship to melancholia but an even more important question is: how does he avoid fragmentation of the ego and schizophrenic illness?

Before embarking on an attempt to throw light on this, I want to refer to my own observations on cases of hysterical character. These patients believe one can be a successful hysteric, and they are obsessed with other people getting away with it either by:

1 Pretending to be well and good when they are not.
2 Pretending to be ill and incapable when they could be perfectly well and pull themselves together.

With this goes the feeling that other 'successful hysterics' manage to procure love, admiration, sympathy, etc., and get the best of all possible worlds without the inevitable conflict which is the truth of psychic life. In other words, they have a concept of avoiding psychic truth and the consequences of psychic catastrophe.

Now to my theme of the use of live external objects to avoid catastrophe. Bion (1962) has described a mechanism of an early infantile relationship as follows. The baby has unbearable anxiety such as fear of death and communicates this to the mother. In a good relationship, the mother bears this intolerable anxiety, shares it with the baby and helps to modify the fear. A mother, however, may be overwhelmed by the anxiety and communicate back to the baby that the anxiety is unbearable. At the same time, she may provide material food partly for comfort or as some form of panacea to deny the anxiety. In a similar way the analyst may supply a so-called interpretation to explain away and obviate the anxiety.

I see that such a mechanism covers a whole range of psychopathology; but say a mother has a combination of: (1) being overwhelmed by anxiety and conveying that it is catastrophic; (2) providing a panacea designed to make the baby believe everything is perfectly all right and she is absolutely secure; (3) at the same time attending to the baby with excessive indulgent attention, over-devotion, omnipotent idealization and excessive sensuous stimulation. Then I believe we have the ingredients of an hysterogenic mother – providing herself both as a model that encourages the negation of psychic reality and as an external love object to avoid catastrophe. There is, then, an attack on psychic reality and at the same time a live external mother who offers a pseudo-relationship. Hence a *modus vivendi* is established, plus a defence against catastrophe.

Now if at the same time the mother resents this devotion and simultaneously provides the infant with everything and makes the infant feel guilty whilst conveying that the infant has no right to complain, then we have this confusing collection of experience that may produce an hysterical character in an infant because: the object is always there; anxiety is conveyed by behaviour and by unconscious communication as catastropic; there is a pretence that everything is ideal and a denial that there is a problem; guilt is used for projection and avoidance of responsibility; psychological provisions to help deal with life are not given and pseudo-understanding is given instead; the infant can only identify with a phantasy unreal object. If we refer to the dream of mother washing her hair, we see some of these elements.

It does seem to me that the severe hysteric presents the analyst with problems of: a greedy dependency, forever present devotion and worship; the realization that there is a catastrophe which is utterly unbearable; pressure that this should be denied and the patient told all is well and they are lovely; pressure that guilt and responsibility should be carried by the analyst; pressure for love and appreciation of pseudo-virtues without really examining and questioning them.

Such a state of affairs interferes with the achievement of real understanding and prevents the creation of two people getting together in order to know each other and develop something meaningful and capable of further development.

I have tried to show how what I call an hysterogenic mother can facilitate the development of an hysterical character. Equally, an infant unable to bear pain with excessive greed and envy could 'hallucinate' such a mother and reject the 'good enough mother' and make the mother feel guilty and worthless if she failed to provide these 'ideal requirements'. Furthermore, I can visualize the infant being attached to such a phantasy picture and constantly seeking such an object as the mother's nipple or a later transfer to the male penis as 'the answer to the maiden's prayer'.

I can also visualize both systems in infinite combinations – all we can say is that clinically this seems to be the picture of the internal mother, in which there is a hatred of clinging to her and an attempt to relive this in the transference.

I think there is evidence of patients clinging to the 'hysterical aspects' of the mother and denying and rejecting the mature helpful aspects of the mother and reliving this in the transference. So the problem is a complex one.

The next point I wish to make is that hysterics, when relating to reasonably normal people who are on the whole kind, helpful and understanding, do not make proper use of them and benefit from them. This point concerns us because we believe we can supply some love and understanding which is useful. We are only allowed to be good and helpful and understanding if we fit in with the patient's machinations and accept their version of the truth – though we have reason to believe we are really despised if we do.

If we do not achieve anything more than a pseudo-relationship, we do not help patients to deal with their problems. When we fail to fit in with their demands we become like the rest of their objects and the hysteric is 'let down' and disappointed and treats us to the life they think we deserve – yet we have reason to believe they may be relieved as well.

If we ask ourselves why the hysteric does not use real, helpful people and only sees us in terms of the internal parents, one explanation is that this is the transference. Also the original *modus vivendi* cannot be given up because: he comforts himself and nurses himself with this 'internal mother'; he yearns for this ideal state and has no body of good experience of a loving 'problem solving' mother who has faith in problem solving; he cannot face the envy of real achieving relationships. Above all, he continues to use the hysterical defence as a means of survival either because his original mother used it, or he fixes on this 'hallucinatory gratification' as a defence, or a combination of both factors.

What I hope I have illustrated is that the analysis of symptomatology is not enough. The object to which the 'hysterical patients' cling prevents real true growth. The aim of the patient is to be a successful hysteric. These features need to be analysed in detail so that a viable alternative of faith in truth-seeking can be demonstrated by the analyst. The analyst needs to show again and again that the truth helps and not the delusional internal object. The analyst needs to show the patient the envious attacks on the capacity to seek the truth and to match this against the alleged supremacy of the delusional baby/child in relationship with the delusional internal mother.

References

Abraham, K. (1924) A short study of the development of the libido, viewed in the light of mental disorders. In *Selected Papers on Psycho-Analysis*. London: Hogarth Press, 1927, pp. 418–501.

Bion, W.R. (1962) A theory of thinking. *International Journal of Psycho-Analysis* 43: 306–310.

Freud, S. (1893–1895) Studies on hysteria. SE 2.

—— (1905) Fragment of an analysis of a case of hysteria. SE 7.

—— (1908) Hysterical fantasies and their relation to bisexuality. SE 9.

—— (1917) Mourning and melancholia. SE 14.

Klein, M. (1946) Notes on some schizoid mechanisms. *International Journal of Psycho-Analysis* 27: 99–119.

7

Meaning and meaningfulness:
touching the untouchable

In this paper I will describe a patient with whom there was enormous difficulty in establishing shared understanding which carried convincing meaning to both analysand and analyst. Vast areas of his life appeared to be untouchable. Whilst he yearned for a relationship, he marshalled his forces to prevent being known. I hope to show a change in which this 'no go' area was reached and modified, so that he could be 'touched'. It was only after he had been in analysis for over two years that he discovered that he had suffered from severe early infantile eczema. In my view, over and above the eczema itself, the way this had been dealt with both externally and internally appeared to have had a profound influence on the patient's capacity to evaluate what was meaningful.

I had seen this 45-year-old man for consultation some three months before the analysis began. He then emphasised that he suffered greatly from a depression, characterised by feelings of futility and meaninglessness in which there was no will to live. He had in the past found refuge in his work which had always remained worthwhile, and in which he had felt appreciated and rewarded by his employers. Now, most dreaded of all, the feeling of meaninglessness was invading his work; he felt that he was plunging into total hopelessness. This fear brought him to analysis. At the time I had told him that I was not certain that I would have a vacancy for him and offered to explore the possibility of an analysis for him elsewhere. He politely pressed me to make room for him.

In this initial interview I learned that he had had two previous analyses, each lasting three to four years, which terminated because of work commitments in another country, as well as two previous marriages which ended in divorce at his instigation. He had recently remarried for the third time, and this was to be the third analysis. I later learned that he frequently fell in love in a totally idealised way, and that when this broke down, the only solution available to him was to cut out the relationship and start afresh. In consequence he was assailed by persecutory guilt as a result of which he felt that he had to give everything he owned to his abandoned wife. His father had died two years previously but he gave no importance to this. I noted that there was a complete blank as to his early years. He had been extraordinarily successful academically and professionally.

On the first day of his analysis, before he lay on the couch, he was acutely anxious and propitiating; he was cautious lest he do anything out of order. He told me that he had been very disturbed when he got into his car that morning to come to his session. He had seen a dark foreigner (he himself is from a country abroad) parking his car in a place which he first called a building site, and later referred to as a demolition site. A huge foreman had rushed over to this man in a manner that was so violent and abusive that he feared that the foreman was actually going to kill this man. My patient had been terrified and the anxiety was still with him. He then told me that when he was filling his car with petrol at the garage close by my house, it had brought back memories of some years ago when a motorist came into a garage and jumped the queue – on that occasion he had feared that anyone who intervened would have killed or been killed. I was acutely aware of his desperate anxiety and of his appeal for help. The fact that I live in a private road which has a large notice stating 'PRIVATE ROAD RESIDENTS ONLY WHEEL CLAMPS IN USE' is obviously significant. After relating all this to me he lay on the couch.

In spite of this overwhelming anxiety, once on the couch he seemed unnervingly calm. He then absolutely repudiated my interpretation that he was feeling anxious in relation to 'parking' himself here, in the analysis. He was very polite, yet there was an implication which became more explicit following that interpretation, that he knew that I would make such trans-ference interpretations, but that as far as he knew there was no evidence to support my interpretation. I tried to use what seemed to me the obvious evidence in the material reported above to validate my interpretation, in the vain hope that I would reach a part of him that would understand. He met this with a complacent rejection. I then felt that any further inter-pretation which I might make would be 'jumping the queue' and would lead at least to 'litigation' (he is partly in practice as a lawyer). I noted to myself his earlier statement that anyone who intervened whilst queue jumping was in operation was in danger of being killed. My interpretation was not experienced by him as a view which could be linked with another point of view. There could be only one right meaning – his own – and correspondingly he perceived me as unable to consider a view other than my own. He did not live in a world in which someone might bring a new perspective and understanding but one in which there is only one, right point of view, which by necessity excludes all others.

On later reflection my interpretation might have dealt with the nearest to conscious manifestations of the split between his feelings on and off the couch. At the time I was astounded by the split affect – the overwhelming anxiety and the unnerving calm once he was on the couch. Yet he presented such compelling material with such 'obvious' transference implications that I felt impelled to believe that my understanding of his persecutory anxiety in the here and now was essential. I believed that I could provide meaning and be meaningful to him. I did not realise then that I was 'programmed' to be part of a re-enactment of a critical situation which I shall describe later, that is, a catastrophic inner situation which needed urgent attention. This enactment bypassed the understanding of underlying crucial emotional issues arising from other parts of himself feeling abandoned. In one way, I was, I believe, correct in my interpretation; in another way I was totally out of touch. He too was partly right, and partly in my view, totally absented himself from another area.

Some developments in the analysis

Quite early on he reported that his wife had returned an unsatisfactorily treated suit to the dry-cleaners. He said that he would be terrified to do so, as he would fear the rage of the dry-cleaner and believed that he would be 'blackballed' even from the services of other dry-cleaners if he complained, though he knew this to be absurd. He came to realise that he believed that any person who offered him faulty service, if challenged, could only take revenge; he had no belief that anyone would listen with concern for his complaint. He then modified this, saying that this did not occur in the institution in which he worked. When I linked this with the analysis and his disagreements with me and feelings of insufficient understanding, he immediately disagreed with me. He said that he felt secure, we had many disagreements, but he always felt that I tried to understand him and he could see my reasoning and my attempts to be fair with him. Although this appeared to be another sign of his compliance, I felt that he was being truthful about his immediate feelings. Once again the split between overwhelming anxiety and absolute calm was striking.

It was around this time that I realised that he had, very soon after starting analysis, recovered and indeed improved his ability to function with interest and enjoyment at work. This suggested that he was also working in the analysis, yet both these improvements remained unacknowledged. He gave all credit for these changes to the support he received from the institution he worked for, even though this support had indeed been available before the breakdown. What became apparent was that for him it was the institution and process of analysis that he found helpful; he emphasised that it was absolutely nothing personal. He dismissed personal contact as irrelevant and unnecessarily complicating, a threat to the institution.

However, on another occasion, the reverse became apparent. He arrived for a session in a very disturbed state and said that he had been disturbed the whole weekend. He gave me an account of a reproach made to him by a junior administrator in his institution; she complained that he disregarded her and did not say good morning to her; she added, 'I know that you are a very senior person, but I am also a human being.' He was terribly upset and asked the woman to see him. It seemed that she had got over this and accepted his apology. He, however, remained tormented, partly believing that he could not have done something so unforgivable and that the whole world would know of this and shun him. This oscillation between massive denial and hateful vengeful annihilation was a regular feature. That is, although he complacently claimed that personal significance was irrelevant, when his annihilation of personal meaning was revealed to him, it constituted the worst of all crimes, and he felt himself to be at the mercy of a vengeful annihilating superego. Yet in relating this to me he was also turning to me as someone who he hoped would react differently from this superego; he was relieved by the end of the session. Again we see this polarised split between experiences in life and on the couch.

By now there was a long history in the analysis in which any reference to either one of us being personally acknowledged as significant, in separation, was treated as an absurdity.

When I drew his attention to this, he would respond, 'You are quite right, it does not mean anything to me.' He believed that he was being friendly; the contemptuous dismissal of me seemed to be miles away from his capacity to be aware of it. It seemed that there was in operation a perverse practice in which he believed I participated. This involved idealisation of the capacity for dismissal of all thoughts of dependency, a possible repetition of an early experience with his caretakers. The unforgivable crime, in terms of his junior colleague's complaint about him, was that the excluded person was not acknowledged; yet it was impossible for him to acknowledge feeling left out in relation to me. Instead he maintained a separation from feeling, and a denial that I or he were disturbed by issues of separation. Annihilation takes place and it has to be accepted by both sides that this has not happened. He annihilates the knowledge that he has destroyed awareness and tries to convert me to believe that a painful experience ever existed. (And yet, as I will show later, this issue is the fundamental point in his background.)

There were repeated examples of this annihilation of personal significance, with indications both that this was dreadful and that it did not matter. Thus, I had learned that he had been the darling of his grandfather, who especially invited him for weekends, and who, out of devotion to the patient, sat through films which he (the grandfather) did not enjoy. When the grandfather died, when the patient was about 12, my patient felt nothing. The family were very upset and cried. He said, 'It may be of interest to you Doctor, to know that when I heard of his death I wet my bed on two consecutive nights.' I, of course, was interested, whilst he totally dismissed its significance. He maintained that there was no connection between the grandfather's death, the missing tears and his bed-wetting. He conveyed that he was both sub-human and lacked the capacity to feel love and loss; at the same time he again showed superior contempt in which he was 'above it all'. The underlying phantasy was that he could turn tears into urine, pee on that part of himself that valued a relationship with a helpful, loved person, and excrete the idea that loss was of significance.

Similarly, on another occasion he told me that when his father had died two years before he started analysis with me, he had experienced no feelings of loss, though family and friends cried at the funeral. Whilst at this time, he had been aware of his inability to feel, he was dubious of the sincerity of others; only the sorrow of his older sister carried conviction. He felt that the many people who came to comfort the family were all false, yet could not reconcile this with his sister receiving comfort and warmth from the belief that the memory of father was valued and kept alive by so many people. (I will refer later to the importance of this belief in the authentic, caring relationship between his sister and their father.) Equally, as his analyst, I knew how much our daily contact meant to him, yet this was totally repudiated by him. At best only an impoverished meaning survived until well into the second year of his analysis.

In the beginning I was conducting an analysis in which I had a patient who believed neither in the transference nor in dreams (this notwithstanding the fact that he had had previous analyses). When I referred to this, he presented extraordinarily long, detailed dreams. He prefaced this by saying that he knew that dreams were important to analysts; he himself thought that they had no significance. Yet again, I abstracted features of the dream to validate my earlier interpretations, showing him how they demonstrated many features that had arisen in the analysis. This was counter-productive and confirmed his view of his analyst as someone narcissistically obsessed with his own ideas, jumping the queue, and annihilating what was meaningful to him. At that time I had been dominated by the idea that the only way of establishing my significance to him was through persuasion and insistence. This was an important counter-transference experience from which I learned a great deal both as regards his early history and how I repeated it. I had the experience and the conviction that there was a child struggling to be included as meaningful, and this very struggle ensured rejection.

Very significant progress was made when he brought to me the problem for him of his wife's desire to have a baby. He lost his composure, and in agitation said that if there was to be the slightest defect or problem, they should not have a baby. A picture emerged of a continuously demanding, totally unappreciative, inconsolable infant. He seemed to be able to enjoy other parents and their children but this could not be the case for him. He believed and was determined to convince me that he and his wife were absolutely ill equipped for parenthood, and that he alone would have to carry this impossible, unbearable burden. He was not, at this point, seeking understanding or exploration but only my endorsing the affirmation that there must be no baby. This corresponded to the dogmatic way in which he cut out any reference to his own infantile feelings. Working through these problems I began to feel freer and that my hands were less tied. He could now acknowledge that the whole of his infantile life was blocked off and experienced as threatening.

The disclosure of an early infantile trauma

He had previously insisted that his mother was a totally unimportant figure; when I referred to the mother (or the mother in me, in the transference) his first impulse was to dismiss this as meaningless. Any current contact with her was something of a dutiful formality. Now in the course of such a 'dutiful' long-distance telephone conversation he had enquired and learned about his early infancy, having told his mother that this was of great importance to him (note, to him, not just an interest of mine). It emerged that when he was born, as his mother did not have enough milk, his mother's sister (who had plenty of milk) then breast-fed him. In the first week of his life he developed severe eczema. 'Distinguished' doctors prescribed ointments and his body was covered in bandages; his hands too were covered and tied to stop him scratching. This treatment continued until he was 3 years old. Mother said that he was wretched. The doctors insisted that they enforce this regime rigorously. Even after the eczema had cleared up, his mother said that, if he, for example, touched a marble table, he would experience excruciating pain; he suffered from unbearable hyper-sensitivity. The patient himself was now able to link this (and this was in itself quite an achievement) with the near chronic current hyper-sensitivity of his upper respiratory system. Although this condition was a defect he quickly reminded me that this was also a condition he held in common with a very famous man.

This account threw a good deal of light on my countertransference experience in the analysis. I had indeed felt that my hands were tied just as his had in fact been tied. How does an infant (child) experience human containment which forbade human intervention? Understandably he turned for love to a phantasy of undifferentiated mutual idealisation which pre-existed separateness. His dreams were frequently dominated by cruelty and persecution, increasingly dreams of stripping those who looked after persons in need. These dreams in which the carer was reduced to pretentious nothingness were a frequent theme. For example he brought to one session the following two dreams:

1 His father was alive and treated by a famous doctor (he associated to the famous doctor who looked after his eczema; also an allusion to a pretentious analyst/me). In this dream his father was maltreated and asked my patient to give the doctor a suitable reward. The patient provided a small box of chocolates.

This dream in my view shows his dissociation from himself as the maltreated patient (it is his father who is the patient) and the contempt for the doctor/analyst (provided with a small box of chocolates) who instigated the enquiry into his infantile life. These devices kept at bay the disruptive violence expressed in other dreams, which I will report later.

2 He came to a session and I was away. A young woman wearing a white coat stood in for me (the implication was 'dressed in her brief authority'). This woman was initially called an assistant, then not really an assistant but a secretary who was not trained to look after patients; not a doctor, not a psychoanalyst; she did not know how to conduct herself.

Although it was me who was absent, I was given the sweetener. Yet there clearly was also a view of me as pretentious, and devoid of any possibility of a meaningful contribution. Yet at this time he was making desperate efforts (in spite of having to travel abroad) to increase his sessions from four to five times a week as he knew he was being transferred abroad and would have to end his analysis earlier than had been planned. The more he realised and now conveyed how much he valued his analysis, the more intensely the devaluation was reiterated in dreams. Love and hate were now coming closer and dangerously together. The earlier extreme splitting which had been employed as a life saver was now becoming less polarised as he came nearer to the unbearableness of ambivalence.

In a dream of this period the entire resources of psychoanalysis were now to be amassed together with the single purpose of saving him, even whilst he wished to show that my efforts were pretentious and meaningless. For example, in this context he dreamed that:

He was in a place like a barren desert; he felt deprived and desperate. The whole world was 'hotting up' as a result of pollution; there were talks on the radio that the world had neglected to deal with pollution. Listening to the radio he heard that all the countries got together to save his home town (the town where he was born and where his mother and sister live). The town was so hot, some reports said 80 degrees centigrade (this, he added, was obviously incompatible with life though this did not cross his mind in the dream). The world had organised a massive fleet of planes carrying liquid to lower the temperature in his home town; it was as if all the planes in the world were assembled for that purpose; they spawned further planes. The sky was full of them. He added as an aside that of course his home town was too far to be reached, that nothing could be done about a temperature of 80 degrees centigrade; he implied that this enterprise of rescue was a gesture, a show rather than a realistic contribution. (He had recently been highly critical of the British government which had ostentatiously rescued one child from Bosnia while neglecting the holocaust there.)

There were four or five (he implied useless) guide poles to guide the planes (he made no conscious association to the four or five sessions). He was with his wife who said 'let's take one or two of these poles as a souvenir'; he replied that he could not do that, it was quite improper, and in any case they were government property. His wife tried to persuade him to take a pole. He first firmly resisted, then reluctantly acquiesced. (He told me this in a way that implied that I should take note of his correct stance under pressure.) Then a Range Rover appeared; Prince Charles, the owner of the poles, stepped out. (I knew that he perceived Prince Charles as a derisory figure, someone who tried to maintain a public image but had no idea how to live a personal life.)

As he related this dream it was clear that he was very conscious of the denigration and stripping of my worthwhileness as shown in his depiction of the person who is going to save the world as an empty selfseeker. It did not take him long to realise that he pictured the whole world as failing to look after what should be looked after, with consequent terrible retribution – the total destruction of life; pretentious exhibitions of technical caring which were totally inefficacious. The analytic guide poles were on the one hand precious and needed to be saved, and on the other hand reduced to futility. They were anyway the property of someone who did not know how to live but wanted to be in a position of majestic adulation (his view of Prince Charles). The degree of narcissistic omnipotence in which the patient's home town is the selected centre of the world to be rescued and at the same time the centre of absolutely destructive heated retribution for unwarranted neglect and destruction typifies the impasse of his wish both omnipotently to destroy beyond repair and to be nursed, saved and looked after by everyone. Yet the actual carer, the analyst, is reduced to a hypocritical, denigrated puppet.

The barren emptiness portrayed at the outset is replaced by a total hotting up into manic triumphalism which commands total service whilst all the efforts on the part of the 'world' to repair the damage are rendered futile and hollow, destined to be of no avail. He is heated up to fever pitch to the point of death, that is, psychic barrenness in which no meaningful life can survive. It was not possible in this vicious circle for me to explore how much the barren emptiness was the consequence and how much the instigator of rage.

The extent of the primitive forces at work as revealed in such dreams now went together with a genuine attempt at working through some of these issues. He was pained to realise what his dreams revealed about his inner world; the abyss between primitive destruction and genuine appreciation. He saw the Prince Charles figure as also alluding to himself, hollow as a drum, unable to live life. At no point did he see himself (or others) as a mixture of some pretension and some real achievement – it was one or the other, both being totally polarised. This excessive split, as I indicated earlier, is central to my theme. Witnessing the capacity of others to engage in an ordinary enjoyable intercourse created in him unbearable envy, which was dealt with by omnipotent triumphalism, as clearly revealed in the dream. He becomes the centre of the world and all awareness of reality is destroyed.

In his early life he had suffered deprivation, pain and wretchedness, feeling that he did not belong, a permanent outsider. (He had been removed from his mother's breast to his aunt's; his whole body eczematous, his hands tied. Presumably the whole 'world' attended to him, yet was unable to really attend to his emotional needs.) He became extraordinarily gifted at technical care (his work), winning prize scholarships to major universities outside his country. He was his grandfather's 'Majesty', he eventually gained his father's dedicated attention, he had many adoring women who were there only to be discarded by him. He had achieved the repeated involvement of analysts. At one time I pictured myself running after him with a spoon, desperate to get acknowledgement, the fate of many women in his life.

I picture this infant, his eczematous skin, hotting up with a rage which is both intensified by his deprivation and restricted so that it cannot be expressed, only screamed out of him. He is driven by this unbearable situation, maddened and tied up, to resort to his omnipotent defences. But once in his omnipotent position his provider now becomes servant to his Majesty. The object's real wish to provide is denied, and all such endeavours are viewed only as technical and pretentious. The failure to provide the understanding for which he craves is met with such hatred that he insists there is no authentic help available; he seems almost to wish to die rather than to admit that he needs help (it has to be found in an 'under the counter' way – getting the guide poles, keeping them and calling them useless souvenirs at the same time). In the analysis he was meticulous in remembering sessions and dreams, was able to link and became interested in the analytic process. The nearer we came to understanding and experiencing personal intimacy the more this faculty broke down. He hated intellectualisation and yet was a master of it.

Later developments

Gradually, when some integration had developed and he felt that emotional contact was achieved, he ended sessions by saying 'thank you' in a way that was quite genuine. He began to tell me of great improvements in his personal life, as well as a new capacity to develop more human relationships at his work. I had reason to believe that these changes were also noticed by others.

Although at times he looked forward to his sessions he could not acknowledge in a deeply personal way that he wished to see me again or that he had missed me. What he consciously yearned for in absentia was not a creative relationship, which at times he felt he discovered with me, but what he called the experience of 'coming fully alive'; this was always represented by fantasies of love affairs in which there was a vital, lively woman continuously available, adoring and at his service. He could not tolerate any frustration, any delay, without almost immediately replacing the missing object with one that was fantasised as omnipresent and completely fulfilling. Previously he had often told me that in social situations he had to be the perfect host providing total continuous satisfaction; equally when he was a guest the burden fell again totally on him to be the sole perfect provider. He saw no incongruity in these demands. He considered it just that he should be excommunicated if he failed in either position. This new experience of his reaction to separation from the analysis was the beginning of his recognition that it was he who should be provided with continuous perfect service and at the same time be regarded as the provider. The increasing clarity of this new awareness laid the foundations for a more realistic enquiry about give and take. He had been both the relentless superego and the victim of it.

Yet the obliteration had not been a total psychotic obliteration; he had seemed able both to wipe things out and to keep them encapsulated for later use and yet maintain some internal communication. But the crucial facts of his infancy had been consciously sealed off, though, as we see, they governed his life.

In the past he had been convinced that he was totally in touch with unadulterated reality and that I had created a false reality to validate my interpretations; now instead he was disturbingly aware of his own changing reality and he now regarded me as more of a helpmate to deal with this aberration. He increasingly recognised the use of his mind partly to see the world in a realistic way and partly to shape it at the service of his defences and narcissism. The analytic sessions were more fruitful, in both his view and mine. He seemed to bring together primitive and more realistic appraisals. From the dreams, however, we could see how unconsciously, this situation was misrepresented and then used to maintain his omnipotence.

For example, whilst the analysis appeared to be going comparatively well, with the achievement of insight, he produced in one session the following two dreams.

In the first dream:

He is in another part of the world chairing an important international meeting; I am somewhere there, outside the meeting, engaged in writing an academic paper.

As I understand it, I and my work have become of academic interest only, cut off from the place where real life is conducted. But he is capable of achieving integrations on a world scale.

In the second dream:

He is in an exotic place enjoying food; he meets my wife, accidentally knocks over some crockery, whilst I am seen outside on a veranda, completely asocial. He has taken over my position, my capacity to integrate, my wife (he is in an exotic place where he is tasting the special foods), and again I am not there.

These events appear to be flamboyantly obvious, but a new development was his ability now to recognise his own envious and jealous feelings. He feels embarrassed – not regretful. He begins to experience me as a significant person, needed by him. Whereas in the past he had a deep terror of being known, the feeling of being understood was now the basis of some security.

Although from the outset this was known to be a time-limited analysis it was in fact cut even shorter as he was obliged to move abroad at the end of three and a half years. The move was very painful and brought home to him the loss of analytic help, the awareness of separation and of his defences against it. Shortly after hearing about his transfer abroad he dreamed of his father's death and awoke crying and crying. He said 'why should I now be reacting like this to my father's death?' The link to the ending of the analysis had been totally disconnected, but was now easily and speedily recovered in the session.

He told me, somewhat shamefully, that he had not even told close colleagues about his move because he felt that from the moment of telling them he would cease to exist in their minds as a person of any significance. He attributed to them his own ways of dealing with loss and separation, that is, annihilation of the object and replacement of it with its successor who now becomes the only object of significance, all memory of the original object having been erased. He knew that this was mad and was amenable to understanding that it was he himself who practised this 'killing and cutting out' as a defence against feelings of catastrophic loss. He felt compelled to eradicate the past and get on with the future, and would say to me 'What is the use of dwelling on the past; what good can it possibly do?' There was no internal structure that could support an experience of working through and mourning. I believe this was linked to his experience of his illness being denied by his family. They had behaved as though it never happened. Yet there was a wish that I should maintain contact with our past, and a search for reassurance that he would not be overwhelmed by loss and guilt or the void created to obviate these feelings. This was exemplified by progress in the way he used dreams. Segal (1991) has described the different ways dreams can be used, distinguishing between communication and evacuation. This was well illustrated by my patient. His dreams were now less split off from his current feelings in his waking life and more manifestly connected to the work we were doing in the analysis.

His dreams, which earlier on had been extremely long, disconnected and were primarily used for evacuation and to disown aspects of himself, were now shorter, coherent and accomplished dream work commensurate with his current reality state. For example, he now dreamed:

He was in a town house in his own country (at home). It was small with an extension at the back that at one time accommodated servants (my consulting room is now at the back of the house). Now it is a study room. As the dream continued he took his food downstairs to a private part of the house and there he heard my voice expressing affectionate greeting at the return of a woman friend who had been absent. My wife also appeared in the dream as a sympathetic concerned person.

This was now no dry intellectual study; in the dream he has an affectionate and meaningful father and mother, but of course he now has an oedipal problem to face, a new more conscious challenge. His dreams also included references to his wish that I keep him alive in my mind, and his attempt to keep me alive. He was now, in reality, in closer contact with his sister and felt fortified by her, sharing with her thoughts about their dead father – a relationship with someone who understood and could share in the loss of a parent/analyst.

He left analysis expressing deep appreciation but with questions in both our minds about the fragility of this improvement. True to form he said 'If ever you are in X and need anything, however trivial, please do not hesitate to get in touch with me. I'll be only too happy to be of service to you' – hinting at the danger of the re-emergence of his apparent obsequiousness, both hiding and revealing the underlying omnipotent superiority. This expressed both his wish genuinely to reciprocate my care and his compulsion to be the perfect provider, with his analyst placed in a position of need.

Discussion

This relatively brief analysis raises many issues. Was the retrieved information about his infancy authentic and does it have any link to 'recovered memory'? How much did this information illuminate or misguide the analytic couple? How useful was this information in the process of working through in the transference and countertransference interaction?

In the light of the massive splitting in this patient, where opposites could not be allowed to come together (so that incongruities in his life had remained unrecognised), the information about his early history helped patient and analyst to extend awareness. I became more in touch with the problem of his inability to believe in personal intimacy (rather than fusion) and the way in which this intimacy was unconsciously both yearned for and feared. This yearning was suffused with grievance which fuelled and was fuelled by envy so that coming alive not only exposed him to frustration and loneliness but to the fear of a catastrophic tragedy in which vengeful hatred would destroy his world. This realisation made sense of his earlier search for intimacy as an undifferentiated union where 'two hearts beat as one', even though he knew that this would end in tragedy when reality would strike home.

This splitting had served a function of promoting survival. Integration was not possible, as the only outcome for him was a violent meeting of irreconcilable forces, as he so clearly communicated in the first session. Had I been aware of his history earlier I might have given a different emphasis. Not being thus aware enabled me to have the experience in the countertransference of the pain of dependency on an object who negated my meaning. I enacted in vain a demand for understanding knowing that it would be met by a rejection suffused with sadism.

The normal developmental process in which the mother provides a home for the projective identification of the infant, and lays the foundation of a faith that the infant is meaningful, was grossly impaired. This absence of an experience in which the infant is enabled to ascribe personal meaning to the mother resulted not only in the deprivation of mutual meaning-fulness, but exacerbated desperate impulses both to find meaning and to vengefully destroy meaning.

The two dreams which followed the information about his history (one in which the famous doctor is rewarded with a small box of choco-lates, the other in which the analyst is clearly depicted as an impostor) showed his contemptuous dismissal of caretakers, whose contribution he clearly depicted as meaningless. However, as he came to value the analysis more and, for example, radically changed his work schedule to gain an extra session, the conflict between yearning for help and his violent grievances erupted, as was clearly depicted in the 'world catastrophe' dream I reported. The vengeance he felt for the way he was treated, the omni-potent reaction and the depiction of desperate efforts to save the world, with the barren consequence, revealed the extent of the impasse. Yet he made use of this realisation to begin the task of re-evaluating his past and later experiences.

The question which arises is what it was that enabled him now to embark on this new development. In the past he had employed excessive splitting, keeping the early infantile experience totally sealed off from consciousness. This had presumably included a family conspiracy of silence, as though there was a hidden agreement that awareness of those events would be beyond anyone's capacity to manage.

It was only after the understanding of that major dream, which had a considerable impact on him, that he was able more fully to recognise his own violence. This had in the past always been so strenuously repudiated. The experience of an analyst who survived the onslaught and was felt able to perceive and tolerate the violence, without counter-violence, was central. This development had its precursors in the analysis, and in that part of him that had, notwithstanding the splitting, remained able to observe a relationship of love and hate coming together, with a favourable ending. I have earlier alluded to the importance to him of the observed passionate relationship between his father and sister. This had played a significant part in his quest to find persons who were authentically truthful and loving, to counteract the pervasive feelings of there being no real concern, only hypocritical imitation.

He had described violent quarrels between them, in which they had insulted each other, smashed plates, slammed doors; he had feared that they would murder each other. But they would always make up and were pleased to repair and recreate the lost good relationship. This was a different world which contrasted with his anxieties (evidenced from the very first session) that damage was final, irreparable and devastating and should be put out of mind as quickly as possible. This relationship between father and sister seemed to have served as a model, a live and authentic relationship, which had been kept alive by him despite his insistence that this did not exist.

Later, when he was becoming more integrated and more aware of his aggressive rivalry with me, he dreamed (as I wrote earlier) that he was in an exotic place enjoying food, meeting my wife and accidentally knocking over crockery. He now brings the smashed plates (connected to the rows between father and sister) directly into the oedipal conflict with me.

Whereas in the past the meticulous care he had been given formed the basis for his meticulous academic and professional achievements (in which he had felt well, if not excessively, supported by the family), now he had some access to a richer emotional life.

As a postscript I would mention that the patient came to see me very recently, some three years after ending; he greeted me in a warm, affectionate way, expressing much appreciation of his analysis and telling me that I would be pleased to learn of the further changes he had made and that he was now looking forward to the possibility of he and his wife having a baby. He felt confident in their ability to take care of a baby. Professionally, he was working in the same field and had been asked by the parent body of his organisation to undertake the task of reconstructing and modernising the whole organisation. I thought that whatever degree of omnipotent rivalry might be present, this was an apposite description of the predominantly positive sublimation of our work together.

References

Freud, S. (1917) Mourning and melancholia SE 14, p. 246.

Rosenfeld, H.A. (1971) A clinical approach to the psychoanalytic theory of the life and death instincts: an investigation into the aggressive aspects of narcissism. *International Journal of Psycho-Analysis* 52: 169–178.

Segal, H. (1991) *Dream, Phantasy and Art*. London: Routledge.

Steiner, J. (1994) *Psychic Retreats*. London: Routledge.

8

The recovery of the good object relationship: the conflict with the superego

In her 1937 paper 'Love, guilt and reparation', Melanie Klein stresses the power of hate and destruction. These forces are seen as fundamental and universal. Klein goes on to say that love and reparation are equally powerful. Her work is of course built on Freud's views, which she extends to the earliest beginnings of life. Klein explored the basic internal struggle that occurs with primitive forces of love and hate; this Klein called the paranoid-schizoid position; attachment to an idealised object is sought and the destructive forces are split off and projected. Subsequently this paranoid-schizoid position meets a more humanised realistic understanding, a state she called the depressive position, which in favourable circumstances moderates the primitive forces of splitting and projection. There is regret at the primitive damage done and a wish to initiate reparation. The moderation of the primitive forces is made possible by the establishment of an appreciative good object relationship, which comes to carry more weight than the primitive forces.

It is generally accepted that the constant interaction between love and hate occurs throughout life and the balance between these states of mind shapes the character of a person.

Who or what accompanies or deserts one on this journey through life makes all the difference. The nature of the external and internal objects is, of course, of vital consequence. When there is a breakdown in the good object relationship the superego (which I will discuss later) holds sway. My main object in this paper is to address the task of recapturing the good object relationship that helps in the move from the paranoid-schizoid to the depressive position, and the modification of the harsh superego.

94

We are all driven, in varying degrees, by love and hate – feelings which exist in both the patient and the analyst. There is no final resolution between these states, no absolute purity one way or the other. But, crucially, the superego does not recognise this complexity and ambiguity: it maintains that one view is absolutely right and operates like an absolutist monarch (the divine right of kings/gods). No one entirely escapes the force of such superego judgement; it is highly persuasive in its insistence on its own singular 'right minded' judgement. We are all vulnerable and all perpetrators.

The superego is a feared, hated and loved object. It demands blind worship like the god of fundamentalism.

The superego powerfully influences our judgement. It is an internal object/subject, which has a relationship with the ego. However, unlike the internal object one might encounter in the depressive position, which provides help to the ego in making a judgement, which gives food for thought to enable a person to work out what is the best thing to do under the circumstances, the primitive superego is prone to overrule the ego. The power of this superego varies in strength from a nagging sense of guilt, to reproaches of such intensity that a person is left feeling totally worthless and unforgivable, driven to melancholia and even madness. This is usually referred to as the murderous superego.

When Freud first wrote about the superego he differentiated two types of internal objects: the so-called 'good' superego was termed the ego ideal. This contained our idealistic aspirations and yearnings. This 'benign' super-ego is in my view not so benign, as it is still instilled with the belief that one should live up to 'ideals' rather than helping someone to be a person in their own right and make their own decisions. As Hanna Segal has repeatedly argued, the other side of the coin in idealisation is persecution; idealisation really belongs to the paranoid-schizoid world.[1]

In her somewhat neglected paper 'On the sense of loneliness' (1963), Melanie Klein emphasised that in loneliness the main factor was the crippling of the self in pursuit of the ideal, and having to be the ideal. Her clear message was in the direction of the need for a realistic relationship rather than the relationship with the delusional idealised self and object. Although she did not develop this theme in that paper she ended by making the important observation that the worst kind of superego is one that says

---

1 The views that I put forward in this paper rely on Freud and Klein and the 1934 classic paper of James Strachey on the mutative interpretation. However I hope to illustrate these forces as they appear in clinical practice.

that 'it should never have happened in the first place'. I would extend this to include the dictate: 'you were wrong from the start, you should not be you, you ought to be someone else'. Submission to this dictate may result in someone forgoing their own reality and becoming a 'false self' in order to obtain love. This may be felt to be imposed by the superego, whose dictates may be consciously accepted, even whilst grievances are unconsciously nursed; I hope to illustrate this in my clinical example.

We may conceptualise love and hate separately from one another, but Klein invites us to see that there is a constant interaction between them. In our clinical work it is important to see elements of love and hate operating at the same time. Of course in some difficult cases the hate is so strong that awareness of love, even the possibility of love, is destroyed.

In 'Mourning and melancholia' Freud famously described how the mourner comes to know what he has lost; yet the mourner (like the melancholic) may go through mad states of mind before eventually recovering. At the time of his writing that paper, object relations theory was not yet developed, but Freud's move toward his 1923 paper is quite clear. With the discovery and love of the good object, recovery is possible. In fact Freud went further; the object is experienced as giving the mourner permission to say goodbye, and to find a new lease of life on his/her own. Keeping the good object alive, or recapturing it, is the gateway to healthy development. Freud contrasts this with the situation of the melancholic. Here the sufferer has lost the good object but does not know what he has lost and therefore cannot recover in the same way as the mourner. As we know from clinical experience, the good object may be converted and corrupted into hyper-eroticism, mania, drugs, mad idealisations, revenge and so forth, which pervert the capacity for realistic judgement.

The melancholic has destroyed what good object relationships he has had and he has also destroyed, as Bion (in *Learning from Experience*) argued, his perceptual capacity to be aware of the needed good object relationship. Even in less pathological states of mind, something of the relentless superego, derived from the earliest times, remains unmodified by good object relations. Consequently there is always conflict between human object relationships and the superego. Where there is no good object relationship in operation, a powerful superego holds sway.

In the clinical situation, I stress that only a patient with some access to a good object relationship can make use of an interpretation of destructive propensities in a way that helps him/her in the struggle with love and hate. Without sufficient attachment to the good object relationship, interpretations of destructive propensities are experienced as superego reproaches, and as demands that the patient should be ideal and free of hatred. I will try to illustrate, with a clinical example, the difficulties in trying to establish such a process. If you fail to address the destructive forces in the patient, you endorse his feelings of masochistic victimisation; if you fail to address the circumstances which promote this, you make him unfairly totally responsible, and likewise increase the sense of masochistic victimisation. For reflection and insight to become possible, a degree of a good object relationship must be present. The problem is a knotty one.

It seems to me that the question is how far the good object can modify the destructiveness of the superego; conversely, how powerful is the super-ego in overruling the good object? This is further complicated by the fact that the powerful superego can itself be viewed, and indeed worshipped, by slavish devotion, as the all-powerful good god (the essence of funda-mentalist worship). One way of looking at this is to try to gauge how far the patient is 'devoted' to the superego, and how far to the good object relationship that would help to modify its impact. That is the essence of this paper.

As I wrote in the preface to this book, Freud selected Sophocles' play, *Oedipus Rex*, as a basis for his epoch-making discovery of the universality of the Oedipus complex. The dynamic force of the play depends on the statement in the play that the gods have ordained that Oedipus would kill his father and marry his mother. Why did the Greeks in this play create and worship such gods who had overriding control of destiny? It seems that this primitive force is a fact of life. The drama is the conflict between human intervention and primitive forces.

Similarly in the early Old Testament God is perceived as someone who made the world, demands unconditional worship and human sacrifice together with constant service, whilst at the same time has no concern with the difficulties people have in coping with life. This god threatens catas-trophe if he is not obeyed and shows no forgiveness. It is interesting, as I noted in the preface, that Melanie Klein wrote about the *Orestian Trilogy* of Aeschylus; she shows the ever-increasing revenge which takes place. She describes the very delicate balance between the unforgiving vengeance and the human understanding of forgiveness. In this trilogy the gods meet to decide whether Orestes should be forgiven or not for having killed his mother; the goddess Athene casts her vote in favour of forgiveness. In these two plays, *Oedipus Rex* and the *Orestian Trilogy*, we see the operation on the one hand of the unrelenting superego, and on the other hand of human understanding and forgiveness. What a sensitive balance it is with only Athene's casting vote to decide.

How does the superego come about?

Freud in his 1915 paper 'Instincts and their vicissitudes' considered that hate was a much older force than love; I think that the primitive ruthless superego is one of the earliest organisations in the psyche and that the loving human understanding which moderates it is developed by the interaction of love in the earliest feeding relationship. Many analysts have written of the delusional phantasies of the baby. Freud spoke of His Majesty the Baby, Klein and also Winnicott referred to the baby's belief that he owns the breast, even that he is the breast; that is, that he is being the ideal breast, or at least is fused with the ideal breast. The baby splits off his bad impulses into the 'bad breast' to get rid of disturbing awareness; this is a necessary process for psychic survival. At the same time, as part of the survival kit, the baby realistically seeks the nipple/breast to obtain nourishment. The infant, then, has both the delusional belief as well as some realistic assessment of what is essential for life.

How far does the baby corrupt truth in order to survive? He behaves as though he owns everything and yet has the nous to know what is needed for survival. This conduct of the baby corresponds to the superego which overrides realistic judgement – a superego which, like the baby, demands total service, yet is the god-like creature, which has it all and succeeds in persuading others that that is so. If this is so we might have to consider that this incongruous 'madness' is essential to promote life. In this arrangement, in the case of the infant, the parents and family may agree about the length of time that this 'madness' should be supported. As Abraham suggested, over-indulgence can support the delusional omnipotence and deprivation may leave the infant with no other attachment to counteract this belief. The outcome, of course, will depend on the nature of the interaction between the mother and the baby in the negotiation between a primitive process and truth.[2]

The baby's demands for an ideal object cannot realistically be fulfilled; no more can the mother's infantile narcissistic demand to be the perfect mother with the perfect baby. The mother, who draws strength from her own experience of working through depressive disappointment and her own love and gratitude for the infant, feels supported to tolerate her own hateful narcissistic resentment of the real baby, as well as 'oedipal' resent-

2 It is interesting to note that fundamentalists, of any colour, believe that they are justifiably right and are entitled to destroy everything in their struggle against an implacable enemy that demands unconditional surrender.

ment of the baby who 'spoils' her coupling. Such a mother, who it is hoped has appropriate tolerance for the infant's rage, and her own disappointment in and hatred at not finding the perfect baby/mother couple, who is respectful of the primitive forces but nevertheless takes in both what the infant needs, and what she needs, is well placed to support the infant to move from imperious demands to human concern and mutual empathy. The introjection of such a mother, if appreciated by the infant, becomes internalised and promotes security in enquiry and development.

This development is always imperfectly achieved and the murderous superego represents the narcissistic element, which relentlessly campaigns for perfection. This part refuses to be humanised and feeds itself with manic moral supremacy.

This of course has been written about, in detail, by Bion, but I would like here to stress two factors: first, that it is not just the mother doing the right thing, but the helpful mother is mindful of the value of the primitive as well as the value of human understanding, and supports a reasonable compromise. I share the view that we have to go through these processes from madness to sanity; for example, to give a simple analogy in later life: if a young man were to propose marriage realistically, and say: 'I overvalue you as a love object', although true, this would be mad. We consider it appropriate that he initially idealises.[3]

The good object is the one that has worked through a fair amount of the paranoid-schizoid–depressive position process and has become more capable of making human judgements. Yet there is always some primitive residue.

For example: in supervising colleagues exposed to attacks by patients out to prove that the analyst is a total fraud, totally useless and has nothing to commend him/her, it is striking how frequently analysts are deeply affected by this onslaught, and do indeed succumb to feeling totally worthless. In 'Mourning and melancholia' (1917) Freud describes the fraudulence and pretensions of the melancholic and adds 'We only wonder why a man has to be ill before he can be accessible to a truth of this kind', and quotes from *Hamlet*, 'Use every man after his desert, and who shall 'scape whipping?'

I think it is extremely important that the analyst allow himself to know of both his pretentious and his real parts; this mixture is often not recognised and tolerated; the analyst then feels 'found out' by the patient, and is overwhelmed by the onslaught; in the process of denying the fraudulent

---

3 I am stressing that he has to go through the experience of loving idealisation, hateful disappointment, and subsequently, it is hoped, with maturity, value reality.

part of himself, he has lost contact with the creditable genuine parts of himself. It is also essential that the analyst does not unconsciously convey that he (the analyst) is free of this conflict and can be totally rational. Bion described this succinctly when he said that when we learn something we also learn how ignorant we are and need an apparatus to cope with this. (The spell of 'Eureka' should be short-lived.)

I showed in the previous paper on 'Meaning and meaningfulness' the particular way in which a patient was governed by a murderous fundamentalist superego. If we revisit that paper we are entitled to raise questions. As I said, from early infancy on, this patient, bandaged as he was, going on for over three years, whilst provided with meticulous, devoted medical care, was deprived of intimate personal contact. The effect of this was a failure of provision that might have helped develop security and might have provided an opportunity to work through problems of deprivation, greed and rivalry and secure a bond of good relationships with which to venture into life.

From the first session he conveyed that he was living in a world where ruthless egocentric demands of a murderous kind menaced him This menace went hand in hand with a murderous superego which threatened to kill him if he expressed his desires. This situation led to an impasse which restricted him and appeared to bring life to a virtual standstill.

For these reasons, finding a retreat in an academic, professional, scientific world seemed to be a reasonable choice, and confining me to such a world was something which was, in his state of mind, to be recommended. I observed, however, that not only did he feel free to dismiss any interpretations of his human need, he also devalued me and felt quite safe to do so. In this way he had a different experience in which apparently he did not feel constricted; indeed it seemed that it might be safe to come alive.

The question thrown up by this account of his history was – if he was deprived of compassionate human intervention why did he not seek it? At first glance one might think that the traumatic experience he had had must certainly exist in his internal world; the dread of repetition would be paramount. I also knew that one of his aims was to find a totally consuming sexual and personal relationship – an 'ideal love' – two hearts that beat as one, thus insulating himself from the vicissitudes of a relationship between separate persons. The fulfilment of these wishes was compulsively sought; in reality it inevitably failed, leading to quite severe depression. These wishes were not, however, evicted from his mind; instead they operated in so powerful a manner that they obliterated learning from experience.

What had happened to his wish to have a containing mother who might take in how he felt, share his plight and help him to work through some of his problems and mourn what could not be achieved? This, it seemed, was a 'no go' area. During the course of the analysis, an event which had really shaken him was when he realised that he had failed to greet a junior administrator with a 'good morning'; he had been insensitive to her need to find a human home (in my patient). He was shattered, broken and felt that he would be publicly exposed and shamed.

There are two contradictory yet interlocked elements. He was frantic to come to tell me about this; he obviously felt that this was a safe place for this confession. At the same time he was totally convinced, without foundation, that the junior administrator (whom I shall call J) would be mortified at not finding a home in his mind where she would feel that she had a meaningful place. How did it come about that he was so convinced that J would be shattered by this experience and yet he had always maintained that he did not need such provisions from me? His anxieties always seemed to be in the area of what the community or society would think, rather than the personal individual relationship.

He did achieve some intellectual insight from the dream of the events in his home town, which followed upon his learning about his early infancy and childhood. He could see how his home town had been punished for not attending to extremely important matters, and his burning hot reaction. The most telling thing in the dream was that the attempts to extinguish the fires were deemed to be designed to acquire the love of the world, a vainglorious display which was absolutely unhelpful, led by a man who was hollow as a drum – the transference implication was clearly that I was a loveless narcissist.

If the narcissist was able to be appreciative of the love he received, the narcissism might contain the seeds of a potentially loving relationship; this could move through developments from the paranoid-schizoid position. The singularity of simultaneously demanding love and demeaning the provider is a feature very often seen in clinical practice. To some extent it is universal. I referred earlier to Freud's reference in 'Mourning and melancholia' to the fraudulent stealing of love in melancholia, and Freud's question of why a person has to be ill before he can acknowledge his cannibalistic appropriation of all that is good. The true acknowledgement and working through of this cannibalism and the reparative guilt is, of course, the keynote to recovery.

We recall that in his very first session he reported that someone parking his car in the wrong place, or on another occasion jumping the queue, was in danger of retributive murder. Likewise that having his radio on too loud would result in public disgrace, or complaining to a shopkeeper could have lethal consequences. All these, and many other examples, illustrate an uncontained primitive ruthlessness and unforgiving retribution, unmodified by human intervention. He both steals the love and strips others of their capacity to love and therefore lives in a totally primitive and dangerous world. The danger comes from the destruction of appreciative love. This comes close to Melanie Klein's description of envy of the breast, in which the breast is denuded of goodness, and the tragic consequences of living in a loveless world, where reparation is not efficacious.

The murderous superego is autocratic, does not value others, demands to be worshipped and demands to be considered above the realistic ego. It is given this priority in which it is preferred to reciprocal appreciation, when loving intercourse breaks down, rather than struggling to repair the broken-down relationship. Unfortunately we see these features not only in the consulting room but also on the world stage.

From the outset I was struck by the complete security this patient had when lying on the couch and the terror he felt outside; here he was in a special sanctuary where we both became harmonious scientists away from the perils of personal human intercourse. This was an ostensible good object relationship – not one which helped him to deal with the problems of life, rather a sanitised place where human emotions of want and responsibility did not arise. We were both dedicated to truth.

This case well illustrates Freud's description of melancholia. The patient was the victim of lovelessness and false claims of concern. Yet he did exactly the same to his objects. Plaints or complaints, victim or perpetrator, chicken or egg?

In an unpublished paper (referred to by Elizabeth Bott Spillius in 2004) Melanie Klein emphasises the importance of discovering how a patient becomes the character he/she is and why he/she behaves in that particular way. It is my view that without this understanding one does not understand the patient.

In the case I have illustrated I have tried to show how the recapturing of the good object relationship is vitally necessary to recover from illness and to proceed in creative endeavour. The good object to which I refer is the combined (intimate) relationship of the infant and mother and the subsequent development extending to other object relationships, in which persons give personal meaning to each other. I postulated that nothing could be meaningful without this foundation. However, in certain instances I think that this theory is open to partial question.

Further exploration of the constituents of the good object

Charles Darwin's mother died when he was 8½ years old and he had no memory of her. When he was 32 years old and already famous for his work, his cousin wrote to him saying that his (the cousin's) wife had died; Darwin replied saying that he did not know what to say as he had never lost anyone close to him. I have taken this information from John Bowlby's biography of Darwin; Bowlby in fact provides numerous further illustrations of Darwin's obliteration of the concept of 'Mother'.

The dedicated pursuit to find the 'Origin of Species' was conducted, then, by someone who was apparently emotionally unaware of the loss of his mother. Many academics have questioned why Darwin called his book *On the Origin of Species* when it was in their view an account of an adaptation to cataclysmic events. Indeed one might consider that Darwin's pursuit was an unconscious adaptation to a cataclysmic happening! He wiped out his awareness of his origins and he could not leave it alone; he was totally governed by this enquiry. We also know how crippled Darwin was by severe bouts of melancholia, a condition which Freud regarded as a negation of the awareness of the loss of a good object as opposed to the sadness of a mourner.

Isaac Newton's father died before he was born; his mother remarried when he was 2 years old and sent the child to his grandmother. Newton was unable to make a stable human relationship and suffered psychotic breakdowns. Yet he spent his life working out in detail the relationship of heavenly bodies, their attractions and repulsions, and produced mathematical laws that explained planetary motion for the first time – discoveries which held sway for 250 years.

Both Newton and Darwin opened up areas of meaningfulness which expanded our awareness and changed our lives. One is hard put to see the operation of a good object relationship derived from personal experience.

Albert Einstein's life also illustrates this combination of pursuing a cosmic truth endlessly with a corresponding impoverishment of the exploration of a personal intimate relationship. In my view this is not based on a choice which is made, but it appears that irreconcilable forces demand satisfaction. Whilst Einstein was careful not to write an autobiography, his writings are revealing about himself. For example, in his lecture on the occasion of Max Planck's 60th birthday Einstein wrote as follows:

> I believe with Schopenhauer that one of the strongest motives that lead men to art and science is escape from everyday life with its painful

crudity and hopeless dreariness, from the fetters of one's shifting desires A finely tempered nature longs to escape from personal life into the world of objective perception and thought. This desire may be compared with the townsman's irresistible longing to escape from his noisy, cramped surroundings into the high mountains, where the eye ranges freely through the still pure air and fondly traces out terrestrial contours apparently for eternity.

With this negative motive there goes a positive one. Man tries to make for himself in the fashion that suits him best, a simplified and intelligible picture of the world; he then tries to some extent to substitute this cosmos of his for the world of experience and thus to overcome it. This is what the painter, the poet, the speculative philosopher and the natural scientist do, each in his own fashion. Each makes this cosmos and its construction the pivot of his emotional life, in order to find in this way the peace and security he cannot find within the all-too-narrow realm of swirling personal experience.

The supreme task of the physicist is to arrive at those universal elementary laws from which the cosmos can be built by pure deduction. There is no logical path to these laws, only intuition, resting on sympathetic understanding, can lead to them. The longing to behold cosmic harmony is the source of the inexhaustible patience and experience to which Planck has devoted himself. The state of mind that enables a man to do work of this kind is akin to that of the religious worshipper or the lover; the daily effort comes from no deliberate intention or programme but straight from the heart.

One may speculate about what love there was and the role of splitting and sublimation. It is obvious that human values do come into Einstein's life, for example his dedicated wish to curtail the use of the atomic bomb (which of course he helped to discover!) and to help his fellow Jews in their plight in Germany – though most of this he believes occurs in terms of the general conscience which he cannot really express in intimate personal relations.

Einstein was aware of this in his later life and wrote:

My passionate sense of social justice and social responsibility has always contrasted oddly with my pronounced lack of need for direct contact with other human beings and human communities. I am truly a 'lone traveller' and have never belonged to my country, my home, my friends or even my immediate family with my whole heart. In the face of all these ties, I have never lost a sense of distance and a need for solitude – feelings that increase with the years.

104

Einstein also wrote that he was constantly aware when personal love was shown to him that he could not really do justice to it.

He also wrote:

> An uneasy feeling comes over me when the inevitable birthday nears. All year long the Sphinx stares at me in reproach and reminds me painfully of the Uncomprehended blotting out the personal aspects of life. Then comes the accursed day when the love shown me by my fellow man reduces me to a state of hopeless helplessness. The Sphinx does not let me free for a moment, and meanwhile I am troubled by a bad conscience, being unable to do justice to all this love because I lack inner freedom and relaxation.

He knew he did not do justice to the personal human love which moved him so greatly.

On one occasion when Hermann Broch gave him a copy of his book on the poet Virgil, Einstein expressed himself in Faustian terms. 'I am fascinated by your Vergil (sic) and I am steadfastly resisting him. The book shows me clearly what I fled from when I sold myself body and soul to Science. The flight from the I and the WE to the IT.'

There seem to be several truths to consider:

1 The study of our nature and the influence of the external and internal environment.
2 The human factor in which the understanding, under the sway of loving concern and ethical values, includes a sense of responsibility to do right by the others.
3 A cosmic truth about the nature of the world and the scientific way, which can lead to a sense of belonging, shared by scientists with their love of the concept of the cosmos, which takes precedence over intimate personal love and getting to know the other deeply.

Whilst Newton and Darwin respectively suffered depression and psychosis, Einstein felt consciously guilty about not giving precedence to personal intimate relationships, from which he admits he ran away. It seems a price is paid whatever we do; there is a gain and loss. It is impossible to fully integrate these forces in personal living. In human affairs there is a delicate balance between our primitive nature and human understanding. This is brilliantly illustrated in Klein's paper on the *Orestian Trilogy*, as I mentioned earlier.

It does seem to me that psychoanalysis itself, like every other study, has at times, proceeded on the lines of scientific enquiry which runs the risk of neglecting the human condition, and at other times in our clinical work stressing the intricate human relationship; it seems impossible to achieve total integration as a continuous enterprise. We obviously have something to say on this matter; scientists are concerned about these issues. For example, Joseph Rotblatt, who gave up his work on the atomic bomb, said that ultimately scientists have to reckon what they owe to science and what they owe to humanity, and that humanity takes precedence – an issue to which we may contribute from our knowledge of clinical studies.

References

Bion, W. R. (1962) *Learning from Experience*. London: Heinemann.

Bowlby, J. (1990) *Biography of Charles Darwin*. London: Hutchinson, pp. 58–62.

Freud, S. (1915) Instincts and their vicissitudes. SE 14.

—— (1917) Mourning and melancholia. SE 14.

—— (1923) The ego and the id. SE 19.

Hoffman, B. (1975) *Albert Einstein*. London: Paladin Press, pp. 221–222, 253–255.

Klein, M. (1937) Love, guilt and reparation. *The Writings of Melanie Klein*, Vol. 1. London: Hogarth Press.

—— (1957) *Envy and Gratitude*. New York: Basic Books.

—— (1963) On the sense of loneliness. *The Writings of Melanie Klein*, Vol. 3. London: Hogarth Press.

Epilogue

When my love swears that she is made of truth
I do believe her, though I know she lies.

(Shakespeare, 'The Passionate Pilgrim')

Freud in 'Mourning and melancholia' stressed that the recovery of the lost good object relationship through mourning enabled that relationship to live in the internal world and support growth. Klein, whilst she gave the same emphasis, augmented this with her emphasis on the importance of reparation for damage done that reinstated the good elements.

In so many cases of psychopathology there is no accessible memory of the value of the good object relationship; instead that space is occupied by a harsh superego, idealisation and numerous other developments some of which I have mentioned in the papers in this book. What has struck me as common to all these conditions is that the gainful achieving relationship of valuing each other and getting to know each other, needing and helping each other, is overtaken by either omnipotence or the slavish worship of omnipotence.

However this has come about (for example, through deprivation, grievance, rivalry, envy, etc.), what I am underlining is the ubiquitous denial of the need for the good object. The slavish worship of omnipotence is the common denominator. I have described very different patients but they share this delusion. For example, the patient who ostensibly comes for help, but instead canvases the analyst's love and admiration at the same time annihilating any belief that the analyst has anything to offer; or the obsessional who insists that his security in life depends on conforming to certain rituals and nothing else matters; or the schizophrenic who can maintain that he is Napoleon and/or Jesus Christ and in his paranoid delusion is convinced that he is robbed of recognition. In all these cases there is a persistent belief that a single object possesses all goodness and knowledge, etc. It follows that there is no available human understanding (wisdom) that contains and helps to achieve and come to terms with limitations.

When there is no good object available there is nothing to stop the further destruction of the good qualities (that is, no mitigating force), and the secret stealing (looting) of the goodness prevails. Like the primitive god who demands human sacrifice, the single-minded dictator/superego not only triumphs over goodness but appropriates the very source of goodness. It then also claims moral entitlement (equivalent to the rights of conquest) with a new 'ism' in waiting. The more 'truthful' parts, which may seek help from understanding, are contemptuously despised as weak, for a failure of self-sufficiency. These parts are shamed, and seem to be offered only the alternatives of humiliation or death; they are obliged otherwise to identify with (Freud's identification with the aggressor) and become the 'divine' dictator or part of the dictatorship, or face excommunication.

This tragedy is further heightened when the patient moves toward feelings of guilt; having established his ruthless superego values, he is now hoist with his own petard and believes himself to be eternally unforgivable. In the psychoanalytic encounter, the capacity of the analyst, able (partially) to experience and survive these onslaughts, and retain faith in human achievement, rather than retribution and blame, may provide the foundation stones for a different development in which there can be an appropriate valuing of each other in a mutually meaningful relationship.

When this breaks down, as inevitably it will, we create the illusion of being the ones who can cope with all vicissitudes. The reality is that we both cope and pretend we can cope – we look at truth and pervert truth. Psychoanalysis has so often been presented as either the cure for all ills or a grand fraudulent delusion (Freud/fraud); yet the understanding of this very dichotomy is something to which psychoanalysis can contribute. Sadly, the more common way of dealing with these problems personally and socially (like the schizophrenic, the fundamentalist and the romantic) has been to maintain that I (or mine) am the embodiment of truth, and others rob me of this recognition with their pretentious lies. This pattern will repeat again and again; the claims of cosmic or scientific truth and illusion all compete to be entitled to be crowned as the 'good object'. Working through disillusionment and mourning and abstracting the best deserves proper consideration.

Introduction to the clinical seminars

Franco De Masi

Several English colleagues led clinical seminars in Milan in the 1980s and 1990s, and they were very influential in the development of our thinking and clinical practice. I want to use this opportunity to express my enduring gratitude to all of them: Irma Brenman Pick, Betty Joseph, Donald Meltzer, Margaret Harris and Herbert Rosenfeld (whose Italian seminars were published in Italy and were subsequently translated into English).

Many analysts in Italy became interested, during this period, in post-Kleinian thinking. I remember that, at that time, some Italian psychoanalysts came to live in England, or commuted between London and Milan or Rome, in order to have a Kleinian analysis. The people who invited the English colleagues were young associate members, who had a strong desire to listen to and keep in touch with the psychoanalytical ideas which were developing abroad. These ideas helped us to listen more deeply to our patients in our consulting rooms. I think I can say that the professional skills of some analysts of our generation originated more from the teaching of those English colleagues than from that of even the most esteemed and admired Italian training analysts.

The link with British psychoanalysis promoted a change in the traditional connections between our Italian Society and foreign Psychoanalytical Societies. There was a move, for people of my generation, away from the French psychoanalytical tradition towards the British one: strong ties were formed with the Kleinian group. The work, which followed this new interest in British psychoanalysis helped us to grow professionally. For several years now, we have been more active in the international psychoanalytical movement, we begin to have a leading role and are able to present new and original topics to the international community.

What has been the specific help which Eric Brenman has given to the Milanese Psychoanalytical Group? I think that his contribution is engraved in the very texture of our analytical identity. I want to remind you of a book, published ten years ago by Karnac and edited by Luciana Nissim and Andreina Robutti. The title is *Shared Experience* and it contains papers by Di Chiara, Nissim, Robutti, Ferro, Bezoari, Vallino, Gagliardi and me.

It was not by chance that we asked Eric Brenman to write the foreword to this book. The book is the result of the very creative impact which Eric's teaching had on the work of the Milanese colleagues who attended his seminars, and shows how we grew and developed our own distinctive psychoanalytical identity.

I think that Eric Brenman was for us the first psychoanalyst who operated the clinical switch from what Luciana Nissim called *suspicious listening* to a *respectful listening* to the patient. Luciana Nissim's thought was deeply influenced by Eric Brenman and she was one of the most attentive and passionate of his listeners: she was always present and active in Eric's seminars and when we met to discuss his approach, which sometimes seemed to us too original or complex, Luciana succeeded better than any of us in understanding and clarifying Eric's clinical and theorical points of view.

Brenman's main contributions to clinical theory are discussed in full in his papers on narcissism, depression and hysteria, all printed in this book, and I do not want to address them here. I want to underline instead one of his most important contributions to analytical technique, that is, his focus on the specific and intimate meeting between patient and analyst.

Reading his papers and his interventions in the clinical seminars, we can see how Brenman, more than any other analyst, listens to the material in a profound and sensitive way, trying to identify with the patient and to understand his mental coordinates. Interpretations are offered as a way to promote emotional and psychic development. For Brenman the analyst has an eminently reparative task, in the most poignant sense. He has to be a new object, in the sense that the new relationship with the analyst allows the exploration of a different kind of object relationship.

The attempt to communicate the particular atmosphere of Brenman's Milanese seminars was one of the main aims of the book when it was originally published in Italian. As we know, written communication is only one of the tools, and a partial one, for sharing thoughts within the psychoanalytical community. A great number of analytical thoughts and ideas are communicated during clinical seminars, lessons or supervisions through words that, due to their impermanence, risk losing most of their precious intuitions.

By putting together the theoretical papers, where the author expresses himself in scientific written language, and the clinical seminars, where he can develop more freely his spontaneity in meeting his colleagues, this book has tried to fill the gap existing between the written and the 'oral' tradition in psychoanalysis. In reading the seminars we can see how carefully Brenman listens to the interaction between patient and analyst, always very attentive to how the analyst's interpretations are received by the patient and to the quality of their relationship. Brenman anticipated many topics that have been developed later by other colleagues (may I remind you of the *psychoanalytical dialogue* by Luciana Nissim and *l'écoute de l'écoute* of Haideé Fainberg).

The analytical relationship between patient and analyst is a topic which is very present in contemporary psychoanalytical writings, no more so than in the contributions from American inter-subjectivists. The seminars presented in this book show us how Brenman, heir to the most valuable Kleinian tradition integrated with Bion's ideas, avoids the risk of subjectivism, which is so present in this kind of contemporary thinking. Brenman doesn't forget the importance of anxiety and trauma which require a capacity to listen in a sensitive and profound way. He never forgets that trauma produces psychopathological structures which inhibit, seduce or distort the mind of the person who suffered it. For this reason I think that Eric is very attentive to the problem of human destructivity, which he often sees not as an envious or perverse attack on a good object but rather as something which damages or obliterates the psychic and emotional development of the person.

I would like to end my contribution by remembering how I felt about the seminars in Milan. I confess that at the beginning I was a little sceptical about his approach to the patient. He seemed to me to be very different from other English colleagues, whom I understood better. Eric did not want to be idealized and had no interest in reaching an easy success. He constantly preferred to show us how difficult the daily work with our patients was, rather than putting forward brilliant or fascinating solutions. His subtle and intimate approach, his humanistic stance, came over as original even within the Kleinian group.

At that time I was a young analyst with very definite, perhaps slightly rigid, views (possible consequences of the way in which my personal analysis or my training had been conducted), and it was not easy for me to change my 'safe' assumptions and to move towards the more thoughtful, honest and introspective approach which Eric saw as essential in the analytical relationship.

A not too large, self-selected group of people gathered around him and continued to attend his clinical seminars for many years without defections. I began to appreciate him much more, listening to him, and I took a very difficult patient to him in a group supervision, whom he continued to supervise for a very long time. This was a borderline patient, whom I took on with the enthusiasm and the unflinching optimism of a young analyst (I really deeply believed in the curative power of analysis). This patient is the case described in the seminar entitled 'Unbearable pain'.

From the time of his supervision on this case I started to appreciate Eric more fully, and since then I have studied with interest all the papers Eric has published.

I just want to end with a few words of thanks to the people who made this book possible. I would like to mention first Paola Capozzi, who took on the difficult task of editing it, Roberto Basile who frequently travelled between London and Milan, Patrizia Gammaro Moroni, Angela Galli, Dino Lanzara and Federico Rocca. I would also like to thank the colleagues who gave us permission to print their clinical material.

In preparing the seminar transcriptions from the tapes that I have in my possession we continued to think and discuss analytically amongst ourselves and found this task enriching and stimulating. It doesn't seem that fifteen or twenty years have passed since Eric's seminars. His way of gathering the patient's emotional history, anticipating moments of impasse and possible developments, his deep interest in what constitutes the strength and the capacity of the analyst at work, all this seems the stuff of today. Brenman's theoretical and clinical contributions are firmly established in contemporary psychoanalytical thinking and are destined to stay.

9

Unbearable pain

This case raises highly complex problems of technique. The patient is a border-line case, whose mother committed suicide when he was a child. His terror and the dramatization of his mental pain induce a countertransference response that tends to deny anxiety, which, precisely for that reason, becomes even more threatening.

Dr Brenman makes some important points about the capacity to tolerate psychic pain and about the tragedy of life when parents have lacked this capacity.

The need with this patient is to understand whether the drama serves the purpose of making the pain less intolerable or, conversely, of rendering the suffering so agonizing that it is unbearable. As a result, the patient wishes either to disappear himself (by numbing his mind) or to cause the disappearance of the person who speaks to him and who could provide him with an understanding of his pain.

Another complicating factor in the analytic relationship is that this patient seeks to erase the memory of good things, owing to his hatred of the object that also inflicts frustration and pain on him. This is what makes the experience of the relationship so painful for the patient and renders separation unbearable.

On account of this configuration, the transition to the oedipal experience becomes highly problematical, but without it the patient will be unable to develop and mature. The problem is not so much the introjection of objects as his difficulty in separating from a father or mother while preserving them as good objects inside.

ANALYST. The patient is a man of about 30 who lives alone and works for a commercial firm. He has never had a sexual or love relationship either with women or with men. In the affective field, he can conceive of friendships with other men, but he is absolutely terrified by the idea of an emotional and sexual relationship with a female figure.

He has had homosexual fantasies, which make him afraid not so much of doing without heterosexual relationships as of the risk of being discovered and ridiculed for his condition. He had spoken about this with great difficulty to the psychotherapist he had been seeing before he began his analysis. That therapy had been broken off after four years because the therapist moved away.

The patient's history is hard to describe, owing to his lack of childhood reference points and the absence of any development in his inner life. Even in the preliminary interviews he was unable to tell of any important events in his infancy and childhood, nor did he mention – because they had been erased from his memory – things that proved, during the analysis, to have disrupted his psychic development.

At first he spoke about his mother in idealized terms, but I later learned that she had been severely depressed – so much so that she had even had electroconvulsive therapy – and that he had suffered terrible anxieties as a result.

He is the third of three children; he was born when his mother was over 40, and has two elder sisters.

The parental relationship was by no means good. The father, an authoritarian figure, aloof and violent, kept up a privileged relationship with the older sister, who stood in for the sick mother. The mother, who led a more or less isolated life at home, had died suddenly.

At the beginning of the analysis, the patient thought that his mother had died of a heart attack, but she had in fact committed suicide, when he was 12 years old. The family had hidden the truth from him. The discovery that her husband was having an affair might have precipitated her suicide.

The patient may well have had an idealized relationship with her in his early life, as she seems to have been reinvigorated by this late pregnancy. During his analysis, the patient remembered that he had preferred to keep away from his mother owing to the depressive anxieties she heaped upon him. After her death, he had been sent away from the family home to boarding school, where he had felt terribly lonely and anxious. Eventually, owing to his manifestly distressed state (he was refusing food), he managed to get himself sent home again. At this point the older sister had become his reference figure.

The first part of the analysis revealed a persecutory father transference: for the patient, the analyst was not 'like the father', but was 'the father' – a violent, intrusive, cold and indifferent father, interested only in dominating him.

With the gradual development of an affective relationship, the analyst was cast in a maternal role, and his emotions became more overwhelming. Although the mother with whom the patient found himself cared for him, she was fickle, depressed and terrifying.

114

At this point the patient recalled some highly traumatic experiences that had tended to make him keep his distance from her. As her condition worsened, the mother, separated from the other members of the family, used her son as a container for her death anxieties, telling him of the coffin that was ready to receive her and the desperate loneliness he would feel once she had gone. As stated earlier, the mother eventually committed suicide. This experience is relived in the sessions presented in this seminar.

The patient is in the third year of a five-session-a-week analysis; the sessions presented here are the last of the week. He has already been discussed on other occasions in the group supervision with Dr Brenman.

Before I read out the transcript of the two sessions prepared for the seminar, let me briefly summarize the previous session. On arrival, he gave the impression of being totally absent. He did not respond to my greeting; then, once on the couch, he began to complain of feeling ill, and of being unable to speak because, if he did, I would disappear. He complained that he was like his mother and, like her, wanted to die. He said he could see his mother dying (and he concretely visualized her death as he did so). He had begun to feel ill before the session. He mentioned a dream in which he was having an operation: a nun appeared and tied up his legs to immobilize him. He kept on repeating that, if he were to speak, I would disappear.

I found it very difficult to say anything owing to the dramatic, anxiety-laden atmosphere he had created.

I tried to describe to him how he felt compelled to enter into the drama in which he saw his mother die and how he ended up fusing with her. I pointed out that he was creating a scene and not reliving a memory. After all, he did not know how his mother had actually died.

After interpretations of this kind, which I repeated several times, the patient appeared to emerge from his anxiety. Once the drama was over, he said he could remember nothing of what he had experienced or said in the session. When I reminded him of his words ('I am there as my mother dies . . .'), he leapt up from the couch in utter terror. At the end of the session, the patient felt that he had woken up from a nightmare of which he had absolutely no memory.

BRENMAN. What was your state of mind in this session?

ANALYST. I felt that I was not in contact, and even a bit bored, because there was something unreal, almost hysterical, about the patient's attitude. But in the sessions that followed – the ones presented here – I felt more in touch with him. In the session I just mentioned, the patient seemed to be virtually sleep-walking.

BRENMAN. It seems to me that the patient really is terrified, but is at the same time putting on a dramatic performance. Given that both these aspects are present, we need to understand which of the two is the better choice for working on in the session.

We need to understand whether the patient is dramatizing the situation because it is too frightening for him, in which case the purpose of the drama is to make it less frightening. Alternatively, is he trying to make the situation more frightening than it really is?

The patient himself does not know which of these two things he is doing; at any rate, he manages to put the analyst into a remote, indifferent state of mind. So we need to ask ourselves what the patient wants to do in generating this state of mind in the analyst.

One possibility is that he wants to make him conclude that the problem does not exist, that there is nothing to worry about, and that everything is a sham. If that really is the situation, then clearly the patient is inducing a state of mind like that of a doctor who says: 'There's nothing wrong with you, you're fine, there's no need to operate!' That may well be the patient's motive.

Yet at the same time he remains frightened, because, even if he has succeeded in convincing the analyst that everything is all right, that does not reassure him in the least; in fact, it only increases his fear.

The difficulty in analysing a patient like this one lies in being able to think in the here and now of the session.

It seems that in the session the analyst wants to get on with the patient's analysis and not with his theatrical performance. Yet this performance, this dramatization, is part of the patient and must be taken into account. Perhaps the analyst is in effect behaving like a surgeon who says: 'Let's get on with it, let's operate, and never mind the emotional aspects of the operation!'

It's important to note that the patient fails to recognize the analyst at the beginning of the session, as if he really is managing to get things out of his mind – to eliminate them completely. This means that he is experiencing a lot of anxiety and does not want to know what is going on.

When the patient says the analyst will disappear if he speaks, he is describing a catastrophic situation – but it may also mean that the defences he is setting up against his own anxiety are so powerful that they cause anything that might make him anxious to disappear.

The other important aspect of his communication is that he is like his mother when she was dying. She killed herself because she could not endure the pain and suffering of her husband's abandonment; and

116

the patient seems to be saying that, when confronted with pain, he wants either to disappear himself or to make the person who talks to him and can tell him about his [the patient's] pain disappear.

When the patient talks about the dream and the operation, he doesn't seem able to face even the idea of surgery. It's a bit like his mother, who was unable to cope with the pain of being abandoned and died out of sheer anxiety. Whether the operation is real or not – whether or not it is a dream – the patient has to make a drama out of it. He seems to have two ways of dealing with anxiety. One is to forget everything, to forget the session, and to cease to exist. The other is to get someone (in this case the analyst) to tell him 'No, no, there's nothing wrong, there's no problem, let's carry on!' and to deny the anxiety situation for him.

Either he denies it himself, and blots it out, or he makes a parent figure do so for him.

The tragedy of his life was that his mother killed herself because she was unable to cope with psychic pain. The patient needs the help of an analyst who can endure it without disappearing or going mad.

When the analyst tells the patient that he wasn't really there when his mother died – whether or not that is true – it would have been better to say that his mother had been unable to endure the pain, whereas the analyst, saying this, can do so without disappearing or dying as a result.

From earlier sessions [not reported here], we have a picture of some-one who is absolutely incapable of enduring a tragedy, of understanding it, and of feeling sorry for the victims, let alone of helping them.

He must immediately repress what has happened so as not to feel at fault and guilty. Since the patient's attitude is to feel that he is at fault, or that what has happened is so terrible that it must be denied, the analyst must tackle this problem.

If he does not, the patient will experience every interpretation as something to be denied, or as a terrible accusation, or as something so terrible that it is bound to cause the analyst to disappear.

This kind of technique demands great effort from the analyst and puts an enormous strain on him. But if he is not up to it, the analysis becomes a defence against the experiences the patient must confront in his daily life, which he is constantly trying to blot out.

QUESTION. *I wonder if it would have been too persecutory to tell the patient that his attitude was killing both the analyst and the possibility of his helping him.*

BRENMAN. I wouldn't say that, because the patient thinks that pain kills people, as it did his mother. He sees the analyst as someone who cannot endure pain and therefore disappears, or as someone who finds fault with him and thinks he is guilty.

Instead, I would emphasize that for him pain is lethal, as it was for his mother. If we think of a mentally disturbed mother with a small child who is crying, she will have an impulse to kill him or to leave the room; be that as it may, she will be unable to tolerate the resulting pain.

At any rate, it is not enough to interpret only this aspect to the patient.

ANALYST. My approach here was to interpret to the patient that he thought he had a fragile analyst.

BRENMAN. It's more important to interpret the patient's anxiety, because the analyst is then showing that he understands it, without blaming the patient and without collapsing, and that he can endure the pain.

Thursday's session

ANALYST. Let me emphasize that the patient is as usual speaking in a very agitated tone of voice, which makes it impossible to think or reflect.

P. (*arriving slightly late*) As usual, I drank some beer before coming along to the session . . . Yesterday after the session I didn't feel at all bad . . . but it felt like having avoided the operation . . . and still being afraid of having to face it anyway . . . I remember yesterday's session . . . I was full of emotions . . . and then you told me that I was putting on a scene. I felt better, but I didn't have any more emotions. Today as well, I talked about this and that, without emotions . . .

A. When you mention emotions, you talk about surgical operations and fear. What you experienced yesterday seems to have been a nightmare, quite terrifying . . .

P. When things like that happened to me, B. (*his previous therapist*) told me I was making a scene. I felt as if B. was throwing water in my face. That's how it was with you too yesterday. It seemed as though you were giving me an anaesthetic with your words.

BRENMAN. The patient says he has been drinking, as if to anaesthetize himself before the session. After the session he felt better, as if he had avoided the operation. This means he is talking about the temporary denial of pain, which will eventually return. When the patient says he no longer has emotions, he is describing his way of getting rid of all emotions, including painful ones. He projects this behaviour on to the analyst and thinks that *he* is behaving that way.

118

When he refers to B., he is saying that he felt B. used to blame him for telling too many stories. He thinks his present analyst has the same attitude. The analyst uses a violent method, which is like a slap in the face to the patient, but which also feels like an anaesthetic to him – something given to avoid experiencing too much fear.

A. Yesterday I mentioned a scene – a drama that terrified you. What you are describing now is like a sensation of fainting, of losing touch with me and with your capacity to be in contact with reality.

P. Yesterday I was talking . . . I can't remember now what I was saying. (*The patient tries to reconstruct yesterday's session but finds it very difficult to do so.*) I don't remember any more . . . Then you said something to me and I was frightened . . .

A. Yesterday you told me you were there when your mother died.

BRENMAN. The patient says he remembers having been frightened, but doesn't remember what he said – as if he had blotted out what had happened as soon as he felt fear. So we can say he is killing off the consciousness of something that frightens him. And he is erasing the pain from his mind because he thinks that no one – not even the analyst – can possibly face it. He invites the analyst to recall the previous day's session, to find out whether he too has removed it from his mind or has been able to contain and remember it.

P. No, I didn't say that. Perhaps it's me who can't explain myself very well . . . I felt that I had to communicate something to you . . . but I couldn't say it to you.

   Now, though, I can't remember what I was really feeling . . . But if I *had* said that, you would have disappeared . . . it was like the tense atmosphere between my father and mother: one of the two disappeared . . . I thought it was impossible for there to be three people together . . . If I had got into that emotional situation, you would have disappeared . . . But if I had stayed in contact with you, and thought of you, I couldn't have talked about that, and you would have asked me: 'What are you thinking about?' and I wouldn't have known what to answer.

A. What you are describing is the difficulty of getting in touch with a part of yourself, and of staying aware of the contact with me at the same time. When you get in touch with me, you lose the feeling of being in touch with yourself.

119

BRENMAN. The interesting thing is that, when the patient thinks of a row between his mother and father, one of the two disappears. One of the ways a child learns to cope with problems is to watch how his parents cope with them. The patient says his mother could not cope with her problems, or his father with his, so how does *he* cope with his? It is hard for him to face pain if his parents were unable to do so; and on top of that, he has no memory of his parents together. If this patient can't get in touch with his own anxieties, there is nothing for it but to find someone who can help him to do that.

P. I remember what happened when I had to have a kidney operation. I waited for five hours and then they told me that the operation had been postponed until Monday. The effect of the 'pre-med' was wearing off and I was afraid of being operated on in that state. I felt relieved. That's what it was like yesterday. When you told me that I was putting on a scene, that's how I felt.

If I had got in touch with what I had inside me yesterday, I would have been in touch with my dead mother and then I would have been dead myself, and you would have disappeared. I thought: at least he's a man and not a woman; he's a man like my father.

But if I had told you that, you would have disappeared. I only have you. Well, actually I also have my nephew. You told me that when my mother died, I felt there wasn't a father I could turn to.

I can't explain it; I don't know if you can understand. Yesterday I felt emotions, and with these emotions I could have got in touch with you and perhaps had an answer. But for me, feeling emotions means dying, so I must choose to become rational and lose my emotions.

BRENMAN. The patient is saying that his five sessions a week are like an anaesthetic that sends him to sleep for a while so that he can put off dealing with his problems. He is saying that, if he had spoken to the analyst, it would have been like connecting him with a dead mother, and the analyst is the only person he has.

But if the analyst is the only person he has, this person is not alive to face his suffering. So the patient returns to the problem of his mother. Only a very disturbed mother can kill herself. A mother who was just a little less disturbed would not kill herself because she would think of what her child would have to face. The patient also says that when he becomes very rational he stops having feelings. What he needs is an analyst who can talk to him about his feelings, who can perceive them and feel them with him without being too rational.

A. It's terrible to think that having emotions means being in touch with the feeling of dying, of losing yourself and of not knowing where you are. *That* is the terrible feeling – the feeling of getting in touch with the sensation of death and of losing touch with me as a person outside yourself, as a real person. Now you are talking to me, and yesterday you felt that I would be dead. You're telling me about the anxiety you had yesterday, about having an analyst you could not turn to, because you felt that I would disappear.

P. I *hate* reality. Now I don't know who you really are. You're different from everyone else I meet. No one talks to me and I don't talk to anyone in this position (*lying on the couch*).

I just thought of my friend Giacomo. Giacomo has never talked to me about his marriage. Giacomo said he didn't talk to me about it because only what happened between me and him was important. I don't even know who Giacomo's parents are and what they are like. Now I don't remember anything you have said to me so far. You said something about it being impossible for there to be three people together.

A. Perhaps you are telling me that you don't know anything about me, that you have no idea what kind of a person I am. But maybe you are also telling me that you don't even know who *you* are: either it's you who are talking to me, as you have done up to now, or else it's you who are plunging into a dream and losing touch with me and with yourself because the weekend is approaching.

BRENMAN. The interpretation seems right. The patient knows that the analyst is aware of the unbearable situation of a dead mother, and also that the analyst is married and is going to take a weekend break. On the other hand, his friend Giacomo told him that his wife didn't matter and that the two of them could always be together.

In the analysis, someone else comes into the situation at the weekend; that is something he can't accept and tolerate. You need to tell him that he expects his analyst to say: 'There's no one but you; my family doesn't exist.' Yet the analysis must go on with the analyst's family allowed to exist, together with the patient. After all, the patient had no family in his own life.

ANALYST. Once before the patient had recalled that, after his mother died, the older of his two sisters had told him she would never get married so that she could always be with him. But then she *did* get married and the patient was sent to boarding school.

QUESTION. *Perhaps the terrible thing the patient cannot talk about is the demand by his infantile part to have the analyst all to himself. It seems that neither the analyst nor the patient can focus on this point. Perhaps, in mentioning his nephew, he means that he is capable of being one of three people together and that he might therefore be able to endure the separation.*

BRENMAN. Possibly. All the same, there is a contradiction in what the patient says, and you need to choose whichever aspect it is better to take up.

The patient is in fact putting lots of things together. For instance, even though he says there is no room for three people, he is saying at the same time: 'Thank goodness there are three of us: there's also my nephew!'

There's a friend who takes care of him, and he likes that. If the analyst were to say 'No, it isn't true; there are only you and me together here!', that would seriously complicate matters.

Now the patient says the analyst is all he has in the world, and then remarks that there is also the nephew, so both of these statements have to be taken into account. The patient reported that there was no room for two people in his family, and this is something that constantly recurs in the transference. It is important for him to know whether the analyst is happy to accept the third person, or whether he is going to behave like a member of the patient's family and not countenance the presence of three people.

The more a mother and father are able to introduce a third person into a child's life, the better the child will be capable of tolerating oedipal jealousy. This is a very important point in analysis. If the father and mother go out to the cinema together and then invite a little friend or cousin over, they will help the child to endure the separation, to form relationships and to create a life of his own.

So when the mother is physically absent, the image of a mother who looks after him persists. The mother is remembered even in the presence of the friend.

The patient needs to re-create this family model for himself because he did not have it in the past. There should be room for three, four and even five people.

Instead of telling the patient 'I shan't marry and I'll stay alone with you!', his sister ought to have said 'When I get married, you'll come and stay with me!' What he wants to know is whether the analyst will keep him in mind during the weekend or leave him by himself. That's the only way of enduring separation.

QUESTION. *Could it be that, with regard to there being three people together and because he does not know who the analyst is, the patient is asking which of the two images of the analyst (the good one who stays with him and the bad one who leaves him alone) is correct?*

BRENMAN. That's right. The analyst is the good person who can help him, but who then abandons him.

There is no such thing as a mother who always gives help and nothing but help; usually she is with her child, but she also goes away. It is important to be able to keep the two aspects together – to remember that you have had help so that you can tolerate waiting to get it again. A normal mother is someone who ministers to her child's needs but who also disappoints him because she goes away. A normal mother is capable of helping, but also of inflicting suffering, because she can cope with pain without deceiving the child – without anaesthetizing him by telling him: 'Everything's all right, everything's all right.'

She must be able to say 'Yes, I love you, but now I must go out!' and to cope with the pain and sorrow. If she can do this, it will allow the child to start keeping the two experiences together.

When a patient is ill and needs surgery, the doctor tells him: 'Yes, the operation will be painful, but if it succeeds you'll feel better and you won't have any more problems.' That's much better than saying either 'No, there's nothing wrong with you' or 'It's terrible; you'll die under the knife.'

P. Yes, that's right. I myself don't know. I sometimes feel as though I were in hospital being operated on for kidney stones. It's true: I did feel relieved that the operation had been postponed, but at the same time I was angry, because I would have to wait until Monday in any case.

I don't know what you are. I'm thinking of the last break in the analysis, when I went to Rome and read the news about China and Vietnam. For me, you were a terrible communist. I was afraid of being involved in a worldwide conflict and that people would die. You had become a terrible communist – either a suicide or a murderer. Now that this war is going on, I'm not as terrified as I was before. I really must be mad.

A. You are telling me what it means to you to feel bad during the weekend break: you feel not only abandoned, but, even worse, that you are in a primitive, cruel world, and you see me as a terrible, murderous person.

BRENMAN. The interpretation is half-right. The patient keeps repeating that the problem has been put off or that he is afraid of this operation. He associates the operation with the possible war between China and Vietnam, which would be something very serious, and he is afraid the world will be destroyed. The fact that the war between China and Vietnam is far away makes him feel relieved, because it is not the whole world that will be destroyed. He can tolerate even the operation, which he sees as something terrible, if it is localized and therefore not lethal.

The analyst is right to speak to him of a primitive, cruel world – but this world must be better localized, so that the rest of the world can survive. If the war were not localized, no one could survive and there would be no way of enduring such a terrible event. In that case we should all be justified in turning to drink, just as the patient drinks beer in order to forget. It would be terrible if the analyst were to abandon the patient once and for all, but if he does so only over the weekend it becomes tolerable.

It is important to distinguish between the generic reassurance 'Everything's all right, everything's all right!', which leaves the underlying annihilation anxiety intact, and the recognition that something is not all right, but that it is limited and confined to the weekend.

When a child is facing separation and having dreadful and seemingly unbearable feelings, a good mother will convey: 'Yes, I understand this rage, this terrible anxiety of yours; I know you'd like to kill me – but calm down now, because we'll see each other again tomorrow.'

P. I'm always afraid of having kidney stones. Sometimes I feel that I really have them and must be hospitalized right away. I've had three operations and it's quite possible that I'll suddenly need another. I don't go to the doctor because I'm afraid he might look inside me and discover the stones. What happened to me yesterday was like having stones. I think the stones are psychological; if I recover fully, I won't have them any more.

BRENMAN. Having kidney stones is awful and you can sympathize with a patient who has this problem. But stones can be treated. It is also possible that the analysis will stop him having stones in the future. The patient hopes so, but it cannot be guaranteed. He wants everything to be all right in the end and these problems not to arise any more. What the analysis can do is to help him face his problems and anxieties with more strength and hope. The way to help him is precisely to enable him to cope successfully with every eventuality that arises. You cannot treat him in the way he would like, by telling him: 'You'll see, now I'll make sure you have no more troubles.' If it is true that a psychological disturbance can cause stones, it is equally true that the only way of avoiding somatizations is to confront anxiety and suffering head on, without running away from them.

A. What happened to you yesterday is that you were suddenly plunged into a nightmare atmosphere; you had a terrible feeling inside and you wanted to expel it. It is something that happens inside your mind, and you would like to get rid of it. Perhaps you need to distinguish between the fear of having something terrible inside and having stones, which seem not to be of psychological origin.

P. Why shouldn't they be of psychological origin? And what about psychosomatic diseases, like a gastric ulcer? I get spasms in the ureter. I feel tense in my head and then my kidney gets blocked.

It's an established fact that high-flying pilots often get stones.

When I went to the surgeon, he told me I was afraid. But I felt very calm. He said that if I was afraid, I would have passed stones through my nose as well.

Then again, V. (*an analyst from his home town*) said: 'The more you're afraid, the more you'll get.' Before I started therapy with B. (*his previous therapist*), I passed one. When I finished the therapy, six months later I had the operation. I sometimes feel emotions in my brain and then my kidney gets blocked.

BRENMAN. According to the patient's theory, when something happens in the brain, it is somatized and goes into the kidney. If his theory were correct, it would be better for his anxieties to stay in his head and not go into the body. But since the patient is unable to cope with his anxieties in his head, he thrusts them away elsewhere, perhaps into the body. So it is important for him to face his anxieties. And the only incentive for him to face them is the hope that something positive will come of it. That's the kind of experience he needs – an experience he lacked in the past when he was small. He needs an analyst to help him localize the pain precisely, so that he can live a sufficiently normal life outside it. That's the way to confront pain.

When we are suffering, we need a friend to think about it and tell us: 'No, it's not such a terrible thing, it doesn't involve the whole world, it's *that*, there, and everything else carries on.' The patient's mother could have said: 'Yes, my husband is leaving me, but I have the rest of my life to live, I have my family, my children, my friends.' Instead, she was unable to limit the problem and the pain, and to get over the crisis. She could only collapse and blame her suicide on everyone else.

What is the object the patient has inside him, with which he is identified? The object is this kind of mother. It's important to make the patient understand that this is his internal object, to try to get him to face problems in a different way, and to see that there may be a different object that deals with problems by other methods – without disappearing and without thrusting things in his face. You have to beware of interpretations that are like thrusting something in his face. And you must avoid getting too bored and disappearing psychologically. After all, in the transference the pattern is repeated with a pressure to make it really happen.

Friday's session

P. I really must have a serious problem. I had four years of therapy with B., and now I've been with you for three or four years – I don't know exactly how many – and I can't remember anything. Yesterday you gave me some interpretations and I can't remember them. I feel ill. I don't know if the analysis can help me. In Tuesday's session you said: 'I don't understand.' I'm always afraid of having stones; today I feel I could go to hospital from one minute to the next.

Of course there's also a biochemical element to stones. But there's psychological tension and renal spasms too.

My father also had stones, but only colics, and my sister had a kidney operation after a typhoid infection.

A doctor once told me that there were antispastics to prevent spasms, but that if you always took them, they wouldn't work any more when you needed them. I really think I myself am the cause of the stones, and here perhaps I really am omnipotent! On the other hand, I have had two stones – one in the right kidney and one in the left, both very big.

I had one when my father remarried, and the other just before he died: he was in hospital and had gone blind in one eye. I didn't want to go to the hospital. Then I had another after finishing my therapy with B. I think there are psychological reasons for the stones. I feel guilty, as if it was my own fault for getting them.

I imagine I won't have any more stones once the analysis has cured me. You say the analysis should help me to tolerate the stones better. But when I think of the illness I feel terrified, and I'd rather die than go through with the operation.

There was someone who had haemorrhages that stopped after psychoanalysis. I feel ill, and I don't know if the analysis can help me.

On Tuesday you said: 'I don't understand.' You told me I kept on saying: 'Come on, help me, help me.' But I didn't say that – or rather, I couldn't explain myself. I don't know if I am the one who doesn't understand what you tell me or if I get it wrong – or if it is I who can't explain myself and make you understand me.

A. You are telling me about a situation of illness, and you don't know if I can understand what you are experiencing, and give you something useful and suggest a solution. You are also asking whether you are managing to make yourself understood, because you are afraid of confusing me.

P. I'm afraid of doctors. If I think of going to a doctor, I'm terrified. I imagine he'll find that everything's wrong inside me. So I don't go to the doctor any more and I put the idea out of my mind.

A. You are telling me about the doctor you are afraid of: someone who doesn't help you if you are ill, but instead puts something bad inside you.

ANALYST. I'd like to point out that the text of the session as I read it sounds much clearer than the direct communication I had from the patient. What I actually felt was that this was a much more confused communication than it now seems.

BRENMAN. This last point is very important. What the patient says is confused and very difficult to follow. According to the analyst's interpretation, the patient is expressing the fear of confusing the analyst.

I think the patient wants to make him feel what it means to be in a state of confusion and how hard it is to bear. He cannot manage to put things into any kind of order, and so he wants the analyst to know what it means to be in that state.

It's important to remember that the patient says he has a serious problem: he is afraid that, if he goes to a doctor, the doctor will not only find the diseased part, but will discover that everything is diseased and that everything is wrong with him. The patient is right to be very afraid if he thinks that this is how the doctor will behave.

P. I don't think the analysis will cure me. But if I go on, at least I can survive. I don't know what I felt on Tuesday or Wednesday. Today I think I feel ill; I shall go to hospital before tomorrow is out. Today I feel as if I had something similar to my mother. If I am ill and go to hospital, I shall jeopardize the analysis and lose you.

A. What do you mean by: 'I shall jeopardize the analysis'?

127

BRENMAN. The patient says the analysis enables him to survive. We need to understand what this means; it may mean that the analysis helps him to understand only some problems but not others, or it may mean something else.

He says he has had four years of therapy and three years of analysis with his present analyst and cannot now remember anything. It sounds as if he is really saying: 'If I don't think about my problems I can survive, but if I do, then I can't.'

This conviction does not augur well for the analysis, because the analyst expects the patient to be able to think of his problems and to survive.

Here he seems to be still connecting himself with his mother. Perhaps his mother dealt with problems by not thinking about them. She had a very unhappy marriage and perhaps found a way of soldiering on – but then, when the truth came out, it killed her.

The patient's model is of a person who somehow manages to survive by not thinking about her problems, but who dies as soon as it becomes impossible not to confront them. The mother behaved not as if she had a problem, but as if her whole life was a problem and was not worth living.

The object the patient has identified with is very clear here. He would be very relieved if he could get rid of this object, which dominates him and controls his life. So, when the patient doesn't want to go to the doctor because he thinks he will tell him that everything is wrong with him, he is saying that he is behaving like his mother who did not want to look at her problems, as if she knew that everything was wrong and that she would die if she were to realize this consciously.

If that is true, as it probably is, then the patient has to be offered a different model – the model of someone capable of facing suffering, of thinking about it while going on living.

It's hard to understand what the patient means when he says that if he went to hospital he would jeopardize the analysis and lose the analyst. Clearly, for him, going to hospital is equivalent to losing the analyst. Perhaps he has the fantasy that having a physical illness and going to hospital is equivalent to deceiving the analyst, who would then not want anything more to do with him.

In the same way, the mother feels deceived if the father turns his attentions to someone else. But the analyst would not *really* break off the analysis if the patient went into hospital to have an operation. The patient thinks the analyst will say: 'Because you have done this to the analysis, you have got kidney stones, so be off with you!'

Whereas on the one hand that *is* what the patient thinks and fears, on the other he wants the analyst to be someone who thinks and interprets useful things for him, and not to be like his mother, who expected the object to be totally devoted to her and was utterly dependent on its help.

He is afraid that the analyst will tell him that everything is psychological and that the fact that he has this illness proves that he has attacked the analyst and the analysis. And this, for the patient, means the end of the analysis.

Since he has this fear, he wants the analyst to tell him what can help him at this time, and also to find out if the analyst is so narcissistic or hysterical that he feels deceived if the patient has gone to the doctor for treatment for a physical illness.

There are some patients who think: 'It's all psychological, so it's my fault!' The patient says he is omnipotent, but he goes on feeling and thinking in that way. It's pretty clear that this idea has to do with the family environment he lived in.

P. I don't know. (*He goes on complaining that he is ill, that he is going to be ill, and that he will go to hospital.*)

When I was in hospital, the surgeon came round in the morning without looking anyone in the face; he looked only at the diseased organ.

After the operation, I had a catheter inserted into my penis up to the kidney. In the night I called the nurse, who then called a doctor; but the doctor felt bothered, because he wanted to sleep . . . But I wanted to have someone close to me during the night.

The catheter was blocked; the urine was pressing on me inside and I couldn't pass it. Then I learned how to unblock the catheter myself.

The operation . . . imagine waking up with your side torn open . . . Everyone slept after the operation, but *I* didn't . . . I only slept after the operation the first time I was in that clinic.

I don't understand what happened on Tuesday, or what you meant by the word 'scene'. At any rate, I felt very ill, and then I stopped feeling ill . . . I didn't feel anything any more.

You told me that I wasn't there when my mother died; well, you must be right to think I say things that aren't true . . . Yes, now I remember . . . I had come to the session and was feeling ill, as if I was in touch with my mother. But I don't know what my mother stands for . . .

I felt as if you were not there; I wanted to convey this sense of boredom to you . . . No, I didn't mean boredom . . . I meant this feeling.

When I came, I wanted to grab hold of your hand, so as to feel that you were really there . . . I wouldn't have actually done it, but I expected to speak to you and to get this answer from you: 'I am here, here with you' – to demonstrate to me that you really were there. I said to myself: 'He [the analyst] is like a father, or rather, he is a better father than my father.' But it didn't happen and I couldn't say it to you, because you [the analyst] would have disappeared.

A. When you say you are feeling ill and describe what you are feeling, when you talk about your mother and say you don't know who your mother is, and when you tell me about something inside yourself, you are talking about your fear of dying and of vanishing into thin air. You talk about being terrified of dying and you want me to be able to take this fear inside me and to endure it, to be really with you, and to help you to go through this experience. But you are afraid that, if you ask for my presence and my help, I shall run away . . .

P. Yes, that's right, I really am terrified of dying.

A. And when you talk about your mother, you are reliving and remembering the experience with your mother, who talked to you about her fears of dying when you were small.

P. Yes, that's how it was. My mother used to make those scenes . . . she would lie down on her bed . . .

BRENMAN. The analyst's interpretation is correct, but incomplete.

The patient mentions that when he was in hospital the surgeon did not look him in the face, but only examined the diseased organ.

In this case, you should have told the patient that he thought the analyst too was considering only his psychopathology and not him as a person. It is important for the patient to have the experience of being seen by the analyst as a person, a feeling that his psychopathology is less important than the personal relationship and that, at any rate, it is not the only thing.

This experience can be conveyed to the patient through interpretation, without the need for acting out. The patient recalls that when he called the doctor, the doctor was annoyed. So this doctor is indifferent to his anxieties. He remembers how terrible it was to wake up with his side torn open; then he says he doesn't understand how the analyst can possibly have talked about a 'scene'.

As for the scene, it's important to remember that, even if the patient is dramatizing the situation, he really is terrified – so much so that the only way of surviving is to forget everything and blot it all out. He forgets so well that he doesn't know who his mother is. Emotionally he remembers what a mother is, because he wants to seize hold of the analyst's hand for reassurance. He wants the analyst to say to him 'I'm here and I'll look after you!' – to be there and to help him endure the anxiety. His anxiety is about dying and being abandoned by the analyst.

Here the analyst reaches the patient, who acknowledges his fear of dying and links up with his mother's fear of dying. The mother was hysterical, made scenes and lay down on the bed, but even so she was really terrified: she was afraid of dying and also of living.

A. Your experience is of being with a mother who asks you, as a little boy, to keep the fear of dying inside yourself. You have this image inside you. You don't have inside you the image of a mother who tells her suffering child: 'I'm here beside you, so nothing bad can happen to you!' You feel like a child who can't go to his mother and talk to her about his fears. Yesterday you told me that, if you had got in touch with this thing inside yourself, you would have lost me, or, if you had got in touch with me, you would no longer have been able to speak and communicate this terrible thing.

P. *(gets alarmed and touches his leg.)* My leg hurts, but it's nothing to do with the stones. Yes, what you say is true. I couldn't tell my mother anything; my concerns were only for her.

A. You're telling me that when you were small you felt that you had to control your mother, that you were afraid of leaving her alone, and that you couldn't separate from her.

P. So people must be different from how I imagine them. I have no experience of being able to talk to anyone about my own troubles. When I was in therapy with B., he told me that I wanted to put something inside him so as to get rid of it, so as not to see it and not to understand it.

A. Whatever the therapist had said to you, it seems that you would have understood it as: 'I don't want to take this terrible thing of yours inside myself.'

P. It was the same with my sister. I couldn't talk to her about my troubles. She was always sad and depressed. So how can I possibly imagine that people won't disappear if I talk to them about my troubles?

And as for my father . . . once I said to him: 'If someone hits me, I'll come to you and tell you about it, and then you can hit them and defend me.' But he said: 'If you come and tell me anything like that, *I'll* hit you!' After that I never told him anything.

My father hit me twice, and each time I thought I was going to die. Then I ran away – that is, I went out in the morning and came back in the evening – and no one said anything to me. I thought: 'If he hit me for something so trivial, imagine what would happen if I had done something more serious.' Well, even in the novel *Padre padrone* the father hit the son . . . but if he felt bad he looked after him and slept by his side at night. And the son became a linguist, a man of letters . . .

A. When you speak of your father, you say you have in mind only negative experiences with him. When your father hits you, there is no explanation for it. When you talk about the doctor or the surgeon, what comes back seems to be the image of a terrible father.

P. Yes, but you see, I can't remember now what you said. The things you said about my mother were important. I remember only the first (*the mother and being terrified of dying*). Oh yes, the other as well (*being terrified of separation*). There is always the problem of what I say in the sessions and whether I can manage to express what I am feeling . . .

BRENMAN. There's a sentence the patient puts into the mouth of B., his previous therapist: 'You are trying to put something inside me.' The patient may have picked up only the first part of the interpretation, about putting one thing inside another, and not: 'You want to put something inside me so that I can take it in and digest it for you!'

The patient's experience is of an analyst who says: 'You are trying to put terrible things inside me; take them back inside yourself and don't bother me!' It is less important to think over or to know what might have happened with the other therapist than to ask yourself whether the patient feels his present analyst thinks the same way. The patient mentions the business with his father, who hits his son like the father in *Padre padrone*.

We have to consider what this means in this context. The father seems to have been like what the patient says: 'Don't come to me with your troubles or I'll hit you!' In this case, the patient appears to succeed in making a distinction and to see the analyst as a more human person who does not react in this way.

ANALYST. When this patient comes back to analysis on Mondays, he is usually terrified of me.

BRENMAN. For the patient there's another problem too: although the relationship is good, when a separation draws near, another image of the analyst is liable to reappear. So he blots out not only the bad experience but also the memory of good things. It's like a child who is put to bed and then has a nightmare: he remembers only the terrifying experience and loses sight of the good one.

It's important to point out to him that, when he forgets, he forgets not only the painful experiences that make him anxious, but also the positive ones. So, when the patient says he can't remember, he is in fact remembering only the bad experiences.

There must also have been positive experiences with the previous therapist, and even in the hospital he can't have had *only* negative experiences with *all* the doctors and nurses.

Going back over the material, we see that the patient is thinking of a limited conflict between China and Vietnam; this reassures him that there is not going to be a worldwide conflict. Even if the conflict is localized as in this case, he can certainly remember only the conflicts and not the positive experiences.

With this patient it is very important to analyse why the good experiences disappear and only the bad ones remain. After all, if he remembers only the negative experiences, every situation will leave him terrified.

It is only through gradually remembering the positive experiences too that the growth situation can develop, and then the experience of three people being together without one of them dying will be able to mature. That is the basis of the Oedipus complex.

The primitive belief is that one of the three must die: only human intervention can allow the family to survive. It will be very important for this patient to be able to analyse and live this experience.

QUESTION. *I wonder if the patient's difficulties in growing might be due to an inability to introject.*

BRENMAN. The patient *is* capable of introjecting something good: his last words show that. His problem of being unable to remember what is said in the session and to express what he feels has to do not so much with introjection as with his difficulty of separating from a father or mother felt to be good objects.

A number of problems come together here. One is that the patient is unable to face bad things, but can't remember good ones either.

He has enormous difficulty in coping with separation. We hate someone on account of separation or because they have suddenly disappeared just when we needed them. It is a good object that we have lost. If the hate is too intense, it cancels out all the love. As Shakespeare writes in *Julius Caesar*: 'The evil that men do lives after them, / The good is oft interred with their bones.' That is the patient's real problem.

As a child grows up, he is often carried away by rage and hate and tends to forget the good things he has received. The important thing in this case is for the parent not to behave like the child. If the parent sees only the bad part, it is hard for the child to be more mature than the parent and to succeed in seeing the good part as well.

The patient shows some development of good feelings in the session: only if the child succeeds in remembering the good feelings about the parent will he be able to fight against hate and face separation.

We must ask ourselves whether his need to grasp the analyst's hand is an expression only of separation anxiety or also of his love.

If the patient is unable to keep the good experience inside himself because he hates the analyst who inflicts the pain of separation on him, then the analyst must do so and give him back the good experience in subsequent sessions.

Even if not everyone here shares this view, I am profoundly convinced that it is right. Given that this patient did not have enough good experiences in his life to return to, it is important for him to be able to have them in the analysis and to remember them.

QUESTION. *Perhaps the patient thinks his mother died because she could not stand him [the patient] rather than from jealousy of her husband.*

BRENMAN. This idea is certainly there and recurs in the material. Alongside it there is also the omnipotent fantasy that it is he who keeps his mother alive.

The patient needs to be helped to give up this paranoid–schizoid fantasy and to approach the depressive position, which is closer to reality – to realize that it is not he who has to keep his mother and the analyst alive, but the mother who keeps the child alive.

All children at first have this omnipotent fantasy, but then life experiences show them that the opposite is the case.

This raises problems of technique. If the analyst interprets along the lines of 'These things happen because you do this or that', he will end up reinforcing the patient's omnipotence.

Instead, you need to give more realistic interpretations. Such patients often have so much power over the analyst that they bring out the analyst's own infantile parts, so that he reacts by telling the patient: 'You are the one who does this.'

Very probably, so far as we can reconstruct the situation, the patient's mother acted out with him in this way.

10

Deprivation and violence

The interest of this supervision centres on the difficulty of attunement between patient and analyst. The patient's aggressive violence results from a history of deprivation dating back to her birth, as a child who had to relate to sick parents. Never having had any joy in her life, she is so angry and rebellious that she destroys her own good qualities. Guilt-ridden and assailed by feelings of persecution following the death of her mother, the patient must now face the drama of looking after her sick father, who has no consideration for her.

Deprivation gives rise to very primitive anxieties: an infant who cannot find milk at the breast wonders if his mother is really sick or just selfish.

Dr Brenman presents some interesting considerations on the effects of deprivation and on the patient's style of penetrating violently into the analyst and leaving her breathless. This patient necessarily resorts to violent projective identification because she lacks the experience of having been understood. She also fears being indoctrinated by the opinions of others who intrude into her mind; she reacts violently, but must then surrender and submit.

In the sessions reported here, there has been a breakdown in understanding between patient and analyst. The crux of the matter is the patient's demand to be able to enjoy life without feeling guilty; the risk for the analyst is to be perceived as a moralizing superego.

Dr Brenman emphasizes that pleasure is a very important part of life. Pleasure can have a meaning in its own right: it is important to distinguish between genuine joy, which helps one to live, and the flight into pleasure, which is obtained by eliminating anything unpleasurable.

ANALYST. Giulia is now 39 years old and has been in analysis for five years. She is the second of five daughters of a close-knit but rigidly conservative lower middle-class family. She seems to have suffered hunger pangs from birth, as her mother produced little milk and suffered from rhagades, while at the same time (in the immediate post-war years) powdered milk was difficult to come by. Since her teens she had been full of hate, rebelliousness and contempt for her family. Later she had given up her job at a bank – a career her father had wanted her to pursue – and gone to live with a boyfriend. A very confused period had followed: she had found and lost a number of jobs, having been unable to turn to account her talent as a designer and her taste for beautiful, ancient objects. Finding and leaving several partners, she had eventually married a foreigner, but had divorced him on learning of his association with groups engaged in dubious activities. Her illness, as she calls it, dates back to four or five years before the analysis. She had fits of anxiety and depression, and was unable to go out into the street, drive a car or get into a tram.

All she could do was to keep working and come to analysis. In a state of profound sexual frustration, she constantly masturbated with intense sadistic fantasies. She was taking a number of psychotropic medications and had an air of vacancy about her; indeed, she seemed to have fallen completely to pieces. In analysis, she slowly improved. Two summers ago her mother suddenly died, causing her to relapse seriously. She had night anxieties, obsessional thoughts and highly sadistic and persecutory nightmares.

A year ago her father, with whom she had been living again since her mother's death, was diagnosed with lung cancer. His condition had deteriorated appreciably during the summer holidays.

Let me add something about the drugs the patient is taking, because this problem comes up in the session. At the beginning of the analysis, she was taking considerable doses of various antidepressants and anxiolytics. Of her own accord, she had gradually cut down on the drugs as she progressed and came to have more trust in the analytic relationship. In her mind, though, the conviction persists that she can survive only with the drugs: if she does not fall to pieces, it is only because she takes a Tavor[1] pill. She goes on stubbornly taking her Tavor: half a tablet in the morning, another half in the afternoon (which she has now given up) and a whole tablet or half a tablet in the evening.

The sessions reported here are from the second week after the summer holidays, in September. She comes four times a week, between Monday and Friday.

1 Translator's note: the Italian equivalent of Ativan (lorazepam).

Monday's session

P. The last three days have not been so good. On Friday morning my father was worse: he couldn't even get up . . . Then he had an injection and felt better. That evening I made a terrible scene. We were having supper: my father, my aunt – my father's sister who had come to stay for a few days – Claudia, Anna (*two of her sisters*) and myself.

We were sitting at the table and I was talking about things that had happened at the office; my father was giving orders as usual: 'Don't leave the omelettes; give some of this or that to your aunt; is there any meat left?' and so on. Bloody hell! I began to shout that there was never any place for me, to talk about my affairs, that these meals were terrible ordeals and that I was sick and tired of them. My sisters looked at me in horror and indignation. And next morning my father was in a bad way again. Then he had his jab and felt better.

I got absolutely furious, as I felt he was playing games with me. Is he well or is he ill? Will there still be any place for love after all this, I ask myself. It's awful. I can't go on living with this uncertainty, with him being fine one minute and poorly the next! I don't know if he's just moaning, or really in a bad way, or if it's the cortisone injection that makes him feel better. Saturday was the best day because by mistake he had two jabs of Bentelan.[2] He says it doesn't work and cries constantly. I can't stand it any longer!

A. You're bringing me the things you can't cope with yourself: your father's state of need and suffering and your own when you felt there was no place for you at home – or in the analysis either because it was Friday. You're also bringing me the part of yourself that solves problems with drugs and seems confused about what it needs – drugs or whatever.

P. I'm fed up with all these worries and the illness. Everyone had forgotten Anna's birthday because they were thinking and talking only about my father's illness. I'm fed up to the back teeth! And then the business of the drugs! Oh, yes, that little bit of Tavor I take! I need something else! My father is so impatient, it makes me absolutely furious! He's always moaning.

---

2 Translator's note: the Italian equivalent of Betnesol (betamethasone disodium phosphate).

A. Let me remind you how impatient *you* felt on Friday, when you felt that no one was listening to you, and not even I was there to listen to you.

P. (*violently interrupting me*) Impatient, impatient! But what kind of a life do I have! Nothing but illnesses, illnesses and death. Since my mother died, I've stopped living. And why? Aren't I entitled to have a man too? And I've never screwed and enjoyed it! What about that, is that right? I can't go for a walk without feeling bad, and that really upsets me because I like walking. And now I can't even watch television and amuse myself a bit, because it annoys my father. What a loathsome family! They're all in the shit! Three daughters in analysis and I've been in it for five years. And what have you done about it all? I feel awful and you sit there, saying 'impatient, impatient'!

A. (*All this comes out like an explosion. So, as soon as I recover somewhat, I say*) Get a move on, you analyst-mummy! Roll up your sleeves and start clearing up. Sweep away my troubles and rage and all the nasties of this unbearable weekend. What are you waiting for? You don't understand anything, you stupid analyst-mummy.

P. (*much calmer*) No, not in the least stupid. Oh yes, the kind doctor knows how to make herself indispensable. You're cunning. What do you think? I know I missed my analysis at the weekend, but I can't stand it. It's you who go away, and I'm left like this, infuriated.

A. I think the reason you felt so infuriated was not only because you were missing my attention and care, but also because you wanted me to be the drug that sweeps away needs, troubles and rage. That's why you accuse me of making myself indispensable. When you talk about 'having a man', 'making love' and 'amusing yourself a bit', perhaps you're trying to use excitement and sexuality in the same way, to sweep away the painful feeling of not having attention and space in my mind, just as you had none in your parents' minds. So you got more and more angry with your father taking his cortisone – and with me, because you suspected me of using sexuality at weekends like a cortisone injection, to avoid all the difficulties and troubles instead of taking them inside me, while you were left alone to endure anxiety, troubles and rage.

P. (*vehemently*) The fact is that I can't allow myself to suffer! I'm afraid of not being able to let myself do it. Of failing and collapsing.

A. So, when you suffered over the weekend it wasn't only because I didn't see you and listen to you; you suffered even more because you were afraid that your pain and rage might tear you apart and make you collapse. After all, you'd already been upset and humiliated by the scene you made at the table with your father. You felt that you'd ruined the family supper, made your father ill, shocked your sisters, and lost your feelings of love and everything else.

P. (*greatly relieved*) That's absolutely right! And then, for some time now, as you know, I've very much wanted to make up for things, to experience all the things I never experienced in my life – which, I admit, I didn't experience partly because of the way I was. Most of all, I'd like to rediscover certain aspects of my nature. That's why I like walking so much. And now all these illnesses and death! And I'm afraid that if I stop now, I'll miss out on everything. I can't stop. That's why I get so infuriated when things happen.

A. You'd like to have a non-stop relationship with me – to penetrate inside me, your mummy's belly, nature, and go on walking for ever and ever, without painful interruptions, without meeting daddy and your sisters, as in the weekend break. You're afraid that if you come out from inside me, your walking will be interrupted, and you won't be able to stand it, you'll lose everything, explode and collapse.

Tuesday's session

P. (*enters the room red-eyed*) Last night I felt very anxious when I went to bed. My father is always crying. He says he can't stop when these fits of demoralization come over him. I immediately make light of it. I try to comfort him by telling him that what matters is soundness of mind, and other bullshit like that, and I don't know whether I believe it myself or not.

I've had three horrible dreams. I remember two of them, but I didn't want to remember the third because they were so nasty. There was no point.

In the first dream I went to see my mother. There was a funny piece of furniture in the room with IOUs inside it. About the IOUs, my mother said: 'Your father wants to leave you some money.' I answered in a worried voice: 'OK, but who's going to settle these IOUs?' I asked my mother to go and see my father, but she replied that she couldn't. My mother spoke to me very warmly and trustingly. She said she had split up with my father, and that when he was young he had young girlfriends. I asked my mother if she had had lovers. She said she hadn't. Then I got a coach to go home with Rosa (*the eldest sister*). We saw a carefree-looking young woman of about 40, like you (*the analyst*), going by. Rosa said: 'She's a terrible woman: she can make you believe

139

anything she likes, for instance that she's your mother, but it isn't true. Just watch out.'

In the second dream, I was in a house on the stairs, with a big hunting knife in my hand. I felt threatened by a brutish man. I thought it would be easy to strike the first blow, but the second would be harder, because once he was wounded he would be more ferocious. I plunged the knife round the corner of the staircase, because that's where the person who was threatening me was. Then I saw it wasn't a man, but a woman who was chasing me down the stairs, right outside the building, and I was running away. I went back in through another entrance and I was terrified because the blade was full of blood and I might be caught. The blade got smaller and I threw it away, but I still had the handle in my hand and you could see it was pink.

Inside the other entrance I met a woman doctor, who shook her head in disapproval. I said: 'All right, I'll come quietly.' I accepted the punishment and the jail sentence.

(*As the patient speaks, her tone of voice becomes increasingly bitter and ill-tempered. She remains silent for a moment, scratching her arm and elbows as if looking for pimples to scratch off, and tugging at her hair. Resuming, she complains about the doctors who make her father suffer by refusing to give him cortisone.*)

What for? To make him live a bit longer? Instead of having him live a month less but better. That's why I'm angry with you, with all that stuff you tell me about the drugs. And then, at the office, I cock everything up and make one mistake after another! Then I have these ghastly dreams. At the office I get confused and can't think rationally. I think I'm doing the right thing, but it turns out to be all wrong.

A. (*for a moment I feel invaded and overwhelmed by the patient's material and her hostility and fury*) Perhaps you're so tormented because you feel you can't bear your father's suffering and your own at his illness, as well as the fear of his death. One part of you would rather take Bentelan (as your father did) and Tavor to forget your frightening dreams, but another part is uncertain and doubtful. You're afraid that you can't think properly, and that it's like in the office, when things that seem right turn out to be wrong.

P. (*losing her temper*) Right, wrong! Who is to say what's right and what's wrong? I can't accept that there's only one justice, only one logic in life. I'm angry with you for what you said about the drugs. Catholic moralism! *I* am more concerned with the quality of life.

A. Yes, you *are* worried about the quality of life inside yourself. About the condition of your father, your mother and myself (the woman doctor)

140

inside you. Last night you viciously attacked your father and aunt, and me as your father and aunt, daddy and mummy all together, because of what you felt was a mutual 'sweeping'[3] away of pain with their relationship, and in the dream you had set your parents apart from each other. That's why, in your mind, your father became a person in pain, wounded, whom you found terrifying, so he had to be urgently tranquillized with cortisone.

P. (*almost shouting, as if trying to shut me up*) You're a sadist, like all doctors; no one could be a doctor without being a sadist.

A. You accuse me of making you suffer terribly when I show you that you're allied with a drug-analyst-mummy who tranquillizes you with drug-words. Just as you want to use drugs to send your wounded, moaning, frightening parents to sleep and kill them – and you feel you would then get some peace for yourself and shut me up.

P. (*with a kind of sigh of relief*) That's really how it is. I do think that as long as my father is like this, I shall never have any peace, or be able to take a break in peace. Yes, if I imagine a moment of pleasure, I also think that this situation has to be over and done with. And that's absolutely awful, terrible! Surely anyone with parents suffering from cancer would feel like that!

A. You're actually afraid that I don't understand – that I am a mother who doesn't come when you call her to your sick father's bedside. You're afraid I'm a mother who can't contain your fear and death wishes. So having analysis, having these murderous wishes taken care of, and acknowledging them, is the same as being caught, punished, flung into jail and annihilated.

QUESTION. *In the first session you presented, the patient is furious, but then acknowledges what the analyst said. It looks as if there is a pattern to the sessions here. I wonder if the patient is protesting and feeling angry with the analyst not so much, and not only, because of the weekend but also – or even mainly – because the analyst's mind at that moment is cluttered and failing to receive her communications.*

ANALYST. That may be, but the patient's style is to penetrate inside me like that and leave me breathless.

BRENMAN. We don't have the patient's full history, but what we do have shows that she was a deprived child from the moment of her birth. Her mother was ill and didn't have enough milk for her, and the family

---

3 Translator's note: the Italian word *scopare* not only means 'to sweep' but is also a slang term for sexual intercourse.

couldn't afford powdered milk. The patient describes herself growing up as a deprived child relating to sick parents. That's why she feels very angry and rebellious – so much so that she destroys her own good qualities.

She tries to solve her problems by resorting to sex with various men, but it's no use. She always finds the wrong men and gets hardly any satisfaction from it all, so she goes on medication and masturbates. The patient feels guilty and persecuted following her mother's death, and the story continues with the drama of a deprived person who also has to care for a sick father, without even having her mother with her.

If we look at the first part of the session, the patient says she has been deprived yet again: for three days she has been without analysis and has made a terrible scene with her sick father, who still dominates the whole family. The father checks whether there's any meat or omelette left, and she has to shout: 'What about me? What are we to do about me?'

This could mean different things: it might be the problem of the weekend when the analyst leaves the patient by herself, but, on a simpler and more direct level, she says she has to look after a sick person who has no consideration for her wishes. The patient doesn't know if there's really nothing that can be done for her father, if he is ill, or if he is just egocentric.

This is a problem that touches on very primitive anxieties. What does an infant feel when there's no milk in his mother's breast? 'Have I got a sick mother?' 'Have I got a selfish mother?'

That's the dilemma she faces. That's what she is talking about when she says: 'Is my father well or is he ill? Is he really ill?' This is her abiding problem. The analyst interprets the patient's need to have someone; she interprets her needs, the fact that she is suffering and has problems, and at least at that point the analyst is trying to understand something about the patient.

But the patient doesn't feel touched by this, and answers instead: 'Everyone forgot Anna's birthday.' This infuriates her because she says that no one in the family – least of all her father – sets any store by moments of joy.

So in the transference she is somehow saying that it is all very well to talk about enduring suffering and facing anxiety and not taking drugs, but that no one is saying anything about the need to have moments of pleasure too.

The analyst fails to pick up this aspect; instead, she goes on telling her to put up with these painful situations. Yet a woman wants more from life than to be able to endure suffering or to face a sense of guilt.

142

'But what kind of a life is this,' the patient says, 'nothing but illnesses and death; am I not entitled to have a man?' She is in fact correcting the analyst by maintaining that there must also be some pleasure in life. I don't know how far the analyst interpreted this point, but it is surely important to dwell on this need, which the patient clearly expresses, to have satisfactions and pleasures in life. If not, the only pleasure a person can have is sadism. It seems that somehow the analyst didn't feel able to give this kind of interpretation.

ANALYST. I didn't pick this up because that's precisely the patient's family portrait. These aspects of satisfaction and joy in life did come up to some extent in the analysis too. The patient has recently discovered a great interest in her work, which she had up to now seen as a chore that had to be got through to survive, as a duty, so as to be able to pay for her analysis and so on. We even noticed that she has ambitions too. 'Good heavens, you actually have ambitions!' – which both pleased and shocked her.

BRENMAN. Let me add something about the patient's style of penetrating violently into the analyst and leaving her breathless. When a child feels he isn't loved or stays hungry, so long as he does not end up dying or emptying himself out, he must thrust himself forward and physically penetrate into other people in order to survive and go on living. All he can do is to thrust himself inside. He has to resort to a violent projective identification because he lacks the experience of understanding.

This is what the patient is talking about; she has not in the least appreciated the fact that the analyst failed to emphasize and take up her wish to enjoy life. Mark you, when she says 'I want to live, I want to have a man, I want to love', the type of relationship she could have is not a genuine love relationship, but only an intrusive one. It's an illusion, but this particular illusion comes about because there hasn't been a genuine relationship and genuine understanding, and the patient has no experience of this kind. In the session, there has been a breakdown in understanding between patient and analyst. Something good happens and the patient realizes that there is something worthwhile in the analyst. The patient wishes for the analyst, and misses her when there is a break.

It isn't clear why the analyst speaks of love in terms of sweeping away.[4] The patient doesn't understand what the analyst means when she talks about sweeping away, or drugs and medication.

---

4 Translator's note: please see earlier note on the double meaning of the Italian word *scopare*.

I think the patient uses this kind of sexuality because there has been a breakdown in her personal relations, and it isn't clear why she has to bring this up at this point in the session. What the patient is saying, and what she realizes, is that she is fond of her analytical sessions, that she misses the analyst, that she feels infuriated and that she needs to be helped to overcome the void she feels at times of separation. In interpreting the patient's defences against the experience of separation, the analyst ought to ask herself: 'Why am I doing this?' Otherwise the patient may hear her interpretation as: 'You can't face separation, so you're a weak person who can't cope with pain.' But in fact the most important thing is to try genuinely to help the patient cope with life at times of separation and get by. After all, the patient begins the session by saying that her father went on in the same old way, without paying the slightest attention to how she felt.

The way the patient starts the session is very important. In this case one should ask oneself: 'Is there some problem about the fact that I am carrying on in my usual way and not trying to really discover what she felt at that moment?' One of the important problems of analytic listening is the need to attend to how the patient is feeling. You have to interpret how the patient is feeling and at the same time the defences or destructiveness. The choice depends on the sensitivity of the individual analyst.

At the point when the patient makes contact with the analyst and says she has missed her, the analyst chooses to interpret only the defences.

If there are two people and one says 'I missed you a lot; it was so painful that I went to bed and drank some whisky', the other should say 'Yes, I missed you too.' But if you meet someone who says 'I missed you a lot, so I went to bed, and drank a glass of whisky', and the other answers 'You tried to put the pain of this separation out of your mind', what she is saying is true, because that really is what has happened, but it might not be the most useful thing to say to the patient. After all, the patient is getting closer to understanding, and going to the analyst has affective significance for her at that time. The patient is saying: 'I know I miss analysis; I can't bear it, and in any case I think about it and it's very painful.'

Her problem, I think, is that she was deprived from the moment of her birth. The only thing the analysis can do is to help her keep her wishes alive, so that she can find something that will give her satisfaction.

ANALYST. I'd like to know more about the aspects Dr Brenman has pointed out here. During the session I had noticed two things about the

144

patient, who had expressed herself ambiguously. On the one hand, she had declared her need and had approached closer to me, but on the other I had the impression that she also felt I was not such a nice person, because I had inflicted a dose of cunning on her.

BRENMAN. And she really is trying to explain this to the analyst, very carefully and very precisely. In the dream she says she was with her sister Rosa, that they saw a young, self-assured woman, who made people believe what she wanted them to believe. This woman was sure of herself and self-confident like the analyst.

Perhaps the patient is saying that she likes to have someone she can feel intimate with – someone to share things with. This person might be the analyst. 'But you, the analyst,' says the patient, 'are full of yourself, of wanting to be enviable at all costs; you can say anything you like, but you won't be able to understand me, and you'll make me believe whatever you want me to believe.' I think this is what the patient is actually saying.

In her experience, analysis does not provide her with the warm and intimate mother who could help her to find other relationships, but instead makes her think how able, clever and sure of herself the analyst is, so that she feels inferior. The analyst has so much power that she can make the patient believe anything.

At any rate, this is a danger of analysis: there are times when patients agree with the analyst, but one doesn't understand why. The patient may assume there is a relationship in which the analyst succeeds in making him believe anything.

I think this patient has felt deprived of understanding, and indoctrinated by the opinions of others who rape her mind; so she reacts violently, but then has to give herself up like a criminal.

This might well be the story of her life – a deprived little girl, with moralistic parents who made her believe anything: that she was bad, that she was terrible, and that she had to behave how they wanted her to behave. She rebels violently and then the parents say: 'Look what a terrible person you are, a terrible murderer.' That is probably what she is saying.

This moralizing, this putting everything on a moralistic level, has been so powerful and strong in the patient's life! 'What sort of doctors are these if they won't give my father cortisone to make him feel better? They're sadists, because they have no understanding of the quality of life. They're only interested in what they call morality.'

What is more, they can even make people believe that raping the mind is a good form of treatment.

ANALYST. I'm thinking of the problem of pleasure sweeping away suffering and of food. It seems to me that this little girl was unable to suck partly because there was no milk, but also because of her mother's rhagades. So she didn't have the *pleasure* of sucking, apart from actually being fed. An infant sucks not only to be fed, but also to get comfort and to experience pleasure. For me, that is the origin of this idea, and perhaps also of this confusion between food and something that produces pleasure, to sweep away pain – a nipple that isn't food but Tavor, the medication. Tavor, of course, is not food; it's not nourishing. In this patient, it seems to me that the confusion arises precisely here, through not having had the two experiences at the breast.

BRENMAN. I think that pleasure is something very important in life, and that having joy in life is not just a matter of getting rid of unpleasurable things. Pleasure really can have a meaning in its own right: true joy helps one endure the pains of life. It's important to distinguish it from a flight into pleasure.

When a mother feeds an infant, there is not only the necessity of feeding, but also a pleasure for the people mutually involved in the process. The problem is about relative values. It also has to do with the issue of deciding on the moment of death. If someone is dying of cancer, you can do your best to keep him alive in desperate suffering, or else you can help to shorten his life, so that it can have at least some meaning.

The patient, it seems to me, is complaining that sometimes she has a good relationship with the analyst, but on other occasions, for some reason – maybe separation or whatever – the analyst is experienced as someone who rapes her mind with morality. She is like the doctors, who withhold help from the patient for moral reasons, because they are not really thinking of how the patient feels.

When the patient talks about this problem, she herself becomes uncertain; she can't think about it properly and doesn't know what is right and what is wrong.

I think she needs someone who is able to investigate and dissect these difficult problems together with her. For instance, is it right to let a person die or suffer like that, without doing anything?

The patient gets very confused because all she can find inside herself is a rebellion against the moral authorities. But what she is constantly emphasizing is the absence of a mother with whom she can discuss these problems warmly and intimately, as in the first part of her dream.

The danger for the patient is that this relationship, which she needs and wants, can be killed off by an authoritarian person. The proper way of thinking about things, and discussing and examining them, disappears and it becomes impossible to understand life's problems and relationships.

I suspect that during this person's life, she has experienced a mixture of serious deprivation and incomprehension from her mother. If the mother can speak to her and discuss things warmly and intimately, she can put her thoughts in order (as in the first part of the dream), but if moralizing and deprivation predominate, she can become violent and murderous, and then she kills off all the good aspects of the relationship.

In this analysis, this might mean that there are moments when the patient feels understood and others when, for good reasons or bad, the analyst is experienced as a moralizing superego. And when the patient rebels, as she did in her teens against what she felt to be a moralizing superego, and the other person tries to insist that he or she is right, then she is liable to forget the experience of understanding that she has also had.

The experience of being crushed and violently intruded upon is very powerful in this patient and she also manages to make the analyst feel it. After all, the analyst felt suffocated and oppressed; she too had the experience of being raped in her mind, so that she was left unable to think.

QUESTION. *I wonder if the problem is not precisely this — the inability to think. The father too mentions his great sorrow at not being able to use his mind creatively and to think beautiful things — that is, to have thoughts. The patient is forced to think and to be very analytic — to be too lucid, so that her mind hears the analyst's words as though they were stabs with a knife, instead of using them to let herself think creatively. Perhaps the whole thing is also connected with an over-harsh primal experience at the breast.*

BRENMAN. There is some truth in that. Let's consider the fact that the father is dying: a person can't spend their whole life looking after a dying father. In this family there are five daughters, and if they were to take it in turns, they could manage to get out of the house every so often and also have something else for themselves. If the father was a nicer, more human person, he would be the first to say: 'It's not right for you to be with me all the time; why don't you go out and spend some time with someone else as well, and do something for yourself?'

This is a way of thinking about the quality of life: a person has to face sadness and suffering, but can't spend their whole life thinking that that's all there is. The patient is very much taken up and preoccupied by this problem. We may wonder how long ago, and how early on, it became a problem for her.

Now if life is nothing but suffering, or if an over-moralizing super-ego is constantly accusing one, something is definitely wrong. All one can do then is to get violent and destructive. I don't think the patient had only this course open to her, as there is evidence of the good relationship between her and the analyst. She knows the value of the analyst who keeps her together.

The patient has a dream in which she shares an experience with her mother; they discuss things together, and talk about the history and the past, which really does concern the patient. So there are elements of a good human relationship, but unfortunately a murder then takes place and the patient has to give herself up. I think the tragedy is that when she feels overwhelmed by the all-moralizing superego, she feels like a murderer.

QUESTION. *The patient's murderous impulses are directed not only towards the analyst (the woman), but also towards her father (the man). The patient seems to be saying that the dying father is also the father who ruined her life. All he leaves behind him are holes or IOUs that have to be paid. There are actually two people attacking the patient: one is a woman and the other is a man.*

BRENMAN. I think it's important to distinguish the various figures in her life: they are not all transference figures. The distinction between a transference figure and a real one is very important in analysis. One problem at this time is to be able to say who is the dominant, selfish, accusing superego, and who is the understanding part.

Looking at the material, the analyst has told us that at times she is overwhelmed by the patient and can understand what the patient might be feeling because she herself is in the same state. The patient goes on to say: 'I can't imagine there's only one justice, only one logic in life. I'm very angry because of what you said about the drugs; that's just Catholic moralism!'

As for the father, it is right to devote some time and thought to your father, but you can't sacrifice your whole life to him. Something has to be worked out, the patient says, to solve this problem. There must be another way of looking after your father: a balance needs to be struck between two things, the father and her life.

But the patient feels that the analyst is moralizing like a doctor. It's important to analyse this in the transference; the patient might well be in a better state after a while, and be able to distinguish her attitude towards her father from what her father is really like. But for the moment the whole world is the same in her eyes: to her there is no difference between the analyst and the father. What she would like is to be able to distinguish between the analyst and her father. The patient needs to have an experience that will enable her to make this distinction.

She thinks the analyst and doctors are always moralizing. Yet she also thinks there are many different ways of tackling problems. No one considers the quality of life. She probably needs the analyst to understand this, to become aware of it and to make her aware of it.

QUESTION. *Perhaps the analyst ought to say: 'I understand your situation. There are moments when one feels like killing even one's own father. It's terrible, but I understand; it can happen.'*

BRENMAN. If you live in that kind of world, it's very easy to feel like a murderer. If you live in a world in which you are starving to death, and someone starts moralizing to make you feel guilty, you will certainly want to kill them; that's perfectly understandable.

I would interpret along these lines: 'Yes, but the problem is that I can understand you wanting to kill your father, but you mustn't kill me.'

We have an impulse to kill anyone who keeps on accusing us, moralizing and backbiting. The only thing that stops us killing is if we have an alternative relationship. If you have an alternative relationship, you can tell your father: 'I can stay with you for a few hours, but then I must go out with my friends.' That's the only way to calm down, by having someone else with whom you have a better relationship.

This can happen at any level. If an infant gets on his mother's nerves, she may say to her husband: 'Listen, you look after the baby, I'm going out for a bit.' There has to be a better alternative. You may also have murderous feelings, but if you have a bit of help, you will be able to contain them, stand back and save the situation.

The patient at that moment feels that her entire world – the whole world in fact – has a moralizing part. So she explicitly asks the analyst to look at her life in a different way, as there's more than one way of looking at a person's life. The analyst could interpret at this point that the patient's need is to have a more positive analyst who doesn't only moralize and make her feel guilty. Otherwise, if there is only this type of relationship with her too, the patient will have murderous feelings.

You have to supply a valid alternative; that may be the only answer to her question.

QUESTION. *The patient is also concerned that the doctors with her father, like the analyst with her, find it hard to stay in direct contact with this aspect of suffering. When forced to face it openly, they are more likely to get in touch with things of their own. The patient accuses the analyst and the doctors of this: 'You expect me to stay with my pain, but you are not prepared to stay with it even for a moment; you take refuge in your specialist knowledge.'*

BRENMAN. Yes, the patient has the impression that analysts are like that as well: they take refuge in their analytic expertise, but withdraw when faced with suffering. Doctors too behave as if the problem were only one of treatment; it seems not to make any difference whether the patient is or is not suffering. That at least is this patient's impression.

The patient's view of this problem is that suffering can be borne only up to a point. Doctors don't really think the patient should be left to suffer, but the problem is where to draw the line as to how much suffering can be endured. Perhaps it would be better for everyone if the father were to die, or perhaps it would be better for him to be relieved of his suffering a bit, so that his life can still have some value.

It seems to me the patient is saying that there isn't one thing that is right and another that is wrong. She is saying only that she can't accept that there is only one justice and logic in life. I agree with that: there are the two aspects.

When things get too bad, death becomes preferable. Certainly the best solution would be for the painful state to be changed. We need to distinguish between the avoidance of suffering because it is excessive, on the one hand, and, on the other, the amount of suffering that can reasonably be avoided and the amount that can be tolerated.

QUESTION. *Perhaps the patient thinks that the adult world has always imposed responsibilities on her which it has never accepted for itself. The doctor doesn't ask himself what is best for the patient, but what he thinks is best. She may be thinking the same about the analyst. The analyst may do the same thing, sometimes: I must be the good analyst, give the right interpretation, and stay faithful to analysis. Perhaps the patient thinks that, when confronted with moments of intense suffering, the analyst uses analysis as a drug of her own.*

BRENMAN. Consider the example of a mother with a normal child. It would be wrong to say 'Everything for the child', while the mother must suffer; but it would be equally wrong to say 'Everything for the mother', so the child has to suffer.

The right approach is to share things out fairly according to the child's age and development. Now, what the patient sometimes thinks is that the analyst is not humanly involved and avoids empathizing with her, but instead gives interpretations. Many interpretations are indeed given to keep the patient quiet, so that the analyst is not disturbed. But I don't think this patient feels that the analyst is trying to avoid suffering.

150

Wednesday's session

ANALYST. When I open the door, the patient is half-hidden behind the jamb. At first I can't see her and almost have to go and look for her.

P. I have a request: I want you to help me experience the reality of my father's illness on a human level. There were times in the past when I wasn't so anxious and obsessional about it, but felt the pleasure of togetherness.

A. You seem to be looking for a different father from the wounded, terrifying one chasing you down the stairs, as well as an analyst-mummy that doesn't turn into the doctor who looks at you disapprovingly, judges you and throws you into jail.

P. Yes, and the two things really are connected. I've experienced it on a normal, healthy level, with pain day by day, but no more. There's been a deterioration, an upset since the beginning of the analysis, but especially since the weekend. I feel anxious all the time, checking to see if he's coughing or not coughing, sleeping or not sleeping.

I'd like to recover the healthy aspect. Then things would have a meaning, life would have a meaning, and my father's illness would also have a meaning. But these upsets don't have any meaning.

A. You feel that you can't bear to let go of me, that it would disrupt things.

P. I'm angry with you because you're not there to experience my troubles with me. I don't think you can help me, but I also know that if I've been able to live through this summer with my father as he got worse, it's because of the analysis. My father's depressive breakdown in the last few days has unsettled things.

A. Perhaps you are feeling that if you are not fused in with me, as you perhaps hoped after returning from the break, everything will collapse. You collapse, your father collapses, and so does your relationship with me ('You can't help me'). It's upsetting to feel helped, then left by yourself, and then helped again – which, if anything, seems to be your state of mind today.

I also wonder whether your standing behind the door jamb when you arrived might have been a test to see if I would come and look for you in spite of everything.

P. The fact is that I'm losing my bearings and getting mixed up. I must rescue a space of my own where I can be myself, and that's all there is to it. That's why my work is so important to me now. If I get lost in a situation with no reference points and no boundaries, as I do when my father, his illness and myself all merge into one thing, and I'm always thinking and brooding, it's very dangerous. Then I start having fantasies about death, about his death, when it will be, what it will be like, and what I shall feel like afterwards. Then I get mixed up – I mix myself up with my whole world, my work, my father's world, the illness, and so on.

Then I lose everything. Sometimes I even feel that the analysis is vague. If I lose my bearings, I start floundering. Then I can't tell nice things apart from nasty ones, so they're all there together, and I mix everything up with my father's illness.

It's not affection – no, it's something completely different. It's something sick and sticky, like when I felt invaded by the parasites. I need my own things, I need to be myself, but that doesn't fit in with my being angry with you because you're not always there.

A. Well, after all, I wonder if that's another reason why you hid behind the door jamb today: to keep a distance between us.

P. I don't know; it's never happened before. Yes, I *do* feel invaded. Every time lately, I come along suspiciously and fearfully: what will she do for me today, what will happen? Or I think: it's a waste of time, what can she do for me? Or: she'll mix me up, muddle my brain, put me off balance. You're a problem for me. Now I feel that this relationship is one more problem.

A. Either you invade me, get mixed up and lose yourself, or I invade you, and make you suffer by putting the pain and rage of separation into you, as well as the fear of collapsing. It's the fear and rage of feeling yourself to be full of hate, with a bloody dagger in your hand to stab the united parents, which is what you feel like when you accuse me of criticizing you and focusing only on 'the bad things in you'. (*This is a reference to material from other sessions not reported here. The parasites are from dreams she brought some years before.*)

BRENMAN. I'd like to say a few things, starting with the pathological aspects. There's a point half-way through the session when the patient feels invaded; she feels as if the analyst is invading her with her interpretations and taking over her mind. That is to say, the analyst doesn't understand her, doesn't consider her as a separate person and doesn't give her food for thought, but takes her over. The patient is also very angry because the analyst went away, whereas she would like her to be there; she'd like to invade her. At the same time she feels invaded by the analyst, but she also knows that it isn't true – that the analyst is not invading her.

152

She begins the session with a request: she wants to be able to experience the reality of the problems of her father's illness on a more human level. She wants to be helped to keep the good things, so that she can have an adequate identification with her father without feeling overwhelmed by the anxiety of his situation.

All this seems very important to the patient, as she keeps on repeating that she needs it, otherwise life has no meaning. At one point she says: 'I feel lost, I feel mixed up. I must rescue a bit of space for myself. I am myself, and no one else.' This is a very sad feeling. In a way she is hiding herself; she feels that the only way to be herself is to hide.

That is true in part, but not entirely so, because she also comes to analysis.

I think she wants an analysis in which she can be with the analyst and at the same time be herself, because no one wants to be someone else. Instead, there's something that invades everything and stops it becoming a reality. It did happen once, but now she seems to be losing it. It seems that the weekend – apart from the problem of her dying father – is too much for her.

QUESTION. *At the beginning the patient twice repeats that there is an area of reality about her father's illness, for which she seeks help. The analyst gives a transference interpretation, saying that the patient can't bear to let go of her. The patient sees it differently and answers that the analyst is not there to experience things with her. It seems that, on the one hand, the patient has a memory that the analysis has helped her cope with her father's illness, but, on the other, at this moment, when the analyst takes the situation upon herself, it doesn't work. Perhaps this is the cause of the mix-up.*

BRENMAN. The analyst's transference interpretation may be correct. But she should give some thought to how to help the patient during the separation, because the patient cannot tolerate it. Perhaps there are some friends, or other people who could help her or go away with her, or she could talk to someone else.

There's a whole load of points here that need to be developed. When you feel the situation is too difficult for the patient, you might also think of someone else she could speak to – perhaps even another analyst she could talk to when her own analyst is not there. These are the patient's requests, and they are reasonable.

I too think the patient is not only talking about the problem of her difficulties with the analyst not always being with her. She is asking a more general question about what the analyst can give, what she can offer. 'What can you, the analyst, give me to help me with the problem of my dying father?' 'What happens when I'm with my father? I feel as if I'm going completely under in my identification with him, so I can't even help him.' 'I want to really be myself.' The patient is saying all these things. She is also saying that during the separation she needs someone to help her to identify with her father up to a point, but also to keep a part of her life for herself.

QUESTION. *Perhaps the problem that has come to a head here is a theoretical one connected with our tendency to see everything as transference and to set no store by reality. We need a thorough discussion of how to analyse the transference while taking account of the patient's reality. This is a typical case, because there's a dying father and the analyst is in effect saying: 'I'm the one who is dying.'*

BRENMAN. I think transference interpretation is legitimate, but all the same the patient is asking the analyst to think about what help there might be for her outside the sessions when she is faced with problems she can't cope with by herself. Other relational objects must be included when working on the transference. If you interpret only emotions concerning the analytic relationship, it's almost as if no one in the world matters but the analyst.

I believe the transference should be extended to the patient's reality and the patient's need to have a relational life outside analysis too. This probably applies in any analysis. If we take care of the patient, we must think about how he can go on living when we aren't there, and what internal or external resources he has to help him face separation.

How are we to tackle this problem if we don't interpret it in the transference first? We may interpret that the situation at the time is too difficult for the patient, that she can't tolerate it, and that someone else needs to be there when the analyst is away. In this way you discuss the possible solutions to the problem; you discuss them together and pave the way for more appropriate solutions.

11

Transgenerational transmission
of trauma

The clinical material presented here concerns a woman with a traumatic past (violence and early exposure to sexuality by her parents) and an unhappy couple relationship. The predominant theme of the sessions is the physical violence inflicted by the patient on her daughters, as a repetition and continuation of the trauma that she herself sustained in the past.

Unable to cope with life, the patient expects her children to be the providers of positive elements and reassurance for her. Because such a mother can face neither her own despair nor her children's demands, she hates her children and constantly beats them.

Considered in these terms, the patient's hate for her own mother seems to be due not so much to the sexual promiscuity or physical violence to which she was exposed, as to the fact that her mother had been able neither to cope with her own life nor to help the patient learn to cope with hers.

Such families are not uncommon. The children are required to reassure their parents and to motivate them to carry on living; in this way, the trauma is repeated from generation to generation.

The sessions presented here show that, alongside the violence, there is also a suffering part of the patient that seeks help from the analyst.

One of the themes of the supervision is the search for possible ways of breaking the vicious circle of the compulsion to repeat the trauma in subsequent generations.

ANALYST. Anna is a good-looking woman of about 40, married with two daughters. She has three elder brothers and a sister. Her mother is 70 years old and her father has been dead for some years.

Anna was born in a country town and the first few years of her life bore the stamp of promiscuity and violence. Her seriously alcoholic father was constantly making terrifying scenes, which either culminated

155

in physical violence or turned into equally violent sexual approaches to his wife. Anna remembers with a mixture of horror and jealousy how the violence of the glances exchanged between her parents would turn to lust. Sleeping in the same bed as her parents, she experienced intercourse between them and also witnessed her mother's sexual relations with her lover. The youngest of her brothers had also attempted to seduce her.

The mother, too, is described by Anna as an extremely harsh and violent woman. Intolerant of her daughter's rebellious attitude, she beat her regularly, enlisting the help of her eldest-but-one child for this purpose.

On a few rare occasions, Anna has told me that she was her mother's favourite in the first four years of her life. She was the first girl and was pretty. When her sister was born, everything fell apart, because the mother devoted herself entirely to her, while Anna, as she grew up, became 'the one who always does everything wrong'.

However, the final breakdown occurred when the mother abandoned the family and moved to the city to work. Her husband was no longer working, there was no money, and she decided to go and 'look after other people's children'.

The children were farmed out to different, constantly changing people. Anna, then aged 8, felt completely lost, with nothing to hold on to; she was the tolerated guest of people who did not love her, in places that often frightened her (there were images of dark corridors, of the disabled son of a woman who was never there, of sly old men, and of women talking among themselves about exciting and mysterious sex).

The family came together again when Anna was in her teens, but the climate was always very tense. I think she began to feel that she had some grip on her environment when she grew into a beautiful girl who was immediately the object of much male attention. But she never had a happy relationship.

She first had sex at the age of 19, with a much older man, but their intercourse was incomplete owing to his potency problems. Finding herself pregnant, she was forced to have an abortion, and it was only during the operation that she 'lost her virginity'.

The other men who had relationships with her are always described as lacking in affection, ambiguous and wanting her only for sex.

The relationship established with her husband, however, was on the whole positive, with each party's extreme need for help from the other being plain from the beginning. The son of parents who were incapable of empathy and affective support, her husband was, and still is, very disturbed, but has been much better since having analysis.

Anna never managed to concentrate on academic work. She failed her secondary school leaving examination and did not bother to repeat it. She left her family and went abroad, travelling to various countries, where she did casual work.

She spent a year in a country where her eldest brother was living, during which her mental balance seemed to fluctuate dangerously. She fell in with a group of hippies and started using drugs, not so much because she liked them but because they were a way of being with the group and feeling protected.

Soon after returning to Italy, she got married, so as to give meaning to her life.

After the birth of the first daughter, Anna's sex life with her husband became difficult because she felt 'blocked' and, it seems, her husband began to deceive her. The fear of being abandoned always made her life impossible. It was this fear, she tells me, that made her accept compromises in her marital relationship: drugs (cocaine) and sex in a threesome (with her husband and the odd young male friend of his).

The reasons why Anna asked for analysis three years ago were vague even to her: she had been thinking of it for some years and saw that her husband was pleased with his analysis and was benefiting from it. She always felt bad, insecure and unhappy, and felt that her life had no meaning. In particular, though – she told me in tears – she felt that she was a bad mother to her daughters.

Between the first and second preliminary interviews, Anna had a serious car accident, from which she miraculously emerged unscathed. The analysis began a week later, at four sessions a week.

A salient feature of my relationship with this patient is the keen suffering aroused in me by the description of her behaviour with her daughters – in particular, the older of the two. It is characterized by bad temper culminating in hatred, utterly stormy reactions, and cruel intolerance of their difficulties and shortcomings. I sometimes feel that the patient is punishing me for my shortcomings towards her, showing me that these are responsible for her cruelty to her children. In its most intense and difficult phases, the analysis centres on this relationship between the patient, her daughters and myself (with the husband sometimes featuring as the third focal point).

Monday's session

P. (*Arrives on time. A short pause ensues.*) I left home an hour ago . . . because I couldn't stand being there any longer.

(*In a harsh tone of voice*) I beat Fernanda. I hit her over and over again! Without hurting her, but over and over. Because she was constantly watching those cartoons on TV. I don't know. She's always watching these cartoons, like a little girl (*contemptuously*). I don't understand, she's regressing. She *always* has these cartoons on, and if I want to watch the news I can't. I told her she was an imbecile, a little girl, and she answered back: 'You're the imbecile.' Then I hit her because she mustn't say such things to me. Then I felt bad. I wanted to hug her because I could see the frightened expression on her face, but I also saw on her face the expression of someone who doesn't give in, like me . . . someone who rebels . . . and then I wanted to hit her again. On top of it, my mother made me even angrier by saying: 'Leave her alone, the poor little mite!'

A. Perhaps the feelings you imagine Fernanda has when she watches the cartoons on TV make you anxious. You tell me you left home an hour ago; today you're on time. Maybe you had to shake yourself out of the apathy and lethargy you felt at the weekend, which might otherwise have stopped you coming.

P. (*a short pause*) I didn't get anything done at the weekend, especially on Sunday. I did nothing at all. I didn't take an interest in anything . . . But I was able to do nothing because Fernanda was with her grandmother. I had so many dreams, and then I thought: what a lot of material! An hour later I'd forgotten the lot.

A. (*after a pause*) Perhaps you think we should see each other more often . . .

P. How ever did you pick that up?

A. What do you think . . . ?

P. Because I'm getting lethargic and not doing anything any more?

A. Well, also because you forget what you wanted to tell me, as if too much time had passed since the last time.

P. (*a pause*) Now I don't want to go home. I don't want to face Fernanda.

A. These feelings that are so painful to you – we should face them here. There's the lethargy, the forgetting of your dreams, the lack of interest in anything. Then perhaps there's the idea of needing me. These are difficult feelings to bear. You want to beat your daughter for feeling them, and not to see her in front of you any more.

P. (*a pause*) Yeah, but in the end, who gives a toss! If Fernanda is like that,

158

that's her business; let her watch her TV, and if Chiara is clever and likes studying, that's *her* business. If my husband and I go out for a walk, he takes a good look at all the little girls, and the younger and more childlike they are the better; well, that's his business: I don't give a toss!

A. (*disconcerted*) What I said to you seems to have put this idea of not giving a toss into your head. You think that if we don't beat each other it's basically because it doesn't matter. Perhaps beating is intended to shake things up.

P. (*a long pause*) I did something I hoped I would never do again . . . I really hoped I wouldn't do it again . . . I found myself making a gesture . . . the identical gesture to one of my mother's. Today, while beating Fernanda.

A. It's hard to let go, and not stay tied to the usual image of this beating mother.

P. That's right. I thought it would be easy to get rid of it . . . but it isn't. Also because it's not a nice thing; it's nasty . . .

BRENMAN. We're talking about things being handed down from generation to generation . . .

ANALYST. Exactly: that's why I chose this case to present. I was interested in this aspect of the transmission of intolerance, guilt and cruelty. How can the analyst get inside the patient's history so as to change things? What is more, the patient is probably stirring up elements of the analyst's history that are similar to her own . . .

For this session the patient arrives on time; I mention this because she is otherwise always five or ten minutes late.

She says: 'I left home an hour ago because I couldn't stand being there any longer!'

BRENMAN. Looking at the material, it seems to me that the patient sees her little girl as someone who can't face life, who clings to the cartoons like a drug. This makes the patient, like many parents, very angry.

We may get angry with our children for some such reason. But if the child is really unable to face life and drugs herself with all these cartoons, a parent may say to herself: 'That means I haven't helped this child to face life.' That is the feeling that's so hard to bear.

We can all have such feelings and reactions, which make us feel guilty and horrible, as they do with this patient. At the same time, when mothers are very violent to their children, you can see that *they* are in fact unable to face life and expect their children to enable them to face it, to offer them beautiful things, to reassure them and to make life easier for them. Such mothers can't cope with their own despair, so they hate

159

their children and constantly beat them. That's the most disturbing aspect. The patient's hate of her mother *seems* to be due to the sexual promiscuity and to the fact that she beat her – but in reality the main reason why she hates her is that the mother couldn't face life herself and didn't help her to learn how to face it.

The patient knows all this because she too went to America, fell in with hippies and used drugs. And now, with her own daughter, her behaviour is even worse than her mother's.

She can't stand the sense of guilt aroused when she sees that her daughter is unable to face life; at the same time she hopes the daughter will be the one to take the situation in hand and enable *her* to face life. This happens in many families. The children have to reassure the parents and motivate them to carry on living. At one point the patient says that one of the things that angered her most in a quarrel with her daughter was the intervention of her mother, who told her to leave the 'poor little mite in peace'. That could perhaps have been picked up in the transference: the worst thing an analyst can do is to leave the patient in peace – to leave her all by herself.

After all, the beating may make the patient feel better. Beating someone means that you feel something, that you are interested in the person who is beaten. The worst thing for the patient is to find herself alone at the weekend and to feel that she's with an analyst to whom nothing matters, who lets her go without doing anything. In fact, she was terrified, emptied her mind and could not manage to do anything.

The analyst understands this and actually says that perhaps the patient would like to see her more often. Yet this could have been brought out much more clearly, seeing that the patient feels she can only function if the analyst helps her.

When the analyst isn't there, what kind of analyst-as-internal-object remains with the patient? Perhaps it's someone who says 'What the hell, I don't give a damn what happens to you' – and that is what makes her very, very angry.

She actually makes this point many times, for instance when she says 'Who gives a toss about Fernanda! Let her watch TV!' – as if she were asking 'But do you give a toss about what I feel at weekends?'

That's the real question. If the analyst really cares about the patient, then the patient can have positive feelings for the analyst and there can be a creative dialogue between them. If there is a bond between two people who are separated, they can write to each other and stay in touch. When the patient is left by herself, she fantasizes that the analyst doesn't give a damn about her. So she deals with separation by doing exactly the same thing to herself, by not caring for herself in the slightest. And that's also what she does with her little girl when she tells her: 'You're stupid, you're an imbecile!'

So the patient and her daughter spend their whole time running each other down. That's the best way of hurting someone, because if you actually strike them, you are showing some interest. Instead, by saying 'All right, you watch television, I don't care!', you are hurting them and leaving them no hope.

If two people say to each other 'I don't give a damn about you, I don't care if you take drugs, or if you watch television', you are creating a vicious circle in which neither cares about the other.

The patient is trying to care for herself by making light of her own problems: 'My husband is going with other women? So what!' In this way she is killing off the caring, loving parts of herself.

This is a very common dynamic.

Waiting for Godot means that you don't know what to do, so the only way of feeling alive is to make war. Killing off love and meaning is a common form of violence, and I'm sure that this is precisely what is happening with this patient.

ANALYST. This patient is much better than I've been able to show. My perception is that she also has a good relationship with her daughters. Even if this terrible aspect comes out, something else can also be glimpsed, though it's hard to pick it up and demonstrate it.

BRENMAN. We are all familiar with this problem inside ourselves. We too may sometimes behave like this and then find a more loving and creative way of constructing things. We recover the most negative situation by constructing something; it's in our nature. There are bitter conflicts and then we start to construct something.

Why can't this patient show the person she is, with her love and hate, peace and war? Logically, we might expect her to be able to turn to the analyst and show her both of these aspects, so as to get help in strengthening the creative part and containing the more destructive part. If she were to show the good aspect, that might encourage the analyst to set about strengthening her good parts.

I don't know if the patient shows only her bad parts. Perhaps we'll be able to find out from the material. My guess is that patients often need to feel guilty and to beat their chests. For these patients, goodness is a matter of fighting against the bad, as if to say: 'You're bad and I'll beat you into becoming good!' That's very important for this patient.

In the Gospels, Christ suggested that people can have faith in goodness so as to cope with badness. But in adopting his teachings the

Church took them to extremes, by proclaiming that punishing people for their sins makes them good. There are two different systems: faith in goodness as a way of facing the bad, and constant attribution of guilt to the bad, in the illusory hope of making people good. The second is a more primitive system, but it's also more widespread.

QUESTION. *Perhaps the patient believes that, if she makes the analyst beat her, she can become good.*

BRENMAN. If the analyst were to hit her, she might become good; she might think she was becoming good. She could take the veil, say the Lord's Prayer and do the most incredible penances. Perhaps that's what she wants, but it wouldn't work. Her family history proves that. To reach the good parts, you must have faith in goodness, defined as the possibility of moderating the effects of the bad, rather than preferring punishment and revenge, seen as the wages of badness. That's what I think.

Tuesday's session

P. This morning I sorted out the clothes in the wardrobes. I moved the summer things up to the top. I noticed that a blue suit of my husband's was missing. Last night he came home at nine o'clock in casual clothes, as he does every Monday . . . He obviously goes off to the casino in the blue suit he wears at the office, and that way he doesn't have to tell me anything and I don't make a fuss. And on Saturdays he does the football pools and stakes enough to pay for two analyses! Not just one! And more besides.

A. Perhaps you are thinking you would like two analyses, or even more.

P. I feel that when I finish my analysis, my husband will stop gambling.

A. It seems to me that there's a feeling that has to do with my presence. The missing suit is the idea of a secret I'm keeping from you, of a life of my own, and that thought causes you a lot of suffering. You'd like to be able to afford two analyses and even more, but perhaps you feel you can't bear the idea of me having a life of my own without you.

P. I had a dream. I put Chiara in the pony cart. The cart was the same as it is in reality, and so was the pony, but instead of other children there were two vicious-looking dogs. I was afraid, but the old man in charge of the cart seemed to be telling me there was no danger, and so I let them go. Then the scene changed. I was in a house, with lots of people. I'd stolen something and was afraid of being found out. There were different kinds of people – good-looking ones, ugly ones . . . I thought there were more opportunities . . . different opportunities . . . I thought: the thief is basically the same person as before . . . (*a pause*)

A. In the cart there are vicious-looking dogs. Dogs are used to defend against thieves. They respond immediately, quickly and aggressively. They don't look anyone in the face. Perhaps the atmosphere of the second scene implies that this wish to take something more can be seen in a different way, less harshly, more tolerantly or with more respect for different aspects . . .

P. (*a long pause*) This year Fernanda is doing well at school, but she's always preoccupied, so that when she's in the street she could easily get run over by a bus. That's surely not good for her. Yesterday I beat her and I hurt her, but then it's only right and proper for her to be scolded if I can't get her to respect me with words.

A. You're talking about the problem of respect – respect for the limits of the analysis. Perhaps you're wondering how people can respect each other without coming to blows. But you're also wondering if, when someone is liable to get hurt, you ought to do something – take her by the arm, pull her to safety, not let her get run over by a bus . . .

P. (*harshly*) But I *wanted* Fernanda to get run over by a bus. I can't stand her. This morning I took the girls to school because my husband had fallen asleep. Walking along with Fernanda, I didn't say a word to her the whole way. I can't.

A. (*a pause*) You felt left alone with something that was too difficult for you right now.

P. Everything seems too difficult for me right now.

A. Perhaps you felt that I was someone who cared only about your behaviour. As if I cared only that you did well at school and not about what you were really feeling. A person who is so lost in her thoughts that she could easily get run over by a bus is someone who is seriously preoccupied – or perhaps she feels that, because no one understands her, there is nothing for it but to jump under a bus herself.

P. After the business with the suit, I wanted to have a drink, but I didn't. I'm trying to diet. But then I thought; how do I know that my analysis will work? And if it doesn't work, I'm convinced it will be my fault. I think that some things work more or less well . . .

A. We're facing a big difficulty here: the feeling of not being understood and the fear of *never* being able to be understood.

BRENMAN. There's a lot of rage in the patient in this session. And in this case the analyst really needs the patient's help; she needs more communications if she is to understand the situation better. We know that this patient's problem is that she acts out her rage with her children. What she would probably have liked to tell her mother is: 'You call yourself a mother? But you don't know the first thing about being a mother!' And she'd like to tell the analyst: 'You call yourself a psychoanalyst? I have to do everything myself!' You could already sense this from the previous session. It's the rage of a child who has to support her parents.

Here the analyst is afraid of comparing herself with the patient, of trying to understand, of getting information so as to understand the situation better. This is a very important subject that has to be tackled with the patient. When a small child cries, the mother is faced with the problem of understanding why he is crying: is it because he is hungry, because something hurts, or because he is cold? Normally the child cooperates with the mother. Without this cooperation, the mother cannot function properly. A good relationship comes about when they help each other to function.

Let's look at the dream. In the dream the patient takes her beloved daughter Chiara to the park, for a ride in a pony cart. She sees two dogs that frighten her badly and doesn't know if the situation is safe. She asks the man a question. He answers: 'It's all right, there's no danger. It's safe.' The patient is not at all sure yet. What she ought to say is: 'I don't know, I'm not sure.' Instead she allows herself to be robbed of a part of herself – the part capable of saying: 'I don't know.'

In a normal situation, doubting would be obvious; anyone would have doubts when faced with two frightening dogs.

In this case the analyst could have said: 'I don't know.' In reality there are these threatening dogs, which could indeed tear the little girl to pieces – rip the analysis apart. In a normal situation, even if the cart man says there is no problem, one can tell oneself that one isn't sure, take the girl away and say: 'Good heavens! I don't know. I'm not sure, but given my doubts this is what I'm going to do.' The patient makes the analyst too feel unable to say: 'I don't know.' Just as she herself is incapable of saying 'I don't know' to the man in the dream and simply accepts his answer, so, in the session, she induces the analyst to behave in the same way, making her unable to say: 'I don't know. Let us see . . .'

QUESTION. *It certainly isn't easy to guess why the patient doesn't offer any associations, but taking the dream literally, you can see that she leaves the little girl there with the two dogs as if she thought that being bad and cruel was a strength. Then she finds herself stealing . . . It's as if identifying with something bad was a strength, a step forward.*

BRENMAN. Right . . . But it seems to me that the analyst is left with the feeling of knowing nothing. Analysis is based on the belief that, with a bit of luck, by carrying on, asking oneself questions and working together, one will get somewhere in the end. The only association I can make is that the woman who steals is also a nice woman . . . In the dream there are good people and bad people, who must represent different parts of the patient's personality. There's a part of her with a loving, caring attitude and another part with an attitude of contempt and omnipotence. She has these different parts inside herself. The problem is to put them together. She can't even admit that she has mixed feelings of love and hate . . . a fierce dog on the one hand and a loving mother on the other. For her it's impossible to integrate these things – to put them together. Given her background, it's not easy for her to admit that she doesn't know, or that she has different, contrasting feelings, even though both are genuine. She would be hit – beaten.

ANALYST. Yes, that's what I had in mind when I gave my interpretation of the dream.

BRENMAN. When the patient talks about sorting out the wardrobes, she probably means that she's sorting things out in her mind. So I more or less agree . . . What is clear is that it's very easy for her to discover every possible failing in her husband. The fact that her husband has so many failings makes her angry, but it doesn't depress her very much . . . There are a whole load of problems connected with sorting things out . . . In the dream she is trying to understand what might be safest for her daughter Chiara, and when she's awake she wonders what might be safest for her daughter Fernanda, because she has to cross the road . . . Perhaps she realizes that she is confusing her, pilfering something, and would also like to sort things out a bit. She says that Fernanda is not only a bad girl: she is doing well at school now . . . But only the day before, she had yelled at her, telling her she was an idiot capable only of watching television. That's why it seems to me that she's making an effort to sort things out in her mind.

I suppose she is also realizing that Fernanda has a load of problems and needs help. But she can't talk to her daughter; she can't reach her. I would interpret that she is trying to sort things out in her mind – for instance, she is also managing to see good things in Fernanda and acknowledges that she is now doing well at school. But when she sees that Fernanda has anxiety problems, which she defends against by emptying her mind, then she feels very unhappy, because she realizes that she can't get close to her daughter, reach her and help her to solve these problems. All the same, the patient wants her daughter to recover.

Behind this, there is also the wish for the analyst to be able to talk to her about *her* difficulties. I think one of this patient's concerns is her difficulty in getting in touch with the girl's anxiety states. It must be awful for her not to be able to talk to her daughter . . .

QUESTION. *I'd like to point out that the girl uses the same methods as her mother – at least according to Dr Brenman . . . She starts off feeling anxious, then she is preoccupied, and she ends up under a bus . . . The husband is probably also anxious and that's why he gambles . . . Gambling, drugs . . . The patient herself, when she sees her husband's suit, thinks of having a drink . . . It's interesting to see how the whole family group uses the same method of constantly emptying their minds.*

BRENMAN. That's right. Drug addicts and alcoholics also get together in groups – for mutual support and so as not to think. I agree that this is a central issue. The analyst's task is precisely to endure the anxiety that the patient can't endure – for example, the anxiety of not knowing, or of having got something wrong. In these situations, a counter-transference problem may arise. The patient doesn't know what has caused her anxiety and empties her mind. One of the first defences is precisely to empty one's mind . . . Children have no defences, so they become omnipotent, relying on an idealized breast as a means of facing the anxiety situation. The same thing happens with drug addicts: they fuse in with something wonderful. None of us is immune from this kind of defence. Anxiety can be faced only when there is someone to help.

Now when this patient notices her daughter emptying her mind, she does exactly the same herself: she is invaded by anxiety and can't get close to her daughter. A third person is needed to help. That's what happens to a mother who finds herself in difficulties with her child and doesn't know what to do: she says 'Help! Now what shall I do?' Her husband comes and gives her support. Every one of us has to deal with dangerous situations of this kind. One of the advantages of working as analysts is that we can take part in discussion groups with colleagues. If there is a blocked situation with a patient, the analyst must seek help from colleagues. Being an analyst is a difficult profession, and it can also be dangerous, unless you have friends and colleagues to discuss things with.

ANALYST. While writing up the session, I suddenly realized that I had identified with the gambling husband. The patient was so cruel to him that I felt myself taking his side. At that point I felt like the husband saying: 'My family is so unbearable that I'm off to the casino.'

BRENMAN. Right . . . We all make such mistakes. Frankly, facing life and seeing problems really is hard. To be honest, we must admit that we see some of them and not others . . . That's the truth of the matter. If we are helped, if there are two of us, we may perhaps see a bit more. It's very interesting to see how, when the patient realizes her husband goes to the casino, she suddenly feels that *she* is the one who is able to face life and says 'What are you up to? Look here, I am sorting things out in the wardrobe, while you go off to the casino' – in the manner of someone who *does* know how to cope with life . . . There's such a clear separation when she says 'I'm the one that faces life, while you go off and . . .' – and at this point it becomes cruel. The analyst finds herself caught up in this situation. The truth of the matter is that we face some things and try to avoid others.

The more serious the problem, the more likely we are to be cruel. One might think that the patient, having had such an awful life, could have more sympathy for her daughter. But the tragedy is that things never happen that way. Boys at English public schools are beaten, so they shout and scream, but when they grow up they send their own children to the same schools. Then *they* treat their children in the same way as they were treated.

QUESTION. *Perhaps there's a kind of cruelty in this patient – an envy that her daughter might not face the same kind of suffering . . . What is painful is to accept that we even kill off our own love objects.*

BRENMAN. I don't know if that's true in this case or not . . . Freud maintained that hate is the oldest emotion we have. At any rate, so many people can only survive by killing off their own child part – the part that is able to love. That makes life meaningless and empty, so that hate and violence are the only way of coming alive. I firmly believe that we kill off parts of ourselves, and that only some manage to survive. I wrote a paper on the subject, 'Matters of life and death', in which I said that we kill off parts of ourselves in order to survive. Freud thought so too, and was criticized. I believe that, in order to survive, we kill off a part of ourselves, while another part stays alive. What matters is not how we kill, but how much we kill. That's not a very popular view, but I believe it to be correct. It's not very nice to say that we kill off parts of ourselves and at the same time parts of others in order to survive. This urge to kill is incredibly strong. In the history of the survival of the species, one tribe had to exterminate another in order to survive. But in this destroying to survive, there's an element of truth and an element of lying: sometimes people kill only out of greed, or to triumph. People also have to kill off the parts that are capable of love, so as not to be excessively tormented by the sense of guilt. This is something universal. The best situations are the ones where something good enough remains, so that we can construct. This problem affects everyone to some extent.

QUESTION. *I wonder if it is more frequent in groups or families than in relationships between two people.*

BRENMAN. Usually people kill off the part which has awareness and causes unbearable pain. For instance, people kill off the intolerable awareness of being alone, and the result is delusion – a delusion that we all have in our own way and to our own degree.

If you can establish a positive relationship, this approach to life can be changed, because two people together can support each other.

At the same time, when people are together, the loving part wants to devour the other person. So there is a kind of mutual possession and killing. Sometimes you want to kill the other person because that stops you getting in touch with your other world – the world of delusion. These mechanisms are constantly at work. And the problem is even more complicated than that . . . In analysis, the analyst can do his job only up to a point, because he too needs to sleep at night, to have his weekends and to go on holiday. The patient will see that the analyst can face things better than she can, but cannot face everything: there are some things that not even the analyst can face.

Patients address their problems to an idealized breast – to an analyst they see as a wonderful person, who can cope with anything. They expect the analyst to be everything.

In the present case, part of the analyst's work is to help the patient to cope with problems she failed to cope with when they originally arose. But the analyst must immediately make it clear that, however much she knows how to cope with certain things, she can do so only up to a point. Gamblers may believe that they will one day become millionaires but that is absurd. Drug addicts and alcoholics also imagine themselves on such a high. All we can do is to aim for ordinary reparation. Manic reparation is impossible.

Wednesday's session

P. This morning when I was waking the children, Chiara asked me if I wasn't expecting another child: if so, we could kill Fernanda, who was always hitting her. She said that may have been a dream. Then Fernanda told me a dream of hers. She dreamt that she had caught AIDS after stepping on a syringe in a garden; she was desperate, but managed to get to a woman doctor who treated her AIDS with a very painful injection! She managed to have the injection – the very last one. But her friend didn't get one.

What with all these dreams, I wound up forgetting my own.

A. There's a storm in the family: Chiara is angry with Fernanda, who hits her, and Fernanda gets frightened. But then, things seem to sort themselves out. Perhaps there's the idea that I might be able to help you.

P. (*a long pause*) Yesterday I told my husband that the world really is unfair . . . (*a pause*) Here I am lying on the couch, and you're there behind me, sitting in an armchair! . . . I went through a lot when I was small – all the traumas I had can't be undone. I went through so much; it's not fair.

A. Yes, it's not fair when a child catches AIDS by stepping on a syringe, but why get angry with the doctor? . . . It seems to me that you feel I might be able to help you . . . Perhaps what you feel to be unfair is that the treatment is painful.

P. I'm not angry with you personally; I'm angry in general.

A. But here, there's me personally. It seems to me that you can't accept being cared for, because if you do, you won't be able to show all the horrible things that you went through any more.

P. (*a long pause*) A number of things occur to me. Last night my husband said that over the years his interest in sex has declined – and seriously. So he can understand how someone who finds a woman who really turns him on can go off with her and leave his family. When I heard this, I was horrified! Then I also thought that, when I was a girl, I didn't want to study – in fact, not only did I not want to, but I positively refused. But my mother, who never had a chance to study, set a lot of store by it and did everything possible to get me to go to school, but I refused to study. My mother also wanted me to play the piano; she had already arranged lessons for me, but I didn't go! I also thought that I'm worried because Fernanda is at home by herself with the dog . . . The dog has a habit of jumping on people and resting its weight on their legs . . . just like in sexual intercourse. And Fernanda lets him do it as if . . . Well, last night I slapped her.

A. What I said before made you think that I might leave you, abandon you or beat you. But there's also another idea: you wonder why you refused what your mother was offering you – why you refuse my help here.

P. (*a long pause*) Now look! I was thinking of something else . . . I was thinking of the furniture in my house, of refurnishing it . . . It's ridiculous!

A. Perhaps it isn't so ridiculous at all. You are thinking about changing the arrangement of things inside yourself; and there's also the idea of seeing things from a different point of view.

P. But I can't do anything, because I haven't got anything at all!

A. I don't think that's the only idea. Before, you mentioned how you refuse to take advantage of opportunities that present themselves. The idea of getting new furniture might also mean making room for new things.

P. (*a pause*) I feel utterly blocked. (*In a hostile tone*) I'm wasting time, and time is speeding by . . .

A. You're blocked, but perhaps you're also very angry.

P. Yes, with you, I always am. Like with my mother. But with my mother I can understand it; with you I can't . . .

A. Perhaps I remind you of your mother. You feel that, like your mother, I'm the only source of hope, but the treatment is painful.

BRENMAN. This patient, her family and also the previous generation have all used the same method. Chiara says: 'Let's kill Fernanda because there's a new baby. We'll replace her with something else.' That's her solution. Fernanda dreams of an attempt on her life.

Murder is in the air with this family, in which each member kills the other. They all manage to pluck these feelings out of the air, as if they were infected by them.

The patient says: 'If I talk about my children's problems, I have to blot out the child part of myself. And if I look after the child part of myself, I'll kill my actual children.' From her standpoint and that of her family, there is no room for everyone; someone must die, as there isn't enough room for them all. Logically, then, either some members of the family must be killed off, or their approach and their behaviour must be changed.

Up to a point the patient has enough insight to realize that, however well she is analysed, she will remain damaged by her infantile traumas for the rest of her life. So the best she can hope for is that she'll be able to endure a part of these traumas and, with a bit of luck, to take pleasure in the improvements she can achieve.

But she feels that all this is very unfair. And so it is. Every one of us has to face this problem, and in doing so we have just two choices: either we can bear a grudge and become vindictive, or we can try to make the best of the unfairness.

When the patient feels that she can have better experiences, but that they won't eliminate the bad ones, she is maintaining that, although there is some improvement, it bears no relation to the traumas she suffered when she was small.

This really is a trial for every one of us. Melanie Klein touched on this point in her work.

Agamemnon kills Iphigenia and Clytemnestra kills Agamemnon. There's a whole series of killings. In the myth, it's the gods who decide. Some said they should go on taking revenge, while others thought they could begin to think of forgiving.

This is the problem. Fighting against an injustice you have suffered may become a just cause, and the fight may go on for generations.

But someone has to be bigger and call a halt to the process; someone has to realize that the only thing to be done is to bring about improvements.

The patient thinks it is unfair. And it really is unfair. When she thinks of her daughters, she can't remember her own dream. She is full of hate and the thirst for revenge for the unfairness she has suffered, and this stops her deriving any pleasure from possible improvements. Part of the problem is to be able to think of Chiara, Fernanda and herself at the same time. Revenge for the unfairness is all very well, but what about the capacity to appreciate improvements?

It is very important to accept that a degree of unfairness must be tolerated. It is also worthwhile. If the patient can accept this, she can also be forgiven for what she has done to Fernanda, and Fernanda will be grateful for the help she can give her. If she can't accept it, she won't even be able to forgive her own sins and will always live with a sense of guilt. If one cannot forgive, one cannot be forgiven either.

In the paranoid-schizoid position, there is no such thing as forgiving. The person hates, and behaves like a superego that says: 'This ought not to have happened on any account.' And that is what persists for generations. The more one knows the truth, the more this idea needs to be looked at afresh.

QUESTION.   *It's very difficult for some patients to get better because that would mean giving up the idea of taking revenge on their parents. If the theme of forgiveness and acceptance is introduced, the analyst gets stick. He is told: 'It's all very well for you.' Forgoing revenge also means betraying the child who has suffered so much . . .*

BRENMAN.   It's always easier for someone else . . . That's unfortunately the way of it . . . This is the point . . . the blood tie . . . the Mafia write their signatures in blood to get their own back, their revenge, on every level. Mephistopheles says: 'I'll give you all these things. You will be my master and I will be your servant; I'll give you everything you want. But in reality you will be my slave and I will be your master.'

(The following sessions date from two months later.)

ANALYST. In these two months, one of the problems that came up in the analysis was envy. The patient always shows her envy by talking about her relationships with her female friends, who are always wealthier, better loved and luckier than herself. My impression is that, as soon as the patient senses a good and useful analytic relationship, she compares it with her infancy and attacks the relationship with me, rather as if she was trying to say how terrible it is for her to think that a different relationship from the one she had with her mother is possible. She can't bear it . . .

BRENMAN. Why does she feel it is so terrible?

ANALYST. It makes her feel that the bad relationship she had with her mother is a wound inflicted on her. For example, in one session she said very aggressively: 'My mother was terrible to us and I am terrible to my daughters. That's how things are and that's how they must be, because the past can't be changed.'

On the Wednesday before the session I'm going to present, the patient said: 'My mother had four children because she needed to pour out her rage on them, as she would otherwise have gone mad. I'm doing the same thing with my daughters.' She said that in an extremely cruel voice. At the end of the session I noticed that I was feeling very bad. In the next session, on the Thursday, the patient came in and told me that she had lost her dog – a dog she in fact hates. But, having lost him, she felt desperate; she looked for him everywhere, eventually found him, and when the dog was back she thought: 'But . . . it would have been better if he'd been lost for good . . .' Then she said: 'No . . . I'm pleased to have found him again.' Then she talked about a journalist who had written an article about the district where she lived, in which she reported only the negative side and did not mention anything good. She had telephoned the paper to protest. In the session, she said: '*I* am that journalist. Yesterday you made me see positive aspects of myself as well, whereas I tend to see only the bad.'

On the following Monday, she arrives twenty minutes late. It is the last week before the Christmas holidays.

BRENMAN. The situation has changed slightly . . . Certain things have developed since the last time. She seems more able to see inside herself.

ANALYST. Yes, she's a bit better at this time . . .

BRENMAN. It will also be more painful . . .

Monday's session

P. (*arrives twenty minutes late*) I left on time. I had to take Fernanda to her music lesson first and then come here. But then I was stopped by the police again, and then R— Street was closed to traffic . . . and that's why I didn't get here sooner. For some time now, I haven't wanted to think about my husband having a lover, but . . . since he finished his analysis, he has never had any desire for me. We have sex perhaps every two months, and it's pretty awful!

But I don't have any desires either. Every so often he tells me: 'There are certainly women around who would like to have me!' It's funny, because usually he does what he wants and doesn't tell. But for some time now, he's always been arriving late on Monday nights and today I found the keys to the flat of one of his friends in his raincoat pocket. It's a completely vacant flat! It's furnished, you understand, but no one ever goes there! I found them and didn't say anything. Then I saw him searching everywhere; he became confused, suspecting that I had found them. Then he phoned me: 'Come and meet me at the office; we'll go home together, in two cars . . .' I thought: 'If he's deceiving me, its better that way!' I must get used to living without him . . . but I can't.

A. Perhaps this business also has something to do with us. You arrive late, with a whole load of excuses. We could let things go, knowing that something is wrong and not saying anything. Perhaps you think I don't care . . . Or perhaps you want to suggest to me: 'I'm late, but it doesn't matter to you very much!'

P. But I'd worked out the time; it's not my fault . . .

A. We need to look at the kind of calculation you did. You probably leave home having counted the minutes, so that if everything goes smoothly you arrive on time, but since not everything goes smoothly in this world . . .

P. (*a pause*) Last night I had a dream. I'm in a room with a bed and in the bed is a venomous snake! I cover it with the blanket but I still feel uneasy. Then I go out through the door and close it tight, but I feel just as uneasy as before . . . Then I think: 'What a fool you are, there's no way it can get out through the cracks . . .' (*a pause*)

A. What does this dream suggest to you?

P. The snake . . . is something I feel here too, on this couch . . . There's no point in covering it up; it has to be got rid of . . . It's dangerous, venomous . . .

A. What is really dangerous is if you don't see it: the snake crawls . . . (I'm thinking how quickly a snake can strike if you don't know where it is).

When you're watching out through the cracks, perhaps you're asking me to look at the snake with you from outside; you're afraid to look at it directly. So you show it to me indirectly, with signs . . . with clues . . .

P. (*a pause*) Yesterday one of my friends invited me to her home for a slice of cake; it was her birthday. It's the friend from Korea . . . I felt envious. She's so much luckier than I am! She is fêted, and has so many friends!

A. You've told me so many things, but now time is up and the session is over.

ANALYST. In this session there were so many things there was no time to look at . . . The Korean friend is one who recently went on a trip to Korea and left her two children with the patient. The children very much wanted to stay with her. So this friend from Korea is connected with an image of the patient as a good mother. But that's as far as it went, as there was no more time.

QUESTION. *What struck me is the patient's communication when she says: 'I must get used to living without him, but I can't.' Doesn't this have to do with the weekend or with the approaching Christmas holidays? And when she arrives late, can't that be seen as an attempt to get used to this situation?*

BRENMAN. I think the problem of her not being able to care about her husband and daughters may also arise in the relationship with the analyst. All this can in fact be applied to the patient's whole life. She is puzzled and feels that life is not worth very much; she always feels that everyone else manages to get much more than she does. Whether that counts as envy or not, I don't know. But the fact is that the patient has never succeeded in enjoying life.

The last time we looked at this case, the patient kept on tormenting her daughter Fernanda: 'Why are you always watching television? Why don't you grow up? Why aren't you more mature?' – much more than a parent normally would. She hated herself for that, and hated her daughter because she failed to live up to her expectations. It seems to me that the patient would like her daughter to gratify *her*. She felt that the daughter was the one who ought to give *her* something rather than that she should help her daughter.

From the material coming up now, it seems that this point has been understood; it seems that the work on this problem has been done, because she says her mother had four children and behaved so horribly with them, expecting the children to be the ones to satisfy *her*. And this was repeated in her life. It's actually something quite common. We discussed this last time too: lots of parents turn to their children for help in bearing their frustrations. It now seems that the patient is recog-

174

nizing this and has established something better with her analyst, but this becomes a problem.

She seems to be saying to herself: 'So it goes on from generation to generation; everyone does the same thing.' So she needn't feel guilty any more. But if she feels that she has a good relationship with the analyst, who takes care of her, she begins to feel guilty about how she treats her children – in particular, Fernanda. The sense of guilt about her treatment of Fernanda is very powerful. I think her greatest difficulty is to face this sense of guilt, about the way she treats her daughters and her life, with her eternal feeling of revenge and rage . . .

When she arrives for her session, she complains about her husband; she reflects on how seldom she manages to have sex with him and that he doesn't turn her on anyway. In a way she enjoys complaining, like the man in a restaurant in one of Woody Allen's films who says: 'The food is awful and uneatable, but the portions are too small . . .'

She takes an almost manic pleasure in saying that her husband is deceiving her. If we think of it, her pleasure is actually to have someone there who can be told off, blamed and made to feel guilty.

I'm sure that this belongs to her protest, her blaming of her mother. It may be a protest about the forthcoming holidays, about being left alone, as the questioner suggested just now. But her emotional reality is not the pain of feeling alone and abandoned. What she feels is *rage* at being left alone and abandoned. She feeds by herself on hate and spite. She wants her husband to be the one to feel guilty, so that she can be the one who is deceived and ill-treated.

When the analyst interprets that everything she has said up to that point has to do with their relationship, the patient replies: 'I worked out the exact time, it's not my fault . . .' What matters for her is to have someone who is guilty, and to attack her, so that she can say it isn't her fault.

And then there is what she does with her daughters and her husband: 'Why are you watching telly? You should be doing your homework! Why have you got home late? Because you've been gambling?' She always has to be blaming someone for something. In this way she satisfies herself with hate; she feeds on hate. And she does so very intensely.

Then she says that this is handed down from one generation to the next.

If she had a good relationship, she would have to stop and begin to feel sorrow, suffering and guilt. It's very interesting to see that when the patient says it isn't her fault – immediately asserting that someone else is the guilty party – she is in fact paranoid.

She had worked everything out so that *others* should feel guilty. In the dream, there's a venomous snake in the bed, but it is covered up. The patient really is venomously vindictive. Her protests may have to do with jealousy and frustration, but the main reason why she did her calculations was to satisfy her hate, precisely so as not to feel guilty and to have someone to blame, like her mother.

If the analyst can empathize and have a good relationship with her, this model breaks down. I feel very confident about this point. It is typical of chronically depressed persons to be like this, to go on complaining and show their dissatisfaction, until they eventually lose their object. Then they are heartbroken. She describes this clearly with the episode of the dog. She hates him, but when she loses him she says: 'My little dog! My poor little dog!' And when she finds him again she says: 'Why did he come back?' In a way, the patient knows this. And it's also true that this is a very old model, which is repeated. It's very hard to break it because of the problem of guilt. The patient's ambition is to accuse someone of ruining her life. It may be her husband, who gambles away all the money, or has another woman and is ruining her life that way. So she can hate, hate, hate. The problem is that the analyst felt very upset about this patient . . .

ANALYST. Yes, it's true. Sometimes I feel desperate . . .

BRENMAN. Desperate because everything goes on in the same old way . . . I think people like that can't face their sense of guilt precisely because they know that they themselves could be accused of being the deceivers and be severely punished, without any possibility of appeal. And this is handed down from generation to generation, for ever and ever . . .

ANALYST. I agree about the problem of guilt. But I wonder if there isn't also something else involved, which plays a very important part: the problem of psychic pain when she is faced with the absence of the object. I think she does make me feel some guilt, but also very much her suffering. Because what she says is true. It's true that her mother would never have become a mother if she hadn't wanted children to pour out her rage on. It's horrible, but true.

BRENMAN. You're raising a really important issue here: the paranoid defence against depression. We know that it's a powerful force – that nations would rather go to war than look at their internal problems. Rather than face sadness, people prefer to kill each other. The sense of guilt is certainly painful, but if one can be forgiven, reparation is possible. On the other hand, if something tells you that you're a sinner, that you're guilty of betrayal, and if that something goes on hammering away at you, eventually you will lash out at someone. That's because, the more you use paranoid defences – unforgiving hate – the harder it is for you to notice things about yourself, as you would then become the sinner yourself: the one who can't be forgiven.

I've told this joke on other occasions: when the woman taken in adultery is about to be stoned, Christ says 'He that is without sin among you, let him first cast a stone at her' – and they all drop their stones. But one woman does start stoning the adulteress, and Christ says: 'Mum, you've ruined everything again!'

All this can go on *ad infinitum*, and eventually you go mad. The only way of changing things is the possibility of being forgiven and of making reparation. It's admittedly a difficult road to travel. If you embark on it by yourself, with a superego that behaves as the patient behaves with Fernanda or her husband, then you end up in a crazy situation. The patient is afraid to face her sense of guilt, because guilt for her means being punished, beaten and accused – just what she does to Fernanda and her husband. This is the difficult problem that makes it impossible for the patient to face guilt. You can show her that that's what she's afraid of.

There's always a part of ourselves that forgives and makes things better through forgiveness, but there's also another part that isn't prepared to forgive and wants to go on punishing and tormenting the culprit for ever. We have to face these two parts of ourselves. If we think we are prepared to forgive and to desist from punishing, we'll always be threatened by the split-off part, which is intent on not forgiving and on tormenting. It's an eternal struggle, which is waged throughout life and is never resolved.

QUESTION. *I'd like to put forward a theory of my own about the betrayal the patient feels she has suffered, which might lie behind her crazy inclination to persecute the object and not to forgive. It's a very old betrayal – the betrayal of a mother who deprived the patient of her position as the favourite daughter when her sister was born. All the horror stories the patient brings, which she is still living through today, mask a kind of paradise on earth that once existed. So the hate and the impossibility of forgiving have to do with the mother's betrayal. She always has to persecute a betrayer, who may be her husband or her daughter who doesn't give her the satisfactions she expected from her mother.*

BRENMAN. I agree, up to a point. But there are other aspects of this patient's mother that suggest that she also had a good side. For example, she wanted her daughter to have the education that she herself lacked. There are some good things about this mother that come out.

177

If one is honest, one has to remember not only bad things but also good ones. But the point is that the mad, narcissistic part believes that one's life could have been perfect if one's parents had not had sex and produced another child: 'No one else has the right to live. Only I have the right to live.'

But to return to the problem of guilt, it can be faced only if someone shares it with you. A child may also cry because his mother goes away, but the mother shares the sorrow and sense of guilt at the fact of leaving him. If no one shares this guilt situation with you, the burden is too heavy. And if, what is more, you have an omnipotent attitude, you feel you are always in the right and you have no sense of empathy or ability to share things with other people. Nor will you then be able to think that there'll be someone there to share things with you.

So you go mad. You can't help going mad if you have no one to share things with. This patient is unable to share; her pleasure is moral supremacy: she is always right and her husband is absolutely wrong. Instead of saying 'What have we done with our lives? What can we do?' and trying to look at things together, she says: 'Look at these horrible things you have done to me.'

In analytic treatment, you need to beware of the patient's tendency to turn the analysis into a manic–depressive situation, in which one of the two parties is absolutely right and the other absolutely wrong. It may be the patient who is right and the analyst who is wrong, or the other way round.

This is a real and very powerful force. Such a defence is very common in war, in which there is one party who is right and another who is wrong. It's only after the war is over that peace is achieved. The same thing happens in a normal relationship or a marriage.

But it's possible to reconstruct and make reparation. This patient, though, goes on in the same old way. Her daughters too will follow the same pattern, and everything will be passed on from generation to generation.

ANALYST. It seems to me that this mother really wasn't capable of coping with the problem of a growing child. She had four children, and when the last daughter – the one who came after the patient – was 4 years old, she moved to Milan and abandoned them all. The patient is very afraid when she notices an improvement in the analysis; she immediately fears that I'm taking on another patient and contemplating sending her away . . .

BRENMAN. That's not unusual. It often happens that a child is seen as wonderful and exceptional, but when he starts getting independent, there is suddenly another little child who is wonderful and exceptional. Some parents carry on that way. They create an idealized image of themselves and of the child, but when there are problems, they are thrown out together with the child and the parents turn to something new. If a man has a roving eye and is a Don Juan, there's a wonderful, beautiful girl and he has a relationship with her, but when the situation gets a bit less idealized and more realistic, he leaves her and finds himself another one. And the same thing is repeated over and over again. He can't stay on a human level, in the depressive position. I imagine the patient possibly having such fantasies; when her daughter watches television, she gets very angry and would like to throw her out. She has never had anyone to help her look at these things. So it's surely very important to interpret this to her. As the interpretative work develops, the patient can be confirmed in the idea that the analyst is looking at her things together with her . . .

QUESTION. *I can understand the analyst must take a lot of trouble with this patient, particularly in case her interpretations are heard as accusations. The first interpretation in the session is absolutely innocuous and kind, but the patient immediately replies: 'It's not my fault!' And her response to the second interpretation is actually to produce a venomous snake that can bite. It's not easy for the analyst to share the sense of guilt with this patient.*

BRENMAN. In such cases, you have to tell the patient beforehand that you are describing a problem but that she might hear what you say as an accusation. So I would show the patient that she is in contact with the image she has inside herself and not with my voice. That's a point that remains to be analysed.

I would say to her: 'Why don't you hear anything that has to do with understanding and would let you forgive? Why do you immediately seize on the punishment aspect?' It's an important question.

The patient sets more store by recrimination than by understanding. She is ruled by a delusional, omnipotent conviction: 'I could have been God in paradise. If it hadn't been for everything that happened, I would be God in paradise.' This must be the voice that actually controls her. The cruel superego is the one she actually listens to, whereas the more generous and helpful superego goes unheard. That's a big problem.

Tuesday's session

(*Arrives seven minutes late, in haste, as if wanting to make up for the lost time by hurrying*)

P. I had only about two hours' sleep last night. I fell asleep at five and woke up at seven. I feel very, very anxious: the holidays are coming up soon and you will have a lovely break and I'll have a ghastly one. There's very little time, and on top of it I'm late. I have a perfectly awful relationship with my husband. There are always these bits of green stuff on his sweater . . . He has another woman, but then, why shouldn't he? It's my fault for neglecting him. But what can I do? If I reject his advances, I can't do anything about it.

A. You wonder what you can do, but you don't seem to expect an answer. You arrive late, in a rush, as if trying to make up the lost time by hurrying through the waiting room. We could ask ourselves why. Wouldn't it be better to accept the fact that you're late and think about it a bit? The relationship with me too is awful; arriving late shows how difficult it is for you to come. We could ask ourselves why this is, and calmly try to understand.

P. I had an uncle and aunt for lunch, and I offered them a brandy at half past two! That's why I'm late . . . I could perfectly well not have done so, but in fact . . . !

A. Perhaps you actually couldn't not have done it; if you did, there must be a reason. Perhaps something made you do it.

P. (*a pause*) I don't know; the first thing that occurs to me is that I'm envious . . . The fact is, I thought: 'Well, just for five minutes!' So, instead of taking my uncle and aunt to my mother's and coming here . . . It's ridiculous! To think that I wanted to be friendly, it's ridiculous . . . to make them feel at home with me . . . and then not to come to analysis.

A. Perhaps you found it hard to let them go, just as you're now finding it hard to let *me* go for the holidays. You wanted to keep them there by giving them something else.

P. (*after a pause*) You are a mature, calm, equable person. You'll have a nice quiet holiday. Whereas I shall feel dreadful, with my husband and Fernanda . . .

A. You see me going off calmly with all my good qualities and abilities, leaving you alone with these difficult relationships of yours.

P. Yes, because you always do the right thing and I always get everything wrong.

A. (*The patient's last two remarks plunge me into despair. I can no longer understand anything; the description of myself that I hear seems to me totally unrealistic and unwarranted. I feel profoundly distressed.*) Whatever makes you think that?

P. Because I always get things wrong; it's always my fault.

A. (*a pause*) Perhaps you think I'm going on holiday because you're a burden on me and make me feel bad. So I want to get rid of you and not think about you any more. And you don't know how to change things; you're full of anxiety and don't know what you can give me to make me feel good with you . . . (*a pause*) Or else, since you mentioned brandy, there's also the idea of putting me off my stroke . . . as you're doing now, given that time was up several minutes ago and I'm going on talking . . .

(*The patient leaves with a smile, and I find myself smiling too.*)

QUESTION. *I wonder if, when the patient mentions brandy, she isn't also referring to a washed-up, alcoholic, manic parental couple – the uncle and aunt . . . She seems to be turning them into alcoholics. She's with them in an intense, excited situation in which she feels that she's the active party. That might be a way of inducing the analyst to share her guilt. Perhaps she could forgive, if she were to realize that she too is an active party – in this scene with three people . . . this love scene with three people . . . She had group sex with her husband. She did so as a victim, but perhaps she wasn't only her husband's victim . . . This anxiety of being in a threesome is probably reactivated by the prospect of holidays with her husband and her daughter Fernanda.*

BRENMAN. I had some difficulty in imagining the kind of interaction between the patient and the analyst here. The patient arrives seven minutes late. It's not the end of the world. Then she launches into a long story . . . She has had only two hours' sleep, the holidays are coming, her husband has another woman, she's a bad wife . . .

I found it hard to understand the first interpretation. It seems that you could have said: 'All right, so you're a bit late. But we still have almost all the session ahead of us.'

The patient says she wanted to offer this uncle and aunt of hers something. She can't do everything, so she arrives seven minutes late. That's reasonable enough. But something happens. The relationship between the patient and the analyst degenerates so much that the analyst feels intense pain.

In a way, the analyst is asking herself something: 'Why do ordinary routine problems turn into unbearable, soul-destroying calamities?'

The patient makes the analyst feel desperate. There are two parts involved here. The accusing part is so strong that it's going to touch the heart of the part that wants to work with her. That's the main thing to bear in mind. It's quite reasonable to think that the patient arrived a little late because she wanted to offer her uncle and aunt a drink, but that breaks her heart.

This must mean something. It has to do with the patient's life and the way she experiences relationships. The patient is probably causing the analyst to feel what *she* is feeling. She too wanted to be kind, friendly and positive. But then she ends up thinking that actually she didn't do anything good. That's a very powerful dynamic.

QUESTION. *It seems to me that the patient is confessing to the analyst that she always gets everything wrong, whereas the analyst is clever and calm. In fact, she makes the analyst feel that she is the one who gets everything wrong. It's the analyst who ends up as the guilty party.*

BRENMAN. I agree. But there's something else. When the analyst tries to make things better, she fails every time. Whatever she does to make things better, it doesn't work. If she tries to repair things, there's nothing to be done. So she ends up feeling compelled to act out – to make a joke, to touch the patient, to reach her. Perhaps this is something we could talk about. She can't share anything good with this patient. I think that what is acted out is the essence of the problem: the good spirit is important – in fact, it can be much more important than the bad one. However stupid it may seem, it's important. What matters is this person's state of mind: the good spirit and the bad spirit.

QUESTION. *I think that, when you have someone who insists on her complaints, if you try to tell her it isn't a catastrophe and can be tackled rationally, it's as if you were depriving her of the object you mentioned before in connection with depressives – an object to torture. If there's something to complain about, everything is all right, but if the object is lacking, the result is a breakdown. In fact, when the patient starts getting angry, she says that the analyst is mature and calm. Perhaps one of the important points is the analyst's attitude towards the patient's complaints.*

BRENMAN. I'm finding it very hard to follow this session . . . to pick up its spirit. Looking at the beginning of the session, the patient seems to be improving. She says: 'However much I have to complain about with my husband, I don't really want to be with him. He's entitled to go off and look for someone else if he wants to.' In a way, her heart is opening up a bit, towards understanding her husband. She can't go to bed with him; she just can't do it. She frankly admits it. At this point the analyst says something. After the analyst's comment, she says in effect: 'Even if I don't succeed, I'm trying to have a good relationship with my husband.' The uncle and aunt who visit her are good objects. The patient can't do everything – look after her uncle and aunt and also come to her session – so she tries to find a reasonable compromise. Well, what happens to this reasonable, good attitude? The analyst suggests:

'Perhaps you couldn't avoid it; perhaps you had good reasons of your own; something made you do it.' It's very important for the patient to know that she's trying to do things for the best. She's trying to understand what she can do to make things better with her husband. How can she reconcile the wish to go to analysis with that of being friendly to her uncle and aunt? The important thing is to recognize and take account of this good attitude. It's this good attitude that has to confront the other – the bad one. If this goes unrecognized, the patient will return to her previous state. The analyst understands this intuitively and tries to restore the good state of mind. It would have been better if the analyst had interpreted – recognized – the good attitude that prevailed until then: that the patient has feelings for her husband, for her children, for this uncle and aunt and also for her analyst, that she realizes she can't satisfy them all, but that she is doing everything she can to make things work out for the best, with her husband, with the analyst and with the uncle and aunt. That's what we call a good mental climate between a mother and a child: 'You can't have all your time to yourself; you can't get rid of the child, so you must work out the best things to have and do for both.' That's what people do to find the best way of coping with different circumstances. To do this, you need someone – a partner. Making order out of chaos is a creative process. You can't do it on your own; there must be two people. One of them has to give something up out of love for the other. If the two people work well together in a creative spirit, they will be able to change the original situation.

QUESTION. *Perhaps the patient and the analyst don't understand each other because the analyst has a good couple in mind, but the patient doesn't. So the patient tells her: 'You are so clean, so good and so honest. I'm dirty because I have a bad, drunken sod in bed, who gets up to all sorts of disgusting things. There are those bits of green stuff. I see them; I'm very watchful. The keys . . . I go and look for the keys . . . I have this rotten sod in mind. You are too honest, too good. I am bad.' The analyst feels sorry. She is good and doesn't understand the patient, who is so bad and dirty.*

BRENMAN. I don't understand . . . The patient tells the analyst: 'You are a calm, equable person. You will have a glorious holiday. But *I* feel terrible.' If someone is trying to solve problems, they can't be perfectly calm, there's anxiety, there's suffering, there's a bit of sadness . . . With a bit of luck, a reasonable degree of peace of mind is achievable. What the patient is actually saying is that the analyst's calmness is too good to be true. So she tries to smash it and bring the analyst to breaking point, because she isn't sharing the problem . . .

The interesting thing is this. If the analyst feels sorry and upset by a whole load of terrible problems facing this patient, and that is never acknowledged, the patient will go on thinking that the analyst has an easy life. I think that here the analyst is carrying on with the analysis as if everything were going smoothly . . . There's no need to despair, to tear your hair out. But at this point, the patient notices that the analyst is always calm, collected and self-controlled, and that this means that there ought not to be any problem. This doesn't actually help her.

I think it's important for the analyst to feel, and make the patient feel, the concern, the anxiety and the toil. There's something in psychoanalysis that can make the patient believe that the analyst's life is so peaceful that his or her own life ought to be equally peaceful.

Yet that's not how things are. This patient didn't have a mother capable of facing problems together with her and so she was forced to turn to an idealized breast that's always composed and calm. So at this point she will hate the analyst. If the analyst is this person who is always calm, the patient will hate her and try to destroy her peace of mind. She does so and she succeeds.

QUESTION. *I wonder if the real problem might be envy – perhaps an excuse to smash this peace of mind . . .*

BRENMAN. The patient feels very deprived . . . She can well understand that her husband, who is equally deprived, turned to another woman . . . The deprivation she suffered from was the lack of someone to share her problems with. If her daughter Fernanda watches television, she might be concerned in case she does so for too long. Instead she gets furious because she doesn't want the child to cause problems. Fernanda has to be a perfect child who doesn't cause problems. The patient lives her life with the idea of a perfect mother and a perfect daughter. It's important for the analyst not to strengthen this conviction.

Let's take a look at the third session . . .

Wednesday's session

(Arrives on time)

P. I've had so many dreams, but I don't remember everything. I remember there was a boy who helped me a lot; he helped me to find a house. Then there were mothers with children.

I think the boy helped me to find a house; in fact, he went along to see the houses before I did, to see if they were OK!

Then there was one of those places where they put newborn babies in clinics. The babies were in cots behind glass windows and each baby had his mother behind him. I wondered whether the babies were drugged or not. In the dream, I imagined them being given a feed with a drug in it. I asked one of the mothers, but she just answered with a smile: it was a riddle.

Now I feel bothered by the noises from the street.

(Lying on the couch, the patient is facing the window – a wide, horizontal window that looks out on to the street. So her situation is very similar to that of the babies in the dream.)

The holidays are coming and I shall feel awful. There's my husband – maybe he has another woman . . . I come along here and do my best to appear on top of things – but I'm not. This morning, when I finished all my chores, I had a drink . . . ! The mothers in the dream were very young . . . a bit neglected . . . Perhaps that's why I thought of drugs.

A. *(After these associations and for the rest of the session, I found it impossible to reconstruct the precise sequence of what I and the patient said.)* What do you think of the riddle?

P. I never understand riddles. People who set riddles make you feel stupid.

A. *(At this point I feel I am understanding hardly anything, but I don't feel stupid.)*

P. I never understand riddles, and then I think I get them wrong.

A. But now you've set me a kind of riddle. You tell me you're not the way you seem, the way you're doing your best to seem . . .

P. There were so many mothers, but perhaps there was only one. The cots . . . they remind me of this couch. I really don't know if the babies were drugged.

A. You're showing me that there are two kinds of relationship with me. There's someone who helps and there's a mother who may be giving a feed to her baby or may be giving drugs. The situation in the dream is similar to the situation here, and you are bothered by the noises in the street. What I seem to be hearing is that you would like more intimacy.

(This is surely a reference to the seminar, which exposes us to the view of a big audience, but I don't know what to do with this other than to confirm the idea of a wish for intimacy.)

There are mothers with children. Perhaps you are wondering if needing a mother is like needing a drug.

P. *(emphatically)* Yes, it is. What's more, addicts call heroin 'mummy'.

A. *(The way she made her last comment makes me feel desperate.)* But a newborn baby really can't live without his mother.

P. But I'm not a newborn baby. When Fernanda and Chiara show they need me – and really do need me – then they bother me. I feel enraged.

A. I wonder if the idea of drugs might also be connected with yesterday's brandy and with my keeping you here for a few minutes over time. Perhaps the neglectful mother is also . . .

P. No, on reflection, she wasn't neglectful, I was wrong . . . You could say she was down-to-earth, in fact. When I left here yesterday, I was happy. I was so happy that I think people could see it. I've never had so many men showing an interest in me lately as I had yesterday. Imagine: one of them even asked if he could get into my car. I thought: 'Careful now!'

A. You were happy because the session went well. But I wonder if things go well for you here only when I get confused . . .

P. Well, your mistake was to give me more time and not less. But it wasn't only that (*in an almost protective tone*). It was the session itself that made me happy. Now I don't know, I'm having trouble remembering, but yesterday afternoon I did without music and TV – the things I always do to deaden myself.

A. So the good relationship with mother is what enables you to feel more or less OK even when you're by yourself; the other relationship is with the drug/analyst, the heroin-drug-mother you can't do without, who leaves you feeling desperate when she's not there.

QUESTION. *Does the patient drink?*

ANALYST. She used to . . . But mainly she used cocaine . . . There's the problem of drugs . . . For her, even food is a drug. Every so often she goes on a diet, and every so often she puts on weight . . .

QUESTION. *The children in the dream seem to be all right . . . They also have a mother . . . Perhaps the patient is asking a question here . . . When she feels good, when she feels better . . . But she doesn't know why. It's odd . . . In the dream there's a calm, good atmosphere. But the associations are: 'The holidays are coming and I shall feel bad.' It sounds as if the part that keeps on recriminating hasn't been properly worked through.*

ANALYST. It's a static, dream-like situation . . . I didn't feel that she was calm . . . She's still, but not calm.

QUESTION. *I'd like to take up the patient's comment that she had never had so many men taking an interest in her. The problem is whether she felt good because the previous session really did make her feel better or whether she was in a kind of drugged state.*

BRENMAN. I agree. The dream has two main aspects: a man looking for a house for her, and babies who might or might not be drugged. The analyst realizes that the patient is saying that one of her experiences is that she feels a bit more at home with her analyst. The analyst provides her with a nice house. That isn't a drug – it's a genuine thought, an attempt to construct something for her benefit.

But then there are the mothers standing behind their babies. Are the mothers trying to drug the babies or will they give them a house? That's the riddle she wants the analyst to solve for her.

I would tell her: 'You'd like to know if I want to understand and construct something with you on the basis of understanding, or if I only want to keep you quiet.'

The patient understands this, because when she talks about her daughters Fernanda and Chiara, she feels unable to construct a situation of understanding with them. She very much wants an analyst-mother to build a house for her, but she's afraid this analyst-mother only wants to keep her quiet. The day before she felt that the analyst was caring, that she thought of her, and that she tried to construct something with her. She left with this feeling of happiness that also radiated from her face. That's certainly much better than having a mother who tells her: 'Just be quiet, be good.' This patient wants to know if the aim of analysis is to construct something or if the analyst just wants to keep her quiet.

Index

Abraham, Karl: cannibalism 2, 43–4; melancholia xvii, 4, 23–4, 25, 30, 58, 71; mother–infant relationship 98
acting out 4, 17; analysts 5, 12, 182; parental expression of emotions 18; repetition compulsion 126; separation 23
aggression 24, 35, 64, 72
alcoholism 155–6, 166, 168
ambivalence 11, 67, 85
analysts: complex interactions with patient 12; coping ability 168; cruelty 60–1; depressive position xvi; narcissism 1–10; patient attacks on 99; patient power over 134; reparative task 110; separation 22, 24, 33; supervision cases 116–23, 127–9, 141–50, 152–4, 160, 181–4, 186–7; support from colleagues 166
analytical relationship xv–xvi, 108, 111, 146, 154
annihilation 73–4, 81–2, 89, 124
antidepressants 136
anxiety 79, 111, 117, 118; analyst's 183, 184; annihilation 124; death 115, 131; mother–infant relationship 74–5; night 136; persecutory 80; separation 26, 29, 30, 31, 32, 134; somatization 125; transgenerational transmission of trauma 165, 166

Bion, Wilfred 39, 100, 111; containment xv, xxii; good object relationships 96;

'human relationship' concept xv; language of achievement 33; mother–infant relationship 74–5; superego xvii
bisexuality 67–8
blame 175, 176
borderline patients 113
Bowlby, John 103
breast: caring historic 15; envy 102; good xxiv, 43–4; ideal 98; idealized 42, 166, 168, 184; identification 69, 70; persecutory 41
Brenman Pick, Irma 109
bullies 6

cannibalism 1, 24, 43–4, 46, 101
Charles, Prince of Wales 85, 86
Christianity 49, 161–2
clinging 18, 24, 25, 58, 59
clinical examples: cruelty 49–56, 57–8; deprivation and violence 135–54; hysteria 65–7, 68–70, 72–3; life and death issues 44–5; meaning and meaningfulness 78–93, 100–2; narcissism of analyst 5–10; reconstruction 13–18; separation anxiety 26–9, 30–1; transgenerational transmission of trauma 155–87; unbearable pain 113–34
compassion 48
containment xv, xvi, xvii, xxii, 18, 100–1
conversion hysteria 63, 73

psychopathology 63, 64, 107
psychosis 62, 63, 71, 103, 105

rage 163–4, 175
recollections 12
reconstruction xviii, 11–21, 22
reparation 12, 22, 176, 177; depressive
    position 44, 94; good object xvi;
    hysterogenic mother 64;
    reconstruction xviii
repetition compulsion 12, 20, 33, 36,
    126
repression 65
revenge 97, 171, 175; *see also* vengeance
Rosenfeld, Herbert xv, xvii, 2, 109
Rotblatt, Joseph 106

sadism 8, 18, 46, 91, 143; doctors 141,
    145; sexual choices 5; sexual fantasies
    136
sado–masochism 18, 24, 25, 29, 32
schizo–paranoid position
    see paranoid–schizoid position
schizoid personalities 38
schizophrenia 63, 74, 107
Segal, Hanna xvii, 47, 89, 95
self-preservative instincts 35
self-understanding 20
separation 22–33, 58, 113, 124, 133–4,
    154; annihilation of the object 81, 89;
    defences 144; enduring 122; lack of
    care 160–1; pain and rage 152
sexual frustration 136, 142
sexual reproduction 36, 37
sexuality 40, 43, 46, 138; deviants 46–7;
    hysteria 65; transgenerational
    transmission of trauma 155, 156, 160;
    see also homosexuality
Shakespeare, William 107, 133
skin 37–8
somatization 125
Sophocles xxiii, 97
splitting 41, 44, 85, 90–2; Einstein 104;
    hallucinatory gratification 74; hysteria
    63; paranoid–schizoid position 94
Spoto, Gigliola Fornari xiii–xix
Strachey, James xvii

suffering 138, 150, 176; *see also* pain
suicide 71, 114, 120, 125
superego xvii–xviii, 94–5, 96–7;
    annihilating 81; babies 98; clinging
    and hating 18; cruelty 49, 53, 56, 59,
    60, 179; harsh 24, 32, 33, 46, 70, 71,
    95, 107; melancholia 23; moralizing
    56, 135, 147, 148; murderous 95, 99,
    100, 102; narcissism of analyst 3;
    paranoid–schizoid position 171;
    persecuting 8, 51; relentless 88, 96;
    ruthless 30, 98, 108; understanding
    54
supervision xv, 112; deprivation and
    violence case 135–54;
    transgenerational transmission of
    trauma case 155–87; unbearable pain
    case 113–34

third person 122
transference: analysis of 12, 13; figures
    148; Freud xxi, 1; hysteria 76;
    melancholic patients 23; narcissism of
    analyst 9; omnipotence of patient 15;
    patient's reality 154; persecutory
    father 114; repetition compulsion 20;
    see also countertransference
trauma: early infantile 83–7;
    psychopathological structures 111;
    transgenerational transmission
    155–87
truth 1, 12, 13, 24, 39, 108; corruption
    of 46, 47; ego strength 3; melancholia
    71; negation of 64

vengeance 32, 59, 91, 97;
    see also revenge
victimization 97
violence 92, 135, 147; killing off
    love and meaning 161; sexuality 46;
    transgenerational transmission of
    trauma 155, 156, 158, 159
Virgil 105

weaning 30
Winnicott, Donald 98
wishful thinking 73, 74